Essential Enterprise Blockchain Concepts and Applications

Essential Enterprise Blockchain Concepts and Applications

Edited by

Kavita Saini
Pethuru Raj Chelliah
Deepak Kumar Saini

CRC Press
Taylor & Francis Group
Boca Raton London New York

CRC Press is an imprint of the
Taylor & Francis Group, an **informa** business

AN AUERBACH BOOK

CRC Press
Boca Raton and London
First edition published 2021
by CRC Press
6000 Broken Sound Parkway NW, Suite 300, Boca Raton, FL 33487-2742
and by CRC Press
2 Park Square, Milton Park, Abingdon, Oxon, OX14 4RN

Library of Congress Cataloging-in-Publication Data
A catalog record for this title has been requested

ISBN: 9780367564889 (hbk)
ISBN: 9780367697655 (pbk)
ISBN: 9781003097990 (ebk)

Typeset in Adobe Garamond Pro
by KnowledgeWorks Global Ltd.

Contents

Editors

Kavita Saini, PhD, is presently working as an Associate Professor, School of Computing Science and Engineering, Galgotias University, India. She received her PhD degree from Banasthali Vidyapeeth, Banasthali. She has 17 years of teaching and research experience, as well as supervising MTech and PhD scholars in various areas.

Her research interests include web-based instructional systems (WBIS), software engineering, blockchain and databases. She has published various books for UG and PG courses for a number of universities including MD University, Rothak, and Punjab Technical University, Jallandhar.

She has published more than 30 research papers in national and international journals and conferences, as well as patents, and delivered technical talks on Blockchain: An Emerging Technology, Web to Deep Web and other emerging areas.

Pethuru Raj Chelliah, PhD, has been working as the Chief Architect in the Site Reliability Engineering (SRE) Division of Reliance Jio Infocomm Ltd. (RJIL), Bangalore. Previously, he worked as a cloud infrastructure architect in the IBM Global Cloud Center of Excellence (CoE), IBM India Bangalore for four years. Prior to that, he had a long stint as TOGAF-certified enterprise architecture (EA) consultant in Wipro Consulting Services (WCS) Division and also worked as a lead architect in the Corporate Research (CR) Division of Robert Bosch, Bangalore. In total, he has gained more than 17 years of IT industry experience and 8 years of research experience.

Dr. Chelliah finished the CSIR-sponsored PhD degree at Anna University, Chennai; and continued with UGC-sponsored postdoctoral research in the Department of Computer Science and Automation, Indian Institute of Science, Bangalore. Thereafter, he was granted a couple of international research fellowships

(JSPS and JST) to work as a research scientist for three years in two leading Japanese universities. He has published more than 30 research papers in peer-reviewed journals such as IEEE, ACM, Springer-Verlag and Inderscience. He has contributed 35 chapters for various technology books edited by highly acclaimed and accomplished professors and professionals.

 **Deepak Kumar Saini, PhD,** is a Project Manager and associated with ST Microelectronics, a French-Italian multinational company in Greater Noida, India. He has 16 years of experience with the IT industry.

He has a keen interest in emerging technologies in the field of computer science and handling various cloud-based live projects. Dr. Saini has in-depth knowledge of blockchain and its various applications.

Contributors

M. Vivek Anand is a Research Scholar in the Department of CSE, Galgotias University, Greater Noida, Uttar Pradesh, India. He received an ME degree in Software Engineering from Anna University, Chennai, Tamil Nadu, in 2013, and Bachelor of Engineering in the stream of Computer Science from Anna University, Coimbatore, Tamil Nadu, in 2011. He has more than five years of teaching experience. His research interests are Internet of Things and blockchain.

K.P. Arjun is a Research Scholar in the Department of CSE, Galgotias University, Greater Noida, Uttar Pradesh, India. He received an MTech in Computer Science and Engineering from the University of Calicut, Kerala in 2016. His research interests are big data analytics, cloud computing, artificial intelligence, machine learning and deep learning. He has authored over five research papers in various national and international journals and conferences. His publications are indexed in SCI, Scopus, Web of Science, DBLP and Google Scholar.

B. Balamurugan completed a PhD at VIT University, Vellore and is currently working as a Professor in Galgotias University, Greater Noida, Uttar Pradesh. He has 15 years of teaching experience in the field of computer science. His areas of interest lie in the fields of Internet of Things, big data and networking. He has published more than 100 international journals papers and contributed book chapters.

S.A. Bragadeesh is a Junior Research Fellow since July 2016. He is pursuing his PhD at SASTRA Deemed to be University, India. He has a Bachelor of Engineering degree in Electronics and Communication Engineering and an MTech in Embedded Systems. He has three years of industrial experience working as an R&D engineer. He is currently working on the domain of Internet of Things. His research interests include data analytics, information security, wireless sensor networks, Internet of Things and blockchain.

Rajesh Kumar Dhanaraj is an Associate Professor in the School of Computing Science and Engineering at Galgotias University, Greater Noida, U.P., India. He holds a PhD degree in Information and Communication Engineering from Anna University Chennai, India. He has published 33+ articles and papers in various journals and conference proceedings, and contributed chapters to books. His research and publication interests include cyber physical systems, wireless sensor networks and cloud computing. He is an Expert Advisory Panel Member of Texas Instruments Inc., USA.

A. Ilavendhan is presently working as an Assistant Professor, Department of Computer Science and Engineering, Galgotias University. He received his BTech degree from Pondicherry University and ME degree in Computer Science and Engineering from Pondicherry University, Bhopal. He has overall experience of seven years. His research interests include game theory, VANET, blockchain and big data. He has published papers in international journals and conferences.

R. Indrakumari is presently working as an Assiatant Professor, Department of Computer Science and Engineering, Galgotias University. She received a BE degree from Madurai Kamaraj University in 2001, and an MTech degree in Computer Science and Information Technology from Manonmaniam Sundaranar University, Tirunelveli. She has overall experience of 15 years, out of which 4 years in industry and 11 years in the teaching field. Her research interests include data mining, big data, data warehousing and tools like Tableau and Qlikview. She has published papers in international journals and conferences.

L. Abirami is presently doing research in VIT, Vellore, under the domain of Machine Learning in the health care field. She finished her undergraduate in Ramakrishna College of Arts and Science, Coimbatore in 2012 and PG at the same institution in 2014. She has overall experience of two years in teaching field. Her research interests include machine learning, blockchain and big data. She has published papers in international journals and conferences. She has filed a patent in the field of machine learning.

J. Jayapriya is a PhD (Integrated) student currently pursuing research at the School of Information Technology and Engineering in VIT, Vellore, India. She holds a bachelor's degree in Computer Science and Engineering from Anna University, Chennai, India. Her research interests are primarily in the areas of blockchain, decentralization, consensus mechanisms, security and cryptography.

N. Jeyanthi received a PhD in Cloud Security from VIT University, Vellore, Tamil Nadu, India. She is an Associate Professor in VIT, Vellore, for School of Information Science and Engineering. Her research work was funded by Department of Science and Technology, Govt. of India. A patent has been granted for one of her research projects. She has authored and co-authored over 64 research publications in peer-reviewed reputed journals and 30 conference proceedings. Books and book chapters have also added to her research contributions. She served as the program committee member of various international conferences and reviewer for various international journals. She has been honored by VIT as an active researcher. Her current areas of interest include IoT, cloud, big data security and blockchain.

P. Ashok Kumar is currently pursuing his PhD at the Vellore Institute of Technology (VIT), Vellore, India. He is working as an Assistant Professor (Junior) in the School of Computer Science and Engineering, VIT. His research areas include topic mining and machine learning.

K. Lalitha received a BTech IT degree from CSI College of Engineering, The Nilgris, in 2005 and an MTech IT degree from Anna University of Technology in 2009. Currently, she is working on her PhD in Wireless Sensor Networks and working as an Assistant Professor in the Department of IT, Kongu Engineering College, Erode. She has conducted various workshops and published several papers in the areas of wireless sensor networks, mobile computing and network security. Her research areas of interest include wireless sensor networks, mobile computing and Internet of Things. She is a lifetime member of CSI and IAENG.

Vinay Reddy Mallidi is presently working as a Software Developer at Hexagon Capability Center, Hyderabad. He received a BTech in Computer Science and Engineering from VIT University, Vellore, in 2019. He has an overall experience of three years, out of which he spent one year in the industry and two years in the teaching assistance and research fields. His research interests include network security, cyber security and data analytics.

M.R. Manu is currently working as a Computer Science Teacher in Ministry of Education, Abudabi, UAE. He worked as an Assistant Professor in the School of Computing Science and Engineering, Galgotias University, NCR Delhi, India. He has an ME in Computer Science and Engineering from Anna University Taramani Campus, Tamil Nadu, India and is currently pursuing a PhD in Computer Science and Engineering from Galgotias University, NCR Delhi, India. His areas of interest include data, networks and network security. He has undergone different research projects in networks specialization and published 16 papers in various international and national journals. He is currently writing a monograph and chapters in books to be published by CRC Press, Springer and Elsevier.

Iyapparaja Meenakshisundaram is an Associate Professor in the School of Information Technology and Engineering, VIT, Vellore. He has 12 years of experience in the teaching field. He received his PhD at Anna University, Chennai, BE degree from Anna University, Chennai and ME degree from Anna University of Technology, Coimbatore. He received the University Rank holder award for his ME degree. His research interests include machine learning, blockchain, software testing and agile testing. He has published 40 papers in reputed journals, conferences and book chapters. He has filed a patent in the field of machine learning. He is a lifetime member of ISTE.

Neethu Narayanan is presently working as an Assistant Professor in the Department of Vocational Studies at St. Mary's College, Thrissur, Calicut University, Kerala, India. She received a BTech in Computer Science and Engineering from Calicut University, Kerala, India, in 2016 and an MTech degree in Computer Science and Engineering from Abdul Kalam Technical University, Kerala, India, in 2018. She has overall experience of two years in the teaching field. Her research interests include image processing, machine learning, network security and theoretical foundations of computer science. She has published papers in international journals and conferences.

S.M. Narendran is a Research Associate, pursuing his PhD at SASTRA Deemed to be University, India, since July 2018. He has a Bachelor of Engineering degree in Electronics and Communication Engineering and a Master of Science degree in Telecommunications Engineering from the University of Trento, Italy. He is currently pursuing his research work in the fields of machine learning and predictive analytics.

C. Poongodi is an Associate Professor in the Department of Information Technology at Kongu Engineering College, Perundurai. She obtained a BE degree in Electronics and Communication Engineering from Bharathiar University, Coimbatore in 2001, and ME degree in Computer Science Engineering from Bharathiar University in 2002, and a PhD in Information and Communication Engineering from Anna University, Chennai in 2013. She has published 20 papers in international conferences and 10 papers in international journals. She is a lifetime member of CSI. Her research areas include wireless networks, delay tolerant networks and Internet of Things.

D. Sathya is an Assistant Professor II in the Department Computer Science and Engineering at Kumaraguru College of Technology, Coimbatore, Tamil Nadu, India. She received her BE degree in Computer Science and Engineering from Maharaja Engineering College, Coimbatore and an ME degree in Computer Science and Engineering from Anna University, Coimbatore. She completed a PhD at Anna University, Chennai in Sensor Networks. She has published 25 papers in both conferences and journals.

Kiran Singh is presently working as an Assistant Professor, Department of Computer Science and Engineering, Galgotias University. She received an MCA degree from Maharishi Dayanand University in 2008 and an MTech degree in Computer Science and Engineering from Rajiv Gandhi Proudyogiki Vishwavidyalaya, Bhopal in 2015. Overall she has 11 years of experience. Her research interests include image processing, big data and IoT. She has published papers in international journals and conferences.

K. Sneha is currently working as Assistant Professor in Computer Science Department of an affiliated college under the University of Calicut. She completed a BTech in Computer Science and Engineering from the University of Calicut and an ME in Computer and Communication from Anna University, Tamil Nadu. Her areas of interest are big data and image processing. She has been a part of many research projects and has published more than 10 papers in various international and national journals with SCI and Scopus indexing.

S. Sreeji received an ME degree in Computer Science and Engineering from Sathyabama University, Chennai, India, in 2014 and a BE degree in Computer Science and engineering from Anna University, Chennai, India, in 2009. He is currently pursuing a PhD in Computer Science and Engineering at Galgotias University, Greater Noida, India. From 2009 to 2012, he worked as a Software Engineer at Tenon Services, Bangalore. Since 2014, he has worked at various universities. Currently, he is working in Galgotias University, Greater Noida, India.

Rishabh Kumar Srivastava is currently a student in the Department of Computer Science and Engineering at Galgotias University. He is very keen on the artificial intelligence field and blockchain industry. His research interests include blockchain, IoT and artificial intelligence. He has published papers in international journals and conferences on blockchain and assistive devices.

V. Sudha is an Assistant Professor II in the Department of Computer Science and Engineering at Kumaraguru College of Technology, Coimbatore, Tamil Nadu, India. She received her BE degree in Computer Science and Engineering from VMKV Engineering College, Salem, and an ME degree in Computer Science and Engineering from CEG Campus, Anna University. She is currently pursuing her PhD at Anna University in Theoretical Computer Science.

A. Umamakeswari received her BE from A.C.C.E.T, Karaikudi, ME from NIT, Trichy, and PhD from SASTRA University, Thanjavur, India. Currently, she is working as a Dean in the School of Computing, SASTRA University. Her research areas include Internet of Things, wireless sensor network, cloud computing, embedded system and blockchain. She has visited Hungary, Japan and Singapore and has published 168 papers in SCOPUS/SCI – SCIE indexed journals and conference proceedings.

S. Vijayalakshmi pursed Bachelor of Science in Computer Science, Master of Computer Application, and Master of Philosophy from Bharathidasan University, Tiruchirappalli, Tamil Nadu, in 1995, 1998 and 2006, respectively. She received her doctorate in 2014. She has been working as an Associate Professor, Galgotias University, Greater Noida, Uttar Pradesh, India. She has 19 years of teaching experience and 10 years of research experience. She has published many papers in the area of image processing, especially in medical imaging.

V. Madhu Viswanatham is currently a Professor at the School of Computing Science and Engineering, Vellore Institute of Technology (VIT), Vellore, India. He has several years of experience working in academia, teaching and research. He received his PhD in Computer Science and Technology from SK University, Andhra Pradesh, India. He has guided four PhD scholars and supervised MTech and BTech students. He has organized several workshops and faculty development programs. His research interests include information security, mobile and wireless systems, image processing, social networks and intelligent systems.

Chapter 1

Blockchain Foundation

Kavita Saini

Contents

1.1 Introduction

Blockchain has gained great prominence over the past years. Blockchain is a decentralized computation and information sharing platform that enables multiple authoritative domains to cooperate, coordinate and collaborate in the decision-making process. It is also termed as an open distributed ledger that can note the transactions among multiple parties productively and in a certain and long-lasting way. This technology also ensures that the transactions are made efficiently in a verifiable and permanent mode [1].

Encompassing a technology behind cryptocurrency exchanges, it has now shown promise in almost every other sector of the economy as it's a secure, reliable and tamper-proof way of recording transactions and exchanging data.

As a decentralized ledger, blockchain keeps recording all the transactions across a peer-to-peer network and helps the participants to keep track and confirm transactions being done in the chain. There is no need of any central authority to keep the track of transactions. Cryptocurrency, settling trades, voting and supply chain management are only a few names of blockchain-enabled applications [2].

A blockchain is a list of cryptographically signed transactional records shared by the participating nodes in the network. Each record has a timestamp and link to earlier transactions, and it is a predominant architectural design of distributed ledger concept. The authorized participants with proper access rights can track the history of transactional events that belong to any participant. However, there is a significant disconnect between the expectation in the market sector and the reality. A blockchain-based approach to the applications will have better control over the transactions, and this can be addressed by establishing a decentralized approach to business model [3].

1.2 Background

Blockchain has a strong leverage in the application development in terms of loosely coupled independence of centralized application control and security by way of smart contract and ledger concepts. The business networks can share the record of transactions and can be updated in the distributed environment with secure, authenticated, verifiable and trusted participants. This chapter focuses on the concepts of blockchain and the identification of opportunities offered by them so that the businesses can take advantage in terms of dealing with the application of blockchain-oriented software engineering, interaction with the intelligent devices and the interoperability with the legacy applications and inter-blockchain [2].

The main hitch to traditional transactions is the loss of personal confidentiality, data protection and ownership of information and transactions. From this time forth, 'centralized' control model of applications media might be a thing of the past blockchain technology [4]. An approach that accommodates blockchain has no single point failure as the data are organized and available in multiple blocks. Hence, blockchain can be adopted for the security of transactions. Some of the significant objectives of blockchain applications are achieving agreement, cooperation, collaboration, participation and activity [5].

Blockchain is a distributed database solution that maintains a continuously growing list of data records that are confirmed by the nodes participating in it. The data are recorded in a public ledger, including the information of every transaction ever completed. The transaction details are shared and available to all nodes. This feature makes the system more transparent than centralized transactions involving a third party.

To develop a blockchain-enabled application, Eethereum brings the next-generation 'decentralized' models [6]. Ethereum is an open software platform that allows developers to build and make available decentralized applications. Blockchain helps with the verification of transactions after applying a pre-defined consensus protocol [7].

1.2.1 Distributed Systems

A distributed and secure ledger resolves almost all the security problems of centralized databases, where a user can see the transactions done by himself. Whereas, a distributed ledger keeps track of all transactions done by all the involved participants. Figure 1.1 depicts the structure of a distributed system.

Blockchain is a decentralized ledger of transactions, where every network participant validates the transaction so that the data stored is immutable and cannot be forged. The main advantage of blockchain is to decrease the time of processing of transaction significantly and reduce the associated costs nearly to zero by locking out multiple risk factors (like double-spending) altogether.

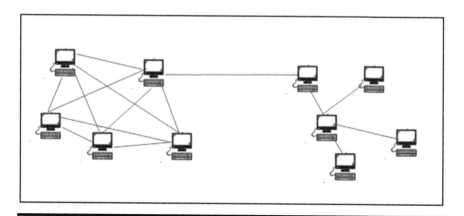

Figure 1.1   Distributed system.

1.3 Principles of Blockchain Technology

Blockchain ensures tamper-proof data blocks that are distributed and connected. Blockchain is essentially a decentralized, distributed ledger-based technology that was originally designed for monitoring financial transactions [7, 8]. Apart from security, the other promising features of blockchain include scalability, effective mechanisms to store, manage, track and coordinate multiple devices, reduce operational and maintenance costs and establish trust between anonymous entities. Recently, extensive focus has been on developing solutions using blockchain across other domains.

The five basic underlying principles for the blockchain technology as shown in Figure 1.2 are distributed database, peer-to-peer transmission, transparency with pseudonymity, irreversibility of records and computational logic. These powerful theories make this technology acceptable all around the world.

1.3.1 Decentralized

Blockchain ensures decentralization which in turn ensures privacy and security through a distributed consensus mechanism. In the present scenario, due to eavesdroppers, there are a lot of issues faced by each and everyone in day-to-day [6, 9]. Each entity on a blockchain has access to the entire database and its complete history. No single entity controls the information and every entity can verify the records of its transaction partners directly, without an intermediary. Blockchain is basically an open and distributed ledger. This ledger records all the transactions between two entities efficiently and in a verifiable and permanent way.

Blockchain technology provides capability to produce a distributed but still unified record and facilitates various industries to use this technology for maintaining secure and distributed applications.

1.3.2 Peer-to-Peer Transmission

Communication occurs directly between peers instead of through a central node. Each node stores and forwards information to all other nodes or entities.

1.3.3 Transparency with Pseudonymity

Each and every transaction in the blockchain has various values associated with it. The information related to each transaction includes who have done the transaction,

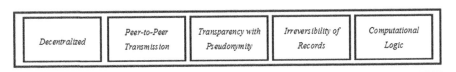

Figure 1.2   Five basic principles for blockchain technology.

timestamp, along with the pervious and the next hash values. Each transaction and the value associated with it are visible to all the participants of the application [10].

1.3.4 Irreversibility of Records

In blockchain, 'chain' means that once any entity performs any transaction, it is entered into the database and the information is updated in all the entities or nodes [10, 11]. Once a transaction is entered in the database and the accounts are updated, the records cannot be altered, as they are linked to every transaction record that came before them (hence the term 'chain'). A number of approaches and technologies are deployed to make sure that the changes made in the database are permanent, available to all the entities involved in the transaction and chronologically ordered.

1.3.5 Computational Logic

The transactions in blockchain can be tied to computational logic as there is a digital ledger and in essence programmed. There is a wide possibility for setting up rules and algorithms where these algorithms could automatically trigger transactions among various entities or nodes. The main aim of blockchain is to keep the transactions transparent, without intervention of any central authority. It is all achieved as the information written on a block can't be changed going to backdate. Here, each transaction has to be authenticated by the community of users, thus limiting the need of government or bank. Ethereum is one of the blockchain-based distributed computing platforms. Blockchain facilitates the most reliable transactions among unreliable contributors in the network, and hence, raised noteworthy attention among scientists, developers and research scholars [12].

1.4 Consensus Mechanisms in Blockchain

Blockchain consensus protocols assure that the nodes in the network are synchronized with each other. Consensus means the nodes in the blockchain network agree on the same state for self-auditing across a distributed network. The main objective of the consensus protocol is to ensure a single chain is utilized and followed, and it is one of the significant revolutionary aspects of blockchain technology. Consensus protocols provide rewards and incentives for the participants who are maintaining the blockchain. The rewards in blockchain are in the form of tokens or cryptocurrencies, and the competition for confirming the next block in the chain is extremely difficult. The complete history of transaction is maintained in digital currencies to check the user's balance at any time.

These consensus protocols are the backbones of the heavily disruptive technology 'blockchain'. Consensus protocols allow a decentralized network to arrive at an agreement about the state of the network. In a centralized system or federal organization, all the decisions are taken by a single elected leader or a board of members. Whereas, in a decentralized network, a leader is not available to take a decision independently; instead, a group of systems/nodes is involved in the decision-making process. This process supports a decision, subject to the interest of all the people involved in the decision-making process, called consensus.

Achieving consensus is an acceptance among nodes on the network for a data value even if some nodes are unreliable. Consensus ensures the correct set of operations in the presence of faulty individuals in a distributed environment. The properties of reliability and fault tolerance of network are determined by consensus mechanisms. All participating nodes agree on a common content-updating protocol for their public ledger to maintain a consistent state. This is known as consensus mechanism. When consensus is reached among the nodes, the blocks are created and added to the existing ledger for later usage [13].

1.4.1 Types of Consensus Protocols

The different types of consensus algorithms are Proof of Work (PoW), Proof of Stake (PoS), Delegated Proof of Stake (DPoS), Leased Proof of Stake (LPoS), Proof of Elapsed Time (PoET), Practical Byzantine Fault Tolerance (PBFT), Simplified Byzantine Fault Tolerance (SBFT) and Delegated Byzantine Fault Tolerance (DBFT). In this chapter, a few consensus protocols are defined.

1.4.1.1 Proof of Work (PoW)

Proof of work is one of the original consensus algorithm used in a blockchain. Nakamoto Consensus can be defined as a probabilistic approach, which is non-deterministic in nature [13]. In this model, all nodes need not agree on the same value; instead, they agree on the probability of the value to be correct. This algorithm is used to confirm transactions and produce new blocks to the chain. With PoW, miners compete against each other to complete transactions on the network and get rewarded.

1.4.1.2 Proof of Stake (PoS)

A new consensus algorithm has been designed to overcome higher use of energy in the PoW protocol to ensure mining activity is conducted in a more cultured manner without wasting energy or computational power. A group of validators will give a specific amount as a security deposit to participate in the block generation process. They will buy cryptocurrencies instead of investing in buying equipment for rigorous computational activity. Each one who wants to participate in the block mining race will deposit some cryptocurrencies as a stake in the network. The higher the stake is, higher is the possibility of the node to become a validator. Based on a random process, the validator is selected to generate a block. The validator who generates a valid block will get incentives for their work. If the block generated is not included in the chain, then the validator will be penalized and lose their stake. In the PoW mechanism, penalty for nodes generating invalid block is only in terms of wasted computational power and resource, whereas in the PoS, nodes lose their stakes if invalid blocks are generated or fraudulent behavior is exhibited. If all the correct or honest nodes in the network follow the protocol and own greater than 50% stake in the network, then the possibility of an already generated block to be revoked from the network drops exponentially.

1.4.1.3 Proof of Elapsed Time (PoET)

It is a consensus scheme working centered on a back-off mechanism that is purely random. Each validator node in the network waits for a time, whose length is random and then backs off after the time is elapsed. Once a node has finished its back-off, it becomes the validator. It is a trusted back-off method for the nodes where each and every validator should be verified and trusted completely. The random back-off is achieved by the use of microprocessors precisely designed for this purpose. A new validator node, while joining the network, gets the back-off program from the peer nodes within the same network [14]. The newly joined validator sends an attestation report to the host network to ensure that the required authentic program for back-off has been loaded successfully. Once the validator fulfills the back-off requirement for a random amount of time, it will generate a new block with the set of all unprocessed transactions it has heard of. A certificate is generated for completing the trusted back-off mechanism and sent along with the block. The back-off mechanism proposed in the PoET algorithm can tolerate any number of faulty validators present in the network. A validator who is rich with a lot of resources can invest in multiple instances to cut short the expected duration of back-off.

1.4.1.4 Practical Byzantine Fault Tolerance (PBFT)

The PBFT model is a fault tolerance algorithm primarily focusing on practical state machine replication, which overcomes Byzantine failures with independent node failures (dishonest nodes) that propagate incorrect or faulty messages. This algorithm works on asynchronous systems with overall optimized performance and very little increase in latency. The system is modeled with one node assumed as a leader and all other nodes considered backups. All the nodes present in the system communicate with each other and the design is likely to bring all the honest nodes to an agreement through a majority. There is a slight overhead in the communication of message since each message has to prove its origin and verify there is no alteration happened in the messages during transmission.

Other than the aforementioned protocols, there are other protocols also available, including, Directed Acyclic Graphs (DAG), Proof of Activity (PoA), Proof of Importance (PoI), Proof of Capacity (PoC), Proof of Burn (PoB), Proof of Weight (PoWeight), etc.

1.5 How Blockchain Works

Blockchain is useful only where multiple entities are collaborating and sharing information. Blockchain maintains local copies in participating node to ensure consistency. The overall functionality of blockchain is depicted in Figure 1.3.

Blockchain applications work in decentralized manner. The nodes that are unknown to each other work together by sharing the data in the form of public ledger. The data could be any historical information of transaction like bank transaction that will be available to everyone for future computation [15]. The public ledger ensures consistency, i.e., the local copies of the data of all the nodes are kept identical and always updated based on global information.

1.5.1 Phases of Transaction among Multiple Parties in Blockchain

This demonstrates that the blockchain is tamper-proof and no transaction can be reversed.

1.5.1.1 Broadcast the Transaction

Each and every transaction is announced to the entire network for verification through broadcasting.

1.5.1.2 Collection and Verification of Transactions

The transactions are verified by the participating nodes and will be added to the block according to the block size (1 MB for Bitcoin).

B L O C K C H A I N

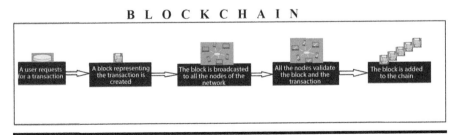

A user requests for a transaction → A block representing the transaction is created → The block is broadcasted to all the nodes of the network → All the nodes validate the block and the transaction → The block is added to the chain

Figure 1.3 Blockchain functionality.

1.5.1.3 *Mining Using Consensus Protocol*

Mining process is to solve the cryptographic puzzle. If a miner is able to solve the puzzle, add this block to the blockchain. This is done using a consensus as PoW as in Bitcoin. There are consensus protocols used in the blockchain like PoS, PoB and PoET.

1.5.1.4 *Updating the Blockchain*

The nodes receive the block and they can accept the block, if the computed PoW is correct and contains valid transactions [15]. Nodes add the block to their copy of the ledger. The hash of the last block is used as the previous hash of the successive block [16, 17]. If solutions are obtained by two miners at the same time, the valid blockchain is the one which is long. If the block of transactions or PoW is invalid, the block is discarded, and the search for a valid block is continued by the nodes. Miners are allowed to earn rewards upon successful mining process. So, blockchain works like a public ledger with the following characteristics:

■ Security enhancement
■ Immutable
■ Distributed in nature
■ Peer to Peer
■ Use of consensus mechanism

1.6 Compelling Use Cases for Blockchain Technology

The most compelling use cases which I believe will greatly reduce inefficiencies and unlock value are in areas of existing industry, where trusted intermediaries are required to record, validate and reconcile transactions without really adding additional value to the original transaction [18, 19].

The areas for improved performance include industries and organizations:

■ Logistics
■ Electronic cash
■ Education and assessment system
■ Cloud security
■ Secure IoT applications
■ Charity
■ Foodchain industry
■ Supply Chain Management (SCM)
■ Healthcare
■ Big data
■ Electronic cash

1.7 The First Application: Bitcoin (₿)

Bitcoin (₿) is the first application of blockchain. Satoshi Nakamoto has described the first cryptocurrency in 2008, but as an open-source software, it came into the picture in 2009. The cryptocurrency must be secured against attacks in the blockchain and it does not rely on a single centralized authority for security, where the users are not having any prior knowledge about the versions of valid record [20]. An attacker may spend some money and the transaction is reverted back with the own version of the blockchain; this is known as double spend. According to a Gartner report, there will be an exponential growth of blockchain by 2020 due to the implementation of smart contract, which includes tokenization and decentralization [21]. Furlonger said, 'Blockchain is not just a technology, it is a societal change'.

The units of this cryptocurrency is called Bitcoin (Figure 1.4). It is used to store and transmit value among all the participants in the Bitcoin network. It is a peer-to-peer technology, which is not governed by any central authority or bank. In comparison to the existing currencies, Bitcoins are secure and virtual. There are no physical coins available; rather, it is entirely a virtual currency [22].

The system is run by the Bitcoin protocol and it is based on mathematics unlike the conventional currencies that are based on the fixed quantity or fiat currencies.

The PoW consensus displayed in Figure 1.5 has been successfully verified by the implementation of the protocol in the 'Bitcoin' blockchain [23].

Transactions are broadcasted to the network and then miners look for transactions and start the mining process. Miners create a block and include the transactions and start PoW [16, 24]. When the PoW is created by the miners by solving the cryptographic puzzle, they broadcast PoW to the network, where the other miners verify the PoW and the process starts over again.

Figure 1.4 Bitcoin (₿).

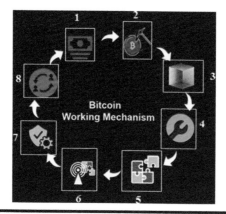

Figure 1.5 Bitcoin working mechanism.

1.7.1 Key Characteristics of Cryptocurrencies

- Decentralized, the ledger is distributed and saved in nodes around the world [25]
- Trustless, meaning that the network as a whole verifies and guarantees the accuracy of the data without the need for a source of trust (normally, this role is played by banks in any money transaction)
- Peer to peer
- Public ledger, all transactions can be verified
- Have mathematical consensus rules (PoW, PoS, etc.)
- Borderless
- Not issued by any government or bank

A cryptocurrency is a tradable digital asset or digital form of money, built on blockchain technology that only exists online [26]. Cryptocurrencies use cryptography to verify and secure transactions, hence the name. There are currently well over one thousand different cryptocurrencies in the world and many people see them as the lynchpin for a fairer, future economy [27]. This chapter discusses the various digital cryptocurrencies using blockchain as an underlying layer.

1.8 Conclusion

In this chapter, we have discussed the basics of blockchain technology. Blockchain as a distributed database provides solution that maintains a continuously growing list of data records, which are confirmed by the nodes (people concerned) participating in it. We have also discussed the effectiveness of the various applications of blockchain such as increased security, transparency and cost reduction of various transactions taking place in real life.

References

[1] N. Gensollen, V. Gauthier, M. Becker, and M. Marot, "Stability and performance of coalitions of prosumers through diversification in the smart grid," *IEEE Trans. Smart Grid*, vol. 9, no. 2, pp. 963–970, March 2018.

[2] Nakamoto, Satoshi, and A. Bitcoin. "A peer-to-peer electronic cash system." *Bitcoin.– URL:* https://bitcoin. org/bitcoin. pdf 4 (2008).

[3] Blockchain technology in India: Opportunities and challenges, April 2017 (ASSOCHAM). https://www2.deloitte.com/content/dam/Deloitte/in/Documents/strategy/in-strategy-innovation-blockchain-technology-india-opportunities-challenges-noexp.pdf

[4] Jesse Yli-Huumo, Deokyoon Ko, Sujin Choi, Sooyong Park, and Kari Smolander, "Where Is current research on blockchain technology?—A systematic review," *PLOS ONE*, Edited by Houbing Song, vol. 11, no. 10, p. e0163477, October 3 2016.

[5] M. Iansiti and K. R. Lakhani, "The truth about blockchain," *Harvard Business Review*, January–February 2017.

[6] Saugata Dutta and Kavita Saini, "Evolution of blockchain technology in business applications," *Journal of Emerging Technologies and Innovative Research (JETIR)*, vol. 6, no. 9, pp. 240–244, JETIR May 2019.

[7] V. Gramoli, "From blockchain consensus back to Byzantine consensus," *Future Generation Computer Systems*, 2017, http://dx.doi.org/10.1016/j.future.2017.09.023.

[8] https://blockgeeks.com/guides/bitcoin-developer/.

[9] H. Massias, X.S. Avila, and J.-J. Quisquater, "Design of a secure timestamping service with minimal trust requirements," In: 20th Symposium on Information Theory in the Benelux, May 1999.

[10] Kavita Saini, "A future's dominant technology blockchain: Digital transformation," In: IEEE International Conference on Computing, Power and Communication Technologies 2018 (GUCON 2018), Galgotias University, Greater Noida, pp. 28–29 September, 2018.

[11] S. Haber and W.S. Stornetta, "How to time-stamp a digital document," *Journal of Cryptology*, vol. 3, no. 2, pp. 99–111, 1991.

[12] H. Suo, J. Wan, C. Zou, and J. Liu, "Security in the internet of things: A review," In: Computer Science and Electronics Engineering (ICCSEE), International Conference, IEEE, vol. 3, pp. 648–651, 2012.

[13] Daniel Kraft, "Difficulty control for blockchain-based consensus systems," *Peer-to-Peer Networking and Applications*, vol. 9, no. 2, pp. 397–413, 2016.

[14] D. Bayer, S. Haber, and W.S. Stornetta, "Improving the efficiency and reliability of digital time-stamping," *Sequences II: Methods in Communication, Security and Computer Science*, pp. 329–334, 1993.

[15] https://www.binance.vision/blockchain/blockchain-use-cases.

[16] Marc Pilkington, "Blockchain works or blockchain technology: Principles and applications," 2016.

[17] W. Dai, "b-money," http://www.weidai.com/bmoney.txt, 1998.

[18] S. Barber, X. Boyen, E. Shi, E. Uzun, "Bitter to Better — How to Make Bitcoin a Better Currency." In: Keromytis A.D. (eds.) *Financial Cryptography and Data Security. FC 2012.* Lecture Notes in Computer Science, vol. 7397, 2012. Springer, Berlin, Heidelberg. DOI https://doi.org/10.1007/978-3-642-32946-3_29.

[19] S. Haber and W.S. Stornetta, "Secure names for bit-strings," In: Proceedings of the 4th ACM Conference on Computer and Communications Security, pp. 28–35, April 1997.

[20] R.C. Merkle, "Protocols for public key cryptosystems," In: Proceedings 1980 Symposium on Security and Privacy, IEEE Computer Society, pp. 122–133, April 1980.

[21] V. Buterin, "A next generation smart contract and decentralized application platform," 2014. [Online]. Available: https://github.com/ethereum/wiki/wiki/White-Paper.

[22] D. Schwartz, N. Youngs, A. Britto, et al., "The ripple protocol consensus algorithm," Ripple Labs, Inc. White Paper, vol. 5, 2014.

[23] W. Feller, "*An Introduction to Probability Theory and Its Applications*," 1957.

[24] B. Alangot, and K. Achuthan, "Trace and track: Enhanced pharma supply chain infrastructure to prevent fraud," In: International Conference on Ubiquitous Communications and Network Computing, Springer, Cham, pp. 189–195. August 2017.

[25] D. S. Baars, "Towards self-sovereign identity using blockchain technology," Master's thesis, University of Twente, Enschede, The Netherlands, 2016.

[26] Saini, K., Agarwal, V., Varshney, A., & Gupta, A. (2018, October). E2EE for Data Security for Hybrid Cloud Services: A Novel Approach. In *2018 International Conference on Advances in Computing, Communication Control and Networking (ICACCCN)* (pp. 340-347). IEEE.

[27] Adam Back, Matt Corallo, Luke Dashjr, Mark Friedenbach, Gregory Maxwell, Andrew Miller, Andrew Poelstra, Jorge Timón, and Pieter Wuille, "Enabling blockchain innovations with pegged sidechains," http://www.opensciencereview.com/papers/123/enablingblockchain-innovations-with-pegged-sidechains, 72, 2014.

Chapter 2

Distributed Consensus Protocols and Algorithms

J. Jayapriya and N. Jeyanthi

Contents

2.1 Consensus Protocol – An Introduction

Consensus protocols allow a decentralized network to arrive at an agreement about the state of the network. In a centralized system or federal organization, all the decisions are taken by a single elected leader or a board of members. Whereas, in a decentralized network, a leader is not available to take a decision independently; instead, a group of systems/nodes is involved in the decision-making process. This process supports a decision, subject to the interest of all the people involved in the decision-making process, called consensus. The mechanism used to achieve consensus in a distributed or decentralized network is defined as consensus protocol. These consensus protocols are the backbones of the heavily disruptive technology 'Blockchain'. Blockchain is a decentralized peer-to-peer system with no centralized authority. By definition, this is a system devoid of any type of corruption from a single point, but it results in some complex problems like reaching a collective decision and scheming mechanisms to get things done in such an environment. Consensus protocol solves the above problems in blockchain by allowing the nodes to collectively reach an agreement on the transactions without relying on a third party. In voting systems, the solution with the majority of vote wins, there is no weightage for emotions or welfare of the minority. In a consensus system, decision is made for the benefit of the whole group scattered around the system, paving the way to create a more democratic and nondiscriminatory society. The famous implementation of blockchain is 'Bitcoin'; a cryptocurrency implemented using consensus protocol. Behind any cryptocurrency in today's world, there exists a consensus mechanism. Consensus protocols also ensure a mutual agreement is reached in the cryptocurrency and there is no double spending. These protocols are implemented in blockchains using algorithms specifically designed for this purpose, known as consensus algorithms.

Due to their usage in distributed environments, they are also known as distributed consensus algorithms.

2.2 Distributed Consensus Algorithms

Distributed consensus algorithms are the algorithms designed for reaching consensus in distributed environment. The reached consensus should be a satisfactory solution supported by all individuals in the network, even though it is not their personal favorite solution. These algorithms make sure the next block/value added to the system is the one and only version of truth [1]. This way we can define consensus as a vibrant way of reaching a general agreement and commonality of faith within the group. Figure 2.1 shows illustration of consensus problem using three nodes: Node 1, Node 2 and Node 3. Node 1 proposes 'value 2', Node 3 proposes 'value 1' to the other nodes, while Node 2 keeps quiet. Consensus algorithms should be designed in a way to address this problem model and reach on some value ultimately [2].

Distributed consensus algorithms have the following properties (see Figure 2.2) to make the system work appropriately and prevent any kind of failure or glitch in the system:

1. Collaboration – All the nodes in the system should work together with the interest of the whole group as the objective
2. Cooperation – System entities should work as a group rather than an individual with personal interests
3. Inclusive – Make sure there is a maximum number of participation from the group

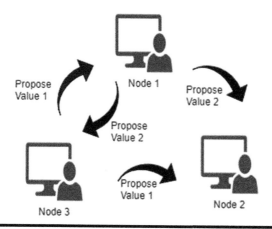

Figure 2.1   Consensus model.

Properties of Consensus Mechanisms

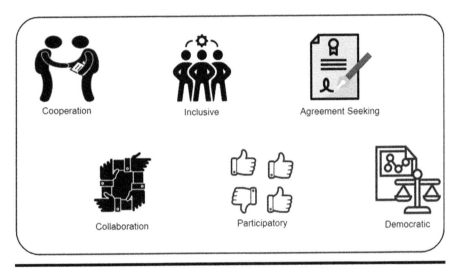

Figure 2.2 Properties of consensus models.

4. Participatory – Active participation by the group is required for being successful
5. Agreement Seeking – Bring as much as agreement from the individual nodes participating in the system
6. Democratic – Each and every vote cast by the individuals should have an equal weightage

Consensus algorithm following the above mentioned properties forms the primary root structure of the revolutionary technology, blockchain. Consensus algorithms deployed in the various blockchains make them differ from each other. This functionality enables millions of nodes to exist in the same space, while they never exist mutually or hinder each other.

The processes highlighted in Figure 2.3 show the application of consensus algorithms in blockchain [1]. Such consensus algorithms reach consensus if the following conditions are satisfied:

1. Agreement – Each one of the non-faulty nodes in the network should decide on the same output value
2. Termination – Each and every non-faulty node should ultimately decide on some output value. This is the termination condition

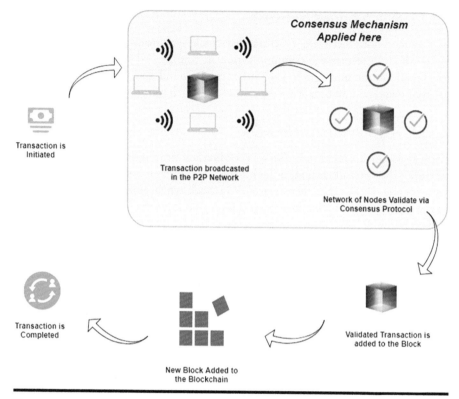

Figure 2.3   Application of consensus in blockchain.

There are a lot of consensus algorithms designed and implemented in real-world use cases, but each of those algorithms may vary in terminology, validity conditions (to achieve the final output value) and procedures of handling the decision-making process.

2.3   Consensus System Model

Consensus systems are message passing systems modeled contingent on the following conditions/assumptions.

2.3.1   Network Synchrony

Network synchrony can be defined as the degree of synchronization between countless components in the system harmonizing with each other [3]. Based on the coordination, networks can be divided into synchronous and asynchronous networks.

2.3.1.1 Synchronous Network

In a synchronous network, a centralized clock synchronization service is used to coordinate the message communication in rounds. All the nodes in the system broadcast the messages to each other in ith round and the nodes process the received messages and broadcast the output in i + 1th round.

2.3.1.2 Asynchronous Network

There is no clock synchronization or coordination procedure in an asynchronous network. The network accomplishes all the tasks without any rule in an opportunistic manner [1, 4]. Since there is no rule or clock synchronization or upper bound on the message transmission delay, there is no guarantee the messages will be delivered properly [3].

2.3.2 Component Faults

The network may have some faulty or dishonest nodes leading to failures in the systems. Depending on the type of fault created, the failure can be classified as the ones listed below.

2.3.2.1 Crash Failure

The node abruptly stops working and does not resume even after a good amount of time. In this case, other components detect such a crash has happened and adjust all the decisions to be made locally.

2.3.2.2 Byzantine Failure

There is no absolute condition resulting in such failure; Byzantine failure occurs arbitrarily. A node with such failure can either remain quiet or send conflicting messages to the other nodes in the network. Such a node will not create any suspicion of the faulty process or malicious activity within the system.

2.4 Consensus Protocols

Consensus protocols are the set of rules defining the working of a consensus system. Two rules are essentially defined as follows for these protocols.

2.4.1 Message Passing Rule

The rule is followed by the components to broadcast or pass on the messages to the other components within the network.

2.4.2 Processing Rule

Once a component receives a message, it should process the message and change the internal state of the system in response to the message.

Message passing and processing is implemented in consensus model by three main type of players:

1. Proposers – Proposers are the leaders elected in the network
2. Acceptors – These actors listen to the values proposed by the proposers and provide response to the values
3. Learners – The nodes which know of the final decided output value and update the state are known as learners

The general framework of consensus model consists of three main steps:

1. Election – All the nodes combined select the next leader, who in turn will have the power to propose the next valid output value
2. Vote – All the honest and non-faulty nodes in the network listen to the output value proposed by the leader, and validate and process it as the next valid value
3. Decide – All the honest and non-faulty nodes must decide and come to a unanimity on the same truthful output value

2.5 Need of Consensus Algorithms

All the nodes present in the network may not be honest or non-faulty nodes. Hence, consensus algorithms are needed for blockchain or any other decentralized network to comply with the required set of functionalities to be implemented in the network mentioned below:

1. All the components in the system decide on a commonly agreed value
2. Every node in the network should behave in the same manner for a certain request
3. There should not be any impact due to faulty or dishonest nodes and unreliable network communication

For the node to be non-faulty, it should be devoid of all the possible failures like crash failure and Byzantine failure. The network is said to be crash fault tolerant if it tolerates at least one crash failure, and Byzantine fault tolerant if it tolerates at least one Byzantine failure. The main problem in Byzantine is to reach on a common value. If there is an event of error or failure in the system, the nodes cannot reach an agreement or the difficulty value might be higher. Consensus systems can work successfully only if all the actors in the network work in harmony. If there is a malfunction even in one system, the entire system may crash. Malfunctioning system can cause inconsistency and it is not ideal for a decentralized network. Thus, consensus algorithms are inevitable to wade through the failure or inconsistency. Consensus algorithms do not face this type of problems and their primary goal is to reach a common agreement by some means making such systems more trustworthy and fault tolerant with better output.

In multi-agent systems or any other distributed systems, the core obstacle is reaching consensus in the system. There is a lot of difficulties involved when a distributed network system tries to come to an agreement or reach consensus on a value much needed for the decision to be taken during the computation process. Any component in such a system is unpredictable and prone to failure making the network untrustworthy as a whole. A number of bad or dishonest nodes trying to tamper the network heavily influence the functioning of the network. If a system has only good actors with good intention and honest behavior, then consensus is not needed for them. Nevertheless, distributed systems in the real-world scenario may have any number of bad actors making the consensus an essential and difficult to implement element.

2.6 Byzantine Generals Problem

A reliable distributed computer system must be able to tolerate the failure of one or more components of the system. In case of failure, the component may send conflicting or malicious information to the other components of the system. To illustrate this scenario, we will consider the famous Byzantine Generals Problem.

Several teams of lieutenants headed by generals are waiting outside a city planning for an attack. The generals will be able to communicate only through messengers and agree on a plan whether to attack the city or retreat. There might be traitors present in the teams who may prevent the generals to agree upon a single plan. This problem is famously known as the Byzantine Generals problem. We need an algorithm to guarantee a solution to the above problem guaranteeing:

1. All the honest or loyal generals agree upon the same decision or plan for action
   a. In this case, we assume loyal generals proceed as per the steps in the algorithm
   b. Traitors may perform the next course of action as per their wish
   c. The algorithm must ensure condition (1) above is met irrespective of the presence of traitors
   d. All the loyal people should agree upon a judicious action plan
2. The presence of few numbers of dishonest people or traitors should not result in the loyal people adopting a bad plan

2.7 Fischer–Lynch–Paterson (FLP) Impossibility

The consensus process involves asynchronous systems, which may be unreliable; such systems may not be able to come to an agreement or terminate even if there exists one faulty node. This nonterminating condition is known Fischer–Lynch–Paterson (FLP) impossibility result.

Consider a synchronous environment, for example, in those systems, messages will be delivered within fixed time duration. If the time frame is expired and the messages are still not delivered, the system terminates, hence there is no possibility of nontermination, whereas in an asynchronous environment, there is no guarantee of the message delivery or no fixed time frame for the message delivery. We cannot make a decision on the maximum time limit for the message delivery; achieving consensus in such an environment is much tougher than in the synchronous systems. Even a single faulty node can make it impossible for the system to reach consensus in asynchronous environments, leading to impossibility result.

Let us consider the Byzantine Generals problem constituting of one general and two lieutenants. In this scenario, even one traitor (general or one of the lieutenants) can cause impossibility results demonstrated in Figures 2.4 and 2.5.

The FLP impossibility resulting in asynchronous system can be bypassed in two ways:

1. Synchrony assumption
2. Non-determinism

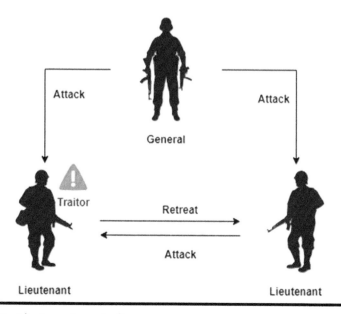

Figure 2.4   Lieutenant as a traitor.

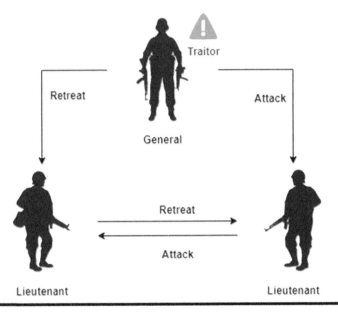

Figure 2.5   General as a traitor.

Various consensus algorithms have been designed using the synchrony and non-determinism assumptions. They are explained in detail in the subsequent sections.

2.8 Types of Consensus Algorithms

With respect to the conventions existing to bypass the impossibility result, consensus algorithms can be broadly classified into categories involving synchrony assumption and non-determinism.

2.8.1 Based on Network Synchrony – Traditional Consensus

A number of algorithms exist to circumvent the FLP impossibility depending on the synchrony assumption like Paxos, Raft, Depth Limited Search (DLS) algorithm and Practical Byzantine Fault Tolerance (PBFT) algorithm. The older algorithms like Paxos and Raft are crash fault tolerant, but not Byzantine fault tolerant, and this makes them an ineligible candidate for consensus on asynchronous networks like blockchain. The DLS algorithm cannot be implemented as well due to partially synchronous network requirement. The PBFT algorithm is the one reliant on network synchrony assumption and works in asynchronous environment as well. Let us discuss the above mentioned algorithms in detail.

2.8.1.1 Paxos

The first real-world implementation of practical and fault tolerant consensus algorithm was Paxos algorithm. It was one of the first and foremost of algorithms, widely adopted by high-tech internet giants for implementing distributed systems.

Let us consider a system with multiple processes proposing different values. The main objective of using consensus algorithm in such a system is to choose a single value among the proposed values. If there are no values proposed by the process, then no value should be chosen. On the other hand, if the system is able to choose a single value, then the processes should be able to learn the chosen value. Multiple assumptions have been made for reaching consensus in those systems as follows:

1. The chosen value must be selected from one of the proposed values
2. Consensus algorithm must ensure only a single value is chosen from the set of proposed values
3. Unless and until a value has been actually chosen, the processes should not be able to learn the value

The ultimate goal is a single value must be chosen from a set of proposed values and the process should eventually be able to learn the chosen value.

Three types of roles are played by actors present in this algorithm. More than one role might be played by a single process:

1. Proposers – Proposers choose new proposal numbers and send requests to other processes within the network
2. Acceptors: Acceptors receive the proposed values from the proposers in the system
3. Learners: Learners gain the knowledge about the chosen value after a majority of acceptors accept the proposed value

Paxos algorithm has three phases implemented in achieving consensus, which are listed below:

Preparation phase

1. The proposer processes choose a new proposal number 'n' and send it to the acceptors in the form of 'Prepare request'
2. If the acceptors receive a prepare request with 'n' greater than the already accepted request, they respond with the acknowledgement stating it would not accept any proposal having number less than 'n' and replies with the highest numbered proposal less than 'n', which has been already accepted

Acceptance phase

1. The proposer receives the responses from multiple acceptors and aggregates the responses
2. It sends an accept request to all of them with number 'n' and value 'v', where 'n' is the number that has been sent in the prepare request and 'v' is the value from the responses having the highest number 'n'
3. As soon as the acceptor receives a request, it will accept it unless it has sent a response already with a number higher than 'n'

Learning phase

1. If an acceptor is going to accept a request, then it will send the accepted value 'v' and number 'n' to all the learners
2. Learners after receiving the value 'v' from a majority of acceptors, will send the value 'v' to the other learners
3. The learners decide on the value 'v' by means of the decide request

Disadvantages

Though Paxos was the first and foremost implementation of fault tolerant consensus, it had multiple drawbacks mentioned below:

1. Some very important processes like election of the leader, failure detection are not defined properly
2. It was very difficult to understand and implement in the real world

2.8.1.2 Raft

Raft is a distributed consensus algorithm as effective as Paxos, but simpler to understand. Multiple servers present in the network are involved in agreeing upon a shared state, even if there are failures. The shared state is primarily a data structure sustained by replicated log. The majority of the systems in the network should be up in order to make sure the network is up and running. A leader is elected by the algorithm that accepts all the client requests and performs the task of replicating the log to other servers present within the network. The flow of data is always from the leader to the other servers, not in the opposite direction.

There are three important steps involved in reaching consensus through Raft algorithm:

1. Leader Election – A new leader is selected once the process starts. The process repeats whenever there is a failure in the existing leader resulting in a new leader being elected

2. Replication of Log – The leader should make sure the logs present in the other servers are consistent with its own copy. This is made possible by applying replication process for the replication of logs to the other servers

3. Safety – Whenever a server commits an entry for a particular index in the log, no other server should enter whatsoever in the same index of the log entry

The below properties of the algorithm should be true all times:

1. Leader Election Safety – At any given term or duration of time, only one leader should be selected

2. Append-Only – A leader can make new entries or append entries on a given index, though it will not be able to reverse, overwrite or delete an entry already present in the log

3. Matching Logs – If two entries at a given index and term are identical between two logs, then all the entries in all the logs should be matching or identical up through the given index and the term

4. Completeness – A log entry committed in the term of a given leader should be present in all the higher numbered terms following the current term

5. State Machine Safety – Once a server present in the network inputs an entry at a given index of its state machine, then no other server should input a different log entry on the same index.

Every server present in the network will be in one of the following states, which are also illustrated in Figure 2.6:

1. Follower – Followers are submissive servers; they do not send any new requests on their own; instead, they work on the requests from leader or candidates. If there is a scenario where a client contacts a follower, the follower will diligently redirect the request to the elected leader

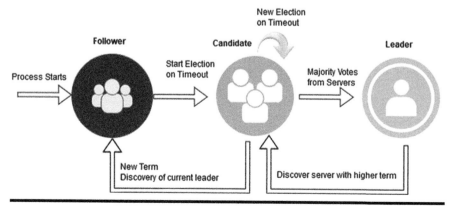

Figure 2.6   Working of Raft protocol.

2. Leader – The leader is the one who is elected newly once per term and handles all the requests from clients
3. Candidate – This state is used to elect a new leader; each leader is a candidate before being elected as a leader

All the terms in Raft algorithm are divided into arbitrary lengths, with each of the term starting with an election of the leader. Voting happens to elect a leader; if a candidate obtains majority, then the candidate becomes the leader for the rest of the term. If there is no absolute majority, then the term will end without a leader. The term number is incremental and each of the servers present in the network stores the term number and sends with each communication. Each server should ensure its current term is not lesser than the other servers. If there is any inconsistency noticed, it will update its current term to a larger value from other server. Once the term of the leader ends, then it will revert to the follower state immediately. If any of the servers receives a request with old term number in the communication, then the request is rejected.

2.8.1.3 DLS Algorithm

The DLS algorithm defines better mechanisms to achieve consensus in partially synchronous systems. This algorithm presents key developments and improvements in Byzantine fault tolerant consensus. In asynchronous systems, there is no definite upper bound for message delays; conversely in synchronous systems, there exists an upper bound on the message delays. A partially synchronous system is an intermediate between these two conditions.

There are two major assumptions in reaching consensus in partially synchronous systems, which are as follows:

1. There exists a fixed bound on how long a message will take to be delivered; nonetheless, it is not known earlier. Consensus should be reached notwithstanding the actual bounds
2. There exists an upper bound for the message delivery, while it can be certainly beginning at some random unknown time. Regardless of when the time window starts, we should be able to reach consensus in the system

The DLS algorithm has two important properties acting as an assurance to achieve consensus in the system:

1. Safety – All the correct or non-faulty nodes in the network should agree on the same value. They must agree on the total order of the transaction logs even in case of failures and presence of dishonest nodes. The system will become inconsistent with two or more valid logs if the safety property is violated.

2. Liveness – This property ensures every correct or non-faulty node in the network agrees on some output value eventually. It will make sure the blockchain is continuously growing and not stalled.

The DLS algorithm divides the working of consensus mechanism into rounds with two phases: 'Trying' and 'lock-release' phases. Let us assume there are 'N' nodes in the partially synchronous network. Following are the steps involved in reaching consensus in the above mentioned system:

1. In each round, there exists a proposer who will accept the value communicated by each process; the processes communicate the value believed to be correct by them
2. If at least N-x process has communicated the same value, then the proposer node proposes it
3. Each of the nodes present in the network should lock on the proposed value and pass on to the others in the network, whenever it receives the proposed value from the proposer
4. If there are x+1 messages from the nodes to the proposer notifying they have locked on some value, the locked value is committed as the final value

Disadvantages

1. We assume timeouts in this algorithm; in case of failure of the synchrony assumption, this will lead to two valid transaction logs resulting in an inconsistent system state. There is nothing useful in having an inconsistent and corrupt system
2. If the nodes are not deciding on some output value, then there is no way consensus can be reached. The system just halts
3. Even if we make synchrony assumptions for termination (timeouts), in case of failure of the assumption, the system will come to a halt

2.8.1.4 Practical Byzantine Fault Tolerance Algorithm

The PBFT model is a fault tolerance algorithm primarily focusing on practical state machine replication, which overcomes Byzantine failures with independent node failures (dishonest nodes) that propagate incorrect or faulty messages. This algorithm will work on asynchronous systems with overall optimized performance and very little increase in latency. The system is modeled with one node assumed as a leader and all other nodes considered backups. All the nodes present in the system communicate with each other and the design is likely to bring all the honest nodes to an agreement through a majority. There is a slight overhead in the communication of message since each message has to prove its origin and verify there is no alteration happened in the messages during transmission.

The PBFT works under the assumption, for a network size of 'N', the number of faulty nodes 'f' should not exceed (N − 1)/3 for the network to be Byzantine fault tolerant. It can be stated in other way as N >= 3f + 1 in a network guarantees to be a BFT system. The PBFT is modeled based on three sub-protocols as listed below.

2.8.1.4.1 Normal Operation Protocol

Normal operation protocol is a 'session-to-session' protocol with various phases like client operation request, pre-prepare phase, prepare phase, commit phase and reply to client. A request from the client to primary is sent in the 'client operation request' phase. In 'pre-prepare' phase, the message is passed on from primary to all the backups present in the system. Each backup will forward the message to all the replicas in the 'prepare' phase. '2f + 1' messages with the same values is required for pre-prepare and prepare phase. A 'commit' phase occurs when each replica sends the message to all the replicas. Finally, a reply is sent to the client if '2f + 1' commit messages are available.

2.8.1.4.2 Checkpoint Protocol

A stable checkpoint is maintained, which the system accepts and safely discards the old transactions in the log. The most recently executed client request is recorded with the sequence number 'n'. Updated checkpoint is broadcasted as a 'checkpoint' message. All replicas update the last checkpoint broadcasted if they receive '2f + 1' checkpoint messages with the same value. All the nodes discard messages prior to the latest checkpoint.

2.8.1.4.3 View-Change Protocol

A view-change happens when there is a fault suspected in the primary node. Whenever any of the backup is in pre-prepare phase of the normal operation protocol for a long time and stops receiving messages, the status is updated to 'view-change'. A view-change request is sent to all the replicas to change the view state to 'v + 1'. The primary node will broadcast a 'new-view' message if it receives 2f view-change messages. The log will be updated and the primary node will proceed to normal operation. The replica nodes after receiving 'new-view' message, validate it, update its state and proceed to normal operation protocol.

2.8.2 Based on Non-Determinism

2.8.2.1 Nakamoto Consensus (Proof of Work)

Nakamoto Consensus can be defined as a probabilistic approach non-deterministic in nature. In this model, every node need not agree on the same value; instead they agree on the probability of the value to be correct. This consensus mechanism is proved to be having the following characteristics through its famous implementation 'Bitcoin':

1. Byzantine Fault Tolerance – There is no leader election in this process; instead, the decision is dependent on the nodes solving the computational puzzle faster and getting a chance to propose its value
2. Incentive Mechanism – When a node solves the puzzle and proposes a value agreed by other nodes, there is an economic incentive rewarded to the winner node
3. Sybil Resistance – Rather than using the conventional PKI (Public Key Infrastructure) authentication scheme or any other scheme, PoW mechanism is involved in the consensus process making sure the process is Sybil-resistant
4. Gossip Protocol – The peer-to-peer gossip protocol ensures messages are routed to all the nodes in the asynchronous network, assuming each node is connected to a subsection of nodes only

2.8.2.2 Protocol Design

Nakamoto consensus is designed on the basis of the principle that each node present in the blockchain network runs an identical protocol and manages its own copy of the decentralized ledger by itself. This protocol depends on the fact that majority of the nodes present in the network are honest or non-faulty nodes.

Important rules applied in the design of the protocol are as follows:

1. Message Broadcasting Rule – All the transactions either they are generated locally or received from other peer nodes within the network should be broadcasted to the identified peers in a timely manner without causing any delay. The same condition applies for broadcasting the blocks as well
2. Validity – All the transactions and blocks received by each node should be validated before broadcasting. Once all the transactions in the blocks are validated along with the block as a whole, it should be appended to the blockchain. Invalid transactions or blocks are discarded in this process
3. Longest Chain Rule – In this consensus mechanism, any longest chain present in the network is considered as the valid chain. Any honest or non-faulty node is built on top of the longest chain by appending the next valid block. Decision on where to append the next block will be reliant on the total amount of computation effort put on the longest chain
4. Mining Process – PoW is the backbone of Nakamoto consensus taking care of valid block generation process. Each node trying to propose a block should be finding a nonce (Number used once) to be inserted into the block header. The difficulty to find the nonce is adjusted periodically to certify the average block generation speed remains constant within the network.

The PoW consensus displayed in Figure 2.7 has been successfully verified by the implementation of the protocol in the 'Bitcoin' blockchain.

Nakamoto consensus is apparently advantageous over the tradition consensus mechanism based on the following points:

1. Nakamoto consensus is Byzantine fault tolerant though most of the traditional consensuses are not
2. Any number of nodes can join or leave the network at any point of time assuring open participation
3. The nodes in the network need not know all the participants in the network, still they will have a finite set of known peers

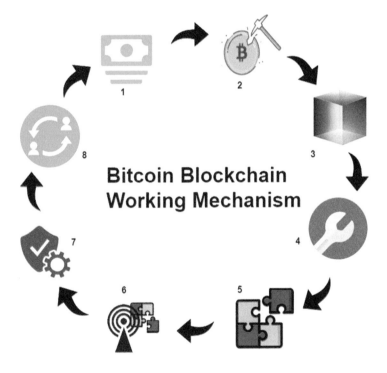

Bitcoin Blockchain Working Mechanism

1. Transactions are broadcast to the Network
2. Miners look for transactions and start the Mining Process
3. Miners create a block and include the transactions
4. Miner starts Proof of Work by using their computational power
5. Proof of Work created by the miners by solving the cryptographic puzzle
6. Successful Miner broadcasts its PoW to the network
7. Other miners verify the Proof of Work
8. The Process starts over again

Figure 2.7   Working of Bitcoin blockchain.

4. There is no communication overhead involved, unlike the traditional mechanisms
5. The leader election process is not required in the Nakamoto consensus

Disadvantages

1. Nodes mining the next block try with brute computing force. Hence, there is higher energy and computational power consumption for calculating the hash
2. The average size of block is limited to 1 MB and the number of transactions processed per block is very less (~7 transactions per second). Other established networks like VISA, PayPal process much higher transactions within the same duration (~10000 transactions per second in VISA)

2.9 Other Consensus Algorithms

2.9.1 Proof of Stake

A new consensus algorithm has been designed to overcome higher use of energy in the PoW protocol to ensure mining activity is conducted in a more cultured manner without wasting energy or computational power. A group of validators will bet a specific amount as a security deposit to participate in the block generation process. They will buy cryptocurrencies instead of investing in buying equipment for rigorous computational activity [2]. Each one who wants to participate in the block mining race will deposit some cryptocurrencies as a stake in the network. The higher the stake is, higher is the possibility of the node to become a validator. Based on a random process, the validator is selected to generate a block. The validator who generates a valid block will get incentives for their work. If the block generated is not included in the chain, then the validator will be penalized and lose their stake. In the PoW mechanism, penalty for nodes generating invalid block is only in terms of wasted computational power and resource, whereas in the PoS, nodes lose their stakes if invalid blocks are generated or fraudulent behavior is exhibited. If all the correct or honest nodes in the network follow the protocol and own greater than 50% stake in the network, then the possibility of an already generated block to be revoked from the network drops exponentially.

Disadvantages

1. An investor who is wealthy enough can invest some amount in the cryptocurrency, bet it as stake, get its rewards and reinvest making themselves richer
2. Nothing-at-Stake Problem – A validator node can bet some value on all the branches existing in the network without any additional cost. These kinds of bets are called 'double bets' where there is no penalty implications

3. Even if a penalty scheme is incorporated in the algorithm, it would not be effective in case if more than 50% of the network stake is owned by a single validator

2.9.2 Proof of Elapsed Time

Proof of Elapsed Time (PoET) is a consensus scheme working centered on a back-off mechanism that is purely random. Each validator node in the network waits for a time, whose length is random and then backs off after the time is elapsed. Once a node has finished its back-off, it becomes the validator. It is a trusted back-off method for the nodes where each and every validator should be verified and trusted completely [1, 5]. The random back-off is achieved by the use of microprocessors precisely designed for this purpose.

A new validator node, while joining the network, gets the back-off program from the peer nodes within the same network. The newly joined validator sends an attestation report to the host network to ensure that the required authentic program for back-off has been loaded successfully. Once the validator fulfills the back-off requirement for a random amount of time, it will generate a new block with the set of all unprocessed transactions it has heard of. A certificate is generated for completing the trusted back-off mechanism and sent along with the block.

The back-off mechanism proposed in the PoET algorithm can tolerate any number of faulty validators present in the network. A validator who is rich with a lot of resources can invest in multiple instances to cut short the expected duration of back-off [5].

Disadvantages

1. The microprocessor used in this mechanism is manufactured by Intel, hence the security of the system is bounded by the security of the hardware and reliability of its servers
2. There is a dependency on a Trusted Execution Environment (TEE) – in this case, Intel's microprocessor
3. This model greatly contradicts the idea of decentralization proposed in blockchain by using a specific hardware making the system centralized and dependent

2.9.3 Ripple Protocol

Ripple consensus protocol is being operated by an organization Ripple Inc., facilitating exchange of currencies and settlements. It is a real-time gross settlement network regulated by a known set of validators. This set of validators generally includes companies and institutions running Ripple servers and programs on their systems. The Ripple programs running in their infrastructure enable the companies to accept transaction processing request from different clients and process them. Each client participating in the network submits its transaction requests to the nominated validators existing within the network. While processing each transaction, a decision is taken centered on the Ripple consensus running in the validators in a distributed manner [6].

Ripple consensus lets each node 'n' in the network to maintain a unique list of nodes (Unique Node List – UNL). The node 'n' along with the UNL forms a sub-network within the network, which needs to be trusted by 'n' partially.

The protocol is designed so as,

1. A list or set of entities with valid transactions is prepared as an initial step. All the new transactions along with the old transactions from the previous cycles constitute the set of valid transactions
2. The candidate set prepared by the node 'n' is combined with the candidate set prepared by the peers in the UNL list
3. All the nodes present in the sub-network vote a 'Yes' or 'No' liable to the validity of transactions available in the combined set
4. Each transaction receives a vote from the UNL nodes within the candidate set. The transactions receiving votes count less than the minimum threshold value are discarded. The discarded transactions are considered for the next cycle of voting consensus
5. The above steps are repeated in the upcoming cycles until the final round is reached where the threshold for the minimum number of votes is increased to 80%. After the final round, all the nodes append the remaining valid transactions and end the cycles.

The transactions are finalized and updated into the list only if 80% of the nodes from the UNL approve [7]. This Ripple consensus protocol is Byzantine fault tolerant making it advantageous to be implemented in the network. There is a special scheme for the authentication of the validators to ensure the true identity of nodes in the UNL is known to others present within the same sub-network.

Disadvantages

1. Any node in the network communicate with the peer nodes within the sub-network (UNL) only. Each individual node in the network may have disconnected or disjoint set of UNLs resulting in network partitioning.
2. Different set of nodes participating in two unique UNLs might agree on different set of transactions and update the ledger in parallel in a conflicting manner. To ensure the above scenario does not happen, Ripple consensus should make sure at least 25% of nodes must be shared between two UNL groups.
3. The protocol is designed and maintained by Ripple Inc., supposedly under its direct supervision. Any changes in the protocol can be done by the company directly, hence the power is in a single hand rather than being decentralized.
4. The above reason makes it unrealistic to be used in public blockchains.

2.10 Comparison of Consensus Algorithms

Table 2.1 shows a comparison among the various Consensus Algorithms.

2.11 Types of Possible Attacks

2.11.1 51% Attack

When a single miner node controls a group of nodes with more computational resources than the rest of the network, i.e., at least 51% or a mining pool has 51% or more of the total network computation resources, then there is feasibility for these miners or pools to undermine the network with a peculiar type of attack known as 51% attack. The miners or group of miners with 51% resources or more will be having the advantage of performing successful mining and claiming reward. The PoW protocol famous for its implementation in 'Bitcoin' blockchain is vulnerable to this kind of attack.

2.11.2 Double Spending

The ability of an individual to use the same coin or funds twice is known as double spending. The possibility of a 51% attack allows a miner to successfully double spend the amount by reversing the already committed transactions. We all know the definition, blockchains are irreversible, immutable transactions, yet the 'longest chain rule' makes reversing and altering the transactions possible [8]. A miner with 51% or more computational resources can create an alternate chain and add blocks on top of it. During a point of time, it will become the longest chain and the actual chain will be dropped making the attack successful. Say for example, a user 'u' orders a high-end laptop from a merchant by creating a transaction. The merchant waits for certain duration to confirm the transaction and ships the product. The user knows the product has been shipped and starts creating an alternate chain now. Once the alternate chain becomes the longest chain, the actual chain containing the transaction to the merchant will be dropped. The transaction is reversed and the merchant loses the money. User 'u' can now happily use the money for some other transactions.

2.11.3 Sybil Attack

When a single person in the network creates multiple identities, they can control multiple IDs, in turn controlling multiple nodes. These IDs are used in an attempt to control the peer nodes in the network, by undermining the network using multiple IDs at the same time. Also, they can influence the decentralized network through additional voting power they acquire with multiple IDs. The main aim of this type of attack is to gain the majority of the influence in the network and carry

Table 2.1   Comparison of Consensus Algorithms

	Permissioned?	Third Party Required	Consensus Finality	Connectivity Requirement	Fault Tolerance	Real-World Implementations
PoW	No	No	Probabilistic	Low	50% Hashing	Bitcoin
PoS	No	No	Deterministic	Low	33.3% Stake	Ethereum
PoET	No	TEE Platform	Probabilistic	Low	50% Instances	Hyperledger Sawtooth
PBFT	Yes	Identity Manager	Deterministic	High	33.3% Voting Power	Hyperledger Fabric
Ripple Protocol	Yes	Ripple Identity Manager	Deterministic	High	20% Nodes in UNL	Ripple

out malicious activities disturbing the integrity of the network. Sybil attacks are difficult to detect and prevent as they involve false identities and hidden motives.

2.12 Consensus Algorithm – Soul of the Blockchain Network

The consensus algorithms are for the systems in a distributed environment to reach a collective agreement. There cannot be any distributed or decentralized system without a consensus mechanism implemented to reach an agreement. The nodes within a network may not trust each other, but they have to comply with the consensus algorithms to decide on a common goal [9]. There may not be a single consensus algorithm common for all blockchain implementations; however, we need some consensus algorithm for the network to be successful and running. Blockchain may build blocks from innumerable transactions forming a database, but they would not be decentralized in nature without the consensus algorithms. Blockchain is predominantly a framework working on decentralization concept, whereas consensus mechanism remains the soul of the network. There are numerous consensus algorithms described in this chapter based on the various assumptions. Much more research is going on in this area and there are developments proposed every day.

References

[1] L. Lamport, R. Shostak, and M. Pease, "The Byzantine generals problem," *ACM Transactions on Programming Languages and System*, vol. 4, no. 3, pp. 382–401, 1982.

[2] M. J. Fischer, N. A. Lynch, and M. S. Paterson, "Impossibility of distributed consensus with one faulty process," *Journal of ACM*, vol. 32, no. 2, pp. 374–382, 1985.

[3] D. Schwartz, N. Youngs, A. Britto, et al., "The ripple protocol consensus algorithm," Ripple Labs Inc. White Paper, vol. 5, 2014.

[4] Nakamoto, Satoshi, and A. Bitcoin. "A peer-to-peer electronic cash system," *Bitcoin.–URL:* https://bitcoin. org/bitcoin. pdf 4 (2008).

[5] Kavita Saini, "A future's dominant technology blockchain: Digital transformation," In: IEEE International Conference on Computing, Power and Communication Technologies 2018 (GUCON 2018), Galgotias University, Greater Noida, pp. 28–29 September, 2018.

[6] V. Gramoli, "From blockchain consensus back to Byzantine consensus," *Future Generation Computer Systems*, 2017, http://dx.doi.org/10.1016/j.future.2017.09.023.

[7] M. Castro and B. Liskov, "Practical Byzantine fault tolerance," In: Proceeding of 3rd Symposium Operating Systems Design and Implementation, pp. 173–186, 1999.

[8] V. Buterin, "A next generation smart contract and decentralized application platform," 2014. Available: https://github.com/ethereum/wiki/wiki/White-Paper.

[9] C. Dwork, N. Lynch, and L. Stockmeyer, "Consensus in the presence of partial synchrony," *Journal of ACM*, vol. 35, no. 2, pp. 288–323, 1988.

Chapter 3

Blockchain Performance

R. Indrakumari, Kiran Singh, Rishabh
Kumar Srivastava and A. Ilavendhan

Contents

3.1 Introduction

Blockchain is attracting many industrial and academic research areas and has gained massive momentum in the recent years. In 2008, Nakamoto proposed the concept of Bitcoin [1] and it forms the basic technology for blockchain. Blockchain or a distributed ledger is an append-only data structure controlled by some sets of nodes that do not trust each other [1]. Blockchain is a log of ordered transactions network that agree on an ordered set of blocks. The conventional database system employs concurrency control techniques and work in a trusted environment [2]. In contrast to this, blockchain nodes do not trust each other and it is intended to achieve Byzantine fault tolerance. Blockchain shares databases among multiple parties and eradicates the need of intermediaries, which are considered as trusted third parties to validate data and coordinate transactions. See Figure 3.1.

The three main characteristics of blockchain which honor it as a trust machine are decentralization, recording the transactions using protocols and tamper-resistant [3].

Bitcoin is considered as the first generation of blockchain that supports peer-to-peer e-cash transactions in its system. The second generation of blockchain is the Ethereum [4] that supports smart contracts and expands its applications to electronic voting, string data processing, digital identity and so on. In addition to Ethereum, Hyperledger Fabric project also supports smart contracts [5].

The blockchain structure is categorized into three categories, namely, the public blockchain architecture, private blockchain architecture and consortium blockchain architecture.

3.1.1 Public Blockchain Architecture

In public blockchain, the data can be accessed by anyone who shows their consent to participate. Some of the public blockchain are Bitcoin, Litecoin and Ethereum.

3.1.2 Private Blockchain Architecture

In contrast to public blockchain, the private blockchain is controlled by specific users or organizations that are holding an invitation to participate.

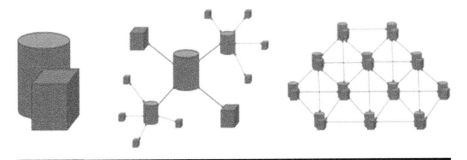

Figure 3.1   Centralized, decentralized and distributed network.

3.1.3 Consortium Blockchain Architecture

In a consortium blockchain structure, protocols are initiated and controlled by the preliminary assigned users.

3.2 Blockchain Application Literature Survey

Blockchain has a wide range of applications, as it provides robust security when compared to other available provisions. In the finance-based applications, there exist some noteworthy cryptocurrencies, an emerging alternative that has created a novel way of payment method and investment. Some of them are Monero [6], Ripple [7], Dogecoin [8], Dash [9], Namecoin [10] and Nxt [11]. Blockchain technology provides a perfect solution for traceability systems. Food traceability project is conducted by top companies like Walmart, Unilever, Nestle and IBM. Blockchain technology is used to store identities by providing an open trusted distributed ledger for identity verification. Many countries have employed blockchain in the field of e-government. For example, in Estonia, e-identity is implemented using blockchain technology [12], in Dubai, for passports [13] and in India, for land registration [14]. In addition, the smart contracts pave the way for a novel industrial revolution in the areas of mortgages, energy, real estate, gambling, music royalty payments, insurance and energy. E-health, cloud storage and education are also using blockchain applications.

3.3 The Roots of Blockchain's Potential

The potential of blockchain is entrenched by four important things: transparancy, immutability, reduced counterparty risk and efficient provisioning of identities [15]. See Figure 3.2.

3.3.1 Transparency

Any blockchain user in the network can see the transaction history in real time and the money trail can be monitored and controlled accurately.

3.3.2 Immutability

Blockchain prevents data tampering, as each and every action in the chain is transparent and the transactions are recorded. Immutability can be applicable in the areas like land title registrations and voter authentication.

3.3.3 Reduced Counterparty Risk

Users can transfer money to anyone in the network without any intermediary, thus reducing the cost. Money transferred to critical zones like natural disaster area or across borders can be sent without any delay.

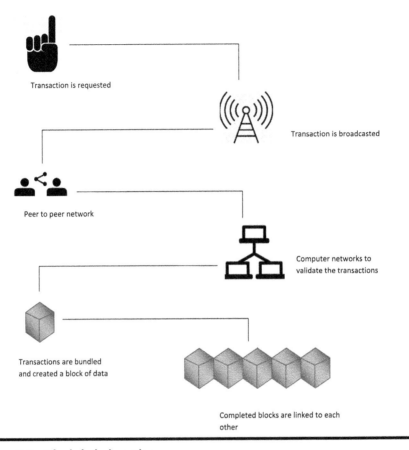

Figure 3.2 Blockchain in action.

3.3.4 Efficient Provisioning of Identities

Through agriculture digital signature technology, blockchain provides the user a public and private key and controls the identities of people in a secure way in lower cost.

3.4 Blockchain Influence on Agriculture and Food

Blockchain application in agriculture industry is in its initial stages. The primary role is to improve the transparency, efficiency and traceability for the users in the whole supply chain from agricultural product producers to consumers. Prior to agricultural supply chain modeling, the data regarding sustainability, safety and certificate status of food are maintained on paper or in the database and audited by trusted third party [16]. This methodology will increase the cost of operational management and decrease the security and loyalty.

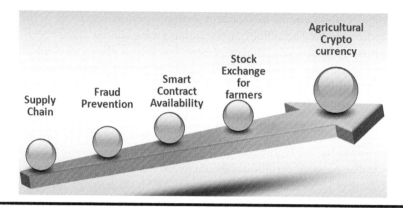

Figure 3.3 Blockchain influence in agriculture.

Food fraud and contamination of food affects both the producers and consumers. The World Health Organization estimates that 1 out of 10 people become ill from consuming contaminated foods [17] and it costs 2–15% of the company's yearly revenue [18].

To increase the efficiency and transparency in food manufacturing while reducing the fraud and contamination, industries are hiring blockchain technology in agriculture. The concept of blockchain replaces the fallible third parties in the collection of data, tracking and manages data in the agricultural supply chains network in an efficient and neutral way. See Figure 3.3.

An Australian company introduced a commodity management platform called AgriDigital, which connects farmers with the value chain actors. AgriDigital creates a token to represent the commodities like tons of rice or wheat. When the commodity is transferred from one person to another, the token is moved among various participants such as from farmer to a purchaser. Every transaction is traceable using the attached token and payment is made in real time through smart contracts. For example, when a producer delivers the goods to a consumer, the digital token associated with the goods is transferred from the producer to the consumer and at the same time, the corresponding amount is transferred from the consumer to the producer.

3.5 Applications of Blockchain Technology in Banking and Finance

Many researches have proved that blockchain technology is well-suited for financial sector, as it eliminates third parties, thereby reduces the costs while increasing the profits for various players in the firm. Both public and private blockchains are involved in the financial application, but private blockchain enables faster transaction and higher privacy when compared to public blockchain, as it is comparatively slower if the number of transaction is high. For example, a USB bank in

Switzerland, a world leading financial consortium, is using blockchain in the inter-bank settlements and backoffice functions, thus saving billions of dollors.

Apart from direct financial management, blockchain plays a vital role in asset management industry, which is a rapidly growing industry, and it is expected to reach $145.4 trillion by the year 2025 [19]. Here, intermediaries play a role to meet shareholder's demands for a global set of products, which makes the process complex and time-consuming. The distributed ledger concept of blockchain allows direct trading across boundaries by increasing the accuracy of data and reducing the costs and delay. See Figure 3.4.

The Indian financial institutions should follow many requirements posed by the Reserve Bank of India. Know Your Customer (KYC) is the leading time-consuming requirement to identify the customers automatically. Blockchain technology automates the bank account opening process by making KYC through a digital source ID while assuring the personal data privacy. The international money transferring process is tedious and lengthy, and many times, it is tedious to trace the agent of the transaction, thus, causes money laundering. Many banks are using blockchain technology, which allows the customer to do safe transaction without any fraud activities, operational cost and human errors.

Sestoft [20] proposes a distributed system – Autonomous Pension Fund – which would be a self-sustaining running autonomous contract-based system to manage

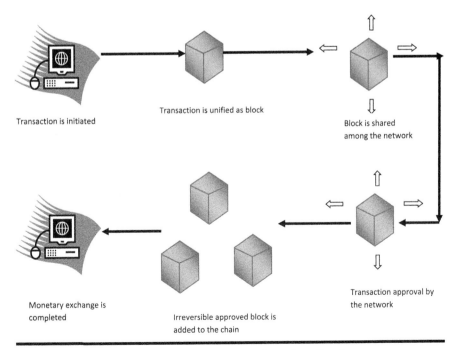

Figure 3.4   Working of blockchain in finance-based applications.

life-based pension funds without a central trusted pension fund. Since a large number of activities related to life-based pension such as receiving payments from active customers, making payments to beneficiaries and payments of taxes on pensions are the main processing of contract-regulated payments.

3.6 Efficient and Cost-Saving Business Operations for Logistics Using Blockchain

Logistics is the ability to manage supply chain along with the flow of information, goods and other resources by connecting people in the origin to destination [21]. Logistics utilizes advanced technologies like business analytics, artificial intelligence, internet of things and blockchain [22]. Blockchain with intrinsic characters like decentralized operation and data integrity is the most promising technology in the logistics field (see Figure 3.5).

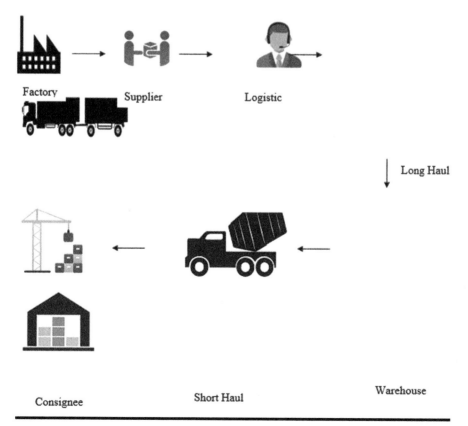

Figure 3.5   Blockchain in logistics management.

Excellence in logistic management depends on collaborative works, which involve physical goods, financial transaction and information. This supply chain can be trapped significantly due to competitors in the logistic field. Many processes involved in the logistic supply are bound to manual data entry and documentation, which makes it difficult to track the origin of the goods and its status as it traverse along the supply chain, causing inconsistency in the world trade. These difficulties can be overcome by blockchain technology, which makes extensive gain in the logistics. Blockchain provides transparency in data, creates a single source of information and increases the trust among the stakeholders to exchange the information securely. Cost management, predictability and visibility are the other features of blockchain in logistics. Features of blockchain like public availability provides the chance to track the goods from the origin to destination, the decentralized structure gives the opportunity for all parties to participate in the supply chain, the immutability and cryptography-based nature provide security [23].

Many companies are practicing blockchain, for example, Ubims is the world's foremost patented 3D supply chain process which connects goods suppliers with the consumers around the world [24, 25]. Ubims is the world's first blockchain-based, decentralized, open supply chain infrastructure system and it is predicted that this technology will disrupt the world supply chain industries. Logistics systems rely on Internet of Things (IoT) devices to be incorporated in the shipments, vehicles, etc. These IoT devices use blockchain technology, which enables smart contracts to pay duties and fees.

3.7 Law Enforcement: Blockchain in Investigations

Increase in the crime rate and the law enforcement are directly proportional to each other. Many police officials have been killed in the line of duty. To avoid this, enforcement of latest technology allows the officials to do their job safely and effectively as possible. Implementing automation allows many crimes to be detected without interacting face to face. Utilizing blockchain technology, the transactions of violent criminality can be monitored, analyzed and flagged, thus reducing the risk of danger. See Figure 3.6.

The third party doctrine has been established by the Supreme Court of the United States (SCOTUS) in 1979 in *Smith vs Maryland* decision, 'a person has no legitimate expectation of privacy in information he voluntarily turns over to third parties'. In 2018, SCOTUS ruling in the case of *Carpenter vs United States* states that mapping a mobile phone location over 127 days is considered as overly intrusive, putting limitations for the third party doctrine as it pertains to cell providers.

The status of blockchain is clear, and hence, it does not require these types of legal battles to follow. Through immutable records of blockchain, it not only provides historical cache of records but also analyzes some criminal activities as the blockchain technology is apart from third party doctrine issues.

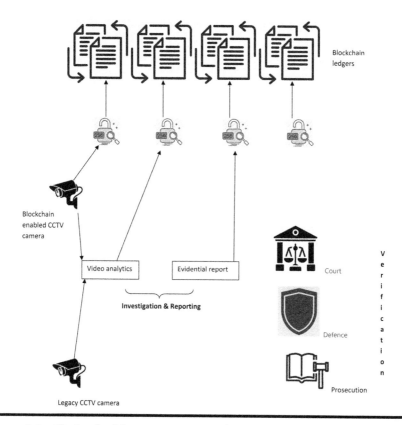

Figure 3.6 Chain of evidence management in CCTV camera.

Cryptocurrency is a safe transaction medium using cryptographic techniques, which works on the blockchain methods. Blockchain allows easy law enforcement by providing a subpoena system. Cryptocurrency technology is based on encryption algorithms, which create finite unique hashes. Users exchange their hashes through a network of computers.

3.8 Case Study: Digital Voting Using Blockchain

Blockchain is a series, or more precisely, a growing sequences of records also known as blocks, which are immutable and joined by some cryptographic principles, which are also known as chains. To keep it simple, let's say that a blockchain is a series of blocks, which are connected to each other by a chain. But that doesn't mean that way; blocks in a blockchain are generally records or data, which are stored in a secure format, and these data or records are linked with some kind of cryptographic principles and functions, which are known as a chain. Each block stores a cryptographic hash of the previous blocks, a timestamp and some transaction data.

According to the design of the blockchains, it is said that a blockchain is resistant to any kind of modifications. The concept of blockchain is said to be brought in by Satoshi Nakamoto in 2008 [26]. Blockchain was introduced to be used widely in cryptocurrencies. It is a kind of open and distributed ledger, which has the capability of storing details related to transactions between two persons in a more efficient and verifiable manner. Though blockchains are used in cryptocurrencies nowadays, they can be used in many other ways also.

We know that voting is the fundamental right of every adult citizen, and there should be a way that this election process can be more secure and transparent. With the use of blockchain, the cost of organizing an election can be cut-off in a very secure and efficient way. By using this modern-day electronic voting system, we can get rid of the old method of conducting these elections, and this new method of conducting elections can be more secure, verifiable and traceable. Thus, the answer to this problem is to use the method of digital voting along with the blockchains.

3.8.1 Requirements for E-voting

1. Privacy: The blockchain uses cryptographic properties to secure any kind of data which are stored in it. A blockchain generates a hash function for the voters who are registered in the block, which is a unique identification of the voter, and it has to be maintained securely from any kind of modifications during the election process [27].
2. Eligibility: All the voters must register themselves using the unique identification document issued by the government, which can prove their eligibility to vote in the elections. For more kind of authentication, a biometric mechanism should be used [27].
3. Convenience: The system should be user-friendly such that the voter faces no problem during the voting system. Biometrics can be used to identify the identity of a person but in such a way that the voter faces no problem [27].
4. Verifiability: The voter should have complete trust in the voting mechanism and should be aware of how the process will take place. The voters may use their transaction ID to track their votes have been counted or not. Another problem which can be faced is the tallying process. There should be complete transparency in the tallying process [27].

3.8.2 Working of Blockchain as a Service for E-voting

The detailed working of the blockchain as a service for e-voting is described below.

Blockchain as a Service: The blockchain is a kind of data structure which can be used as an append-only data structure in which the data are stored in a format

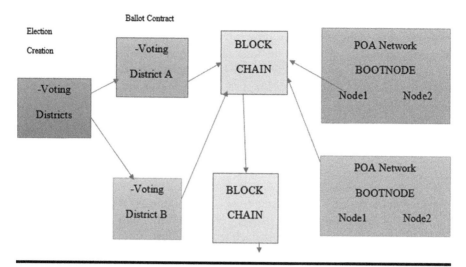

Figure 3.7   Election as a smart contract.

known as a distributed ledger. These data cannot be tampered or deleted. These blocks of data are connected or chained using a hash function, which contains the information of the previous block, thus creating a series of immutable blocks. There are generally two types of blockchains, which have different kinds of restrictions and different read and write properties [28]. A public blockchain is a kind of blockchain in which everyone can read and write. Such kind of blockchain is most popular in the implementations of cryptocurrencies. A private blockchain is a kind of blockchain which has some kind of restrictions with it. These restrictions can be who can read or write, or who can interact with the blockchain. Private blockchains are also known as 'permissioned' blockchains [29].

Another kind of blockchain service is the 'Smart Contract'. Smart contracts are the contracts which are programmable and they execute automatically whenever some conditions are met [30]. A smart contract is used to bind agreements among different parties. This contract is cost-saving, efficient and provides reduced risk. Smart contracts take the definition to the next level as the contracts are visible to everyone using the blockchain, and hence, the contract is verifiable also. Thus, the technique of smart contracts can be used in the digital voting system [31]. See Figure 3.7.

3.8.2.1 Setup

In a democratic election, the major issues faced are privacy and security. We have to maintain the privacy of the voters as well as provide security during the voting process. The voters have to vote in a superintend environment. For this purpose, one can set up 'Go-Ethereum' permissioned Proof of Authority (POA) blockchain.

(Go-Ethereum is one of the original implementations of the Ethereum protocol. It is capable of running application on smart contracts without any kind of fear of downtime, fraud, censorship or any kind of third party interface. The transaction rate is dependent on what kind of blockchain we are using, i.e., public or private.) The structure of this kind of blockchain consists mainly of two types of nodes:

1. District Node: The use of this node is to represent the individual voting district. Whenever the election administrator creates an election, a ballot in the form of a smart contract is created and it is deployed to its corresponding district nodes. After this creation, the smart contract is given the permission to establish an interaction with its corresponding contract. Whenever any individual casts their votes from their corresponding smart contract, the data (votes data) are verified by a majority of the corresponding district nodes and every vote after verification is appended to the blockchain.
2. Boot Node: A boot node is a coordination and recovery service, which is there to help the district nodes to discover and communicate with each other. The boot node does not keep any state of the blockchain and usually runs on a static IP in order to help the district nodes find their peers faster.

3.8.2.2 Election as a Smart Contract

The definition of smart contract basically involves three steps: identify the roles that are involved in the process, election process and voting transaction.

1. Election Roles: The roles here basically symbolize the parties that need to participate in the smart contract agreement. These are the roles in the election:
   a. Administrator: The role of the administrator is to manage the lifetime of the election. The election administration will create the election process, register and verify the voters. The administrator can control the lifetime of the election and can also assign permissioned nodes.
   b. Voter: Any individual who will meet the criteria for voting can be able to register, load ballots, cast their votes and can verify their votes has been counted in the results.
2. Election Process: These are the activities that will be carried out during the election phase:
   a. Election Creation: The election administrator will have the authority to create a list of candidates for the election according to their voting districts, and will load the ballots using the smart contract. Then, these smart contracts are loaded to the blockchain where the district node will get permission to interact with them.
   b. Registration: The election administrator will have to start a process for registering the voters. The election administrator will also have to list down the eligible voters, who can give the vote. This can be done by

taking into consideration any of the government-issued identity. Then, each eligible voter will get a token number, which will uniquely identify them during the election phase.

    c. Results: The ballot smart contract will do the calculations for its corresponding locations in its own storage.

    d. Verifying the Votes: During the voting phase, each voter will be allotted with the transaction identification number or ID after their response is recorded. These voters can afterward use this transaction ID to verify their votes. They can visit an authorized election site and after the verification of their identity, they can use this transaction ID to track their transaction and see whether their vote was counted in the results or not. This will further enhance the transparency of the process.

3. Voting Transaction: In the voting process, the voter will interact with the ballot smart contract according to its corresponding district nodes. This smart contract with the help of district nodes will interact with the blockchain and will append the votes to the blockchain. After voting, the voters will be allotted with a transaction ID with which they can track their votes. With the help of the transaction ID, we can identify the block which has stored the transaction and in turn from which district node, the vote was cast and thus enabling the traceability of the system.

Thus, with the use of this system, one can hold the democratic election without the fear of any kind of privacy, security and tallying. There are many such systems which use the method of blockchain for the digital voting system:

AGORA, which is an end-to-end blockchain voting system, uses its own token on the blockchain for the election purpose. The governments or the institutions purchase these tokens for individual eligible voters.

Netvote is a decentralized blockchain-based digital voting system. It uses decentralized apps (Dapps) to interact with the users. The admin Dapp is used to create the election phase and the ballots. The voters Dapp is used to vote and verify their votes. The tally Dapp is used to tally the results.

Thus, the blockchain in the digital election process can be proved to be more secure and helpful in carrying out a secure and transparent election.

3.9 Conclusion

Blockchain is a promising revolutionary technology that provides trust with mathematics-based security. Decentralization concept is applicable where many parties are willing to transact with each other and do not have any system of trust. This paves the way to make multiple untrusted parties to do cross-border transactions, for example, Bitcoin. Nowadays, many applications are required to uphold huge volume of vital data and metadata on regulated firms. Due to alteration in the industry classification, these data are often in flux, which leads to maintain high data accuracy. Blockchain technology eradicates all these problems and provides solutions in a trusted way.

References

[1] A. Berentsen, (2019) *Aleksander Berentsen* Recommends "Bitcoin: A Peer-to-Peer Electronic Cash System" by Satoshi Nakamoto. In: Frey B., Schaltegger C. (eds) 21st Century Economics. Springer, Cham. https://doi.org/10.1007/978-3-030-17740-9_3.

[2] Q. Lin, P. Chang, G. Chen, B. C. Ooi, K.-L. Tan, Z. Wang, "Towards a non-2pc transaction management in distributed database systems," In: Proceeding of the 2016 International Conference on Management, 2016, pp. 1659–1674.

[3] D. M. Katz, M. Bommarito, and J. Zelner, "The trust machine," The Economist, OTC, 2015. https://www.economist.com/news/leaders/21677198-technology-behind-bitcoin-couldtransform-how-economy-works-trust-machine.

[4] Ethereum Project Homepage, https://www.ethereum.org/.

[5] Fabric Project Homepage, https://www.hyperledger.org/projects/fabric.

[6] Monero, 2017. https://getmonero.org/.

[7] Ripple, 2017. https://ripple.com.

[8] B. Markus, "Dogecoin," 2013. http://dogecoin.com/.

[9] Dash, 2017. https://www.dash.org/es/

[10] F. Schuh and D. Larimer, "Bitshares 2.0: General overview," 2017. Available: https://bravenewcoin.com/assets/Whitepapers/bitshares-general.pdf.

[11] "Namecoin," 2014. https://namecoin.org/. Nxt White Paper, 2014. Available: https://bravenewcoin.com/assets/Whitepapers/NxtWhitepaper-v122-rev4.pdf.

[12] "e-Identity — e-Estonia," e-Estonia, 2019. Available: https://e-estonia.com/solutions/e-identity/.

[13] C. McGoogan, "The end of passport gates? Dubai to test 'invisible' airport checks using facial recognition," The Telegraph, 2019. Available: https://www.telegraph.co.uk/technology/2017/06/13/end-passport-gates-dubai-test-invisible-airport-checks-using/.

[14] "Indian states look to digitise land deals with blockchain," 2019. Available: https://in.reuters.com/article/india-landrights-tech/indian-states-look-to-digitise-land-deals-with-blockchain-idINKBN1AR0PA.

[15] Gsb.stanford.edu, 2019. Available: https://www.gsb.stanford.edu/sites/gsb/files/publication-pdf/study-blockchain-impact-moving-beyond-hype_0.pdf.

[16] H. Kim and M. Laskowski, "Agriculture on the blockchain: Sustainable solutions for food, farmers, and financing," SSRN Electronic Journal, 2017.

[17] https://www.who.int/en/news-room/detail/03-12-2015-who-s-first-ever-global-estimates-of-foodborne-diseases-find-children-under-5-account-for-almost-one-third-of-deaths.

[18] https://www.pwc.com/gx/en/food-supply-integrity-services/publications/food-fraud.pdf.

[19] "Blockchain technology and the financial services market," White paper, Infosys, 2016.

[20] P. Sestoft, "Autonomous pension funds on the blockchain," IT University of Copenhagen, Dagstuhl seminar, March 2017.

[21] M. M. Solomon, "Logistics and supply chain management," Springer Nature vol. 3, pp. 900–907, 2013.

[22] Etp-logistics.eu, 2019. Available: http://www.etp-logistics.eu/wp-content/uploads/2015/08/ALICE-Recomendations-WPs-2018-2020-v161216.01_rev170117.pdf.

[23] "Blockchain has the potential to revolutionize the supply chain – TechCrunch," TechCrunch, 2019. Available: https://techcrunch.com/2016/11/24/blockchain-has-the-potential-to-revolutionize-the-supply-chain/.

[24] UbiMS, "A Global Supply Chain Revolution," 2016 Available: http://www.ubims.com/.

[25] M. Dobrovnik, D.M. Herold, E. Fürst, and S. Kummer, "Blockchain for and in logistics: What to adopt and where to start," *Logistics*, vol. 2, p.18, 2018.

[26] BlockChain, Wikipedia, 2018 https://en.wikipedia.org/wiki/Blockchain.

[27] K. Khan, J. Arshad, and M. Khan, "Secure digital voting system based on blockchain technology," International Journal of Electronic Government Research, vol. 14, no. 1, pp. 53–62, 2018.

[28] J. Jerome Mizzi and F. Inguanez, "Blockchain based e-voting system," Journal of E-Technology, vol. 9, no. 2, p. 44, 2018.

[29] A. Kulkarni, "How to choose between public and permissioned blockchain for your project," 2019.

[30] A. Rosic, "Smart contracts: The blockchain technology that will replace lawyers," A Beginner's Guide to Smart Contracts, 2019.

[31] R. Bulut, A. Kantarcı, and S. Keskin, and S. Bahtiyar. Blockchain-based electronic voting system for elections in Turkey. 4th International Conference on Computer Science and Engineering (UBMK), 2019, pp. 183–188. 10.1109/UBMK.2019.8907102.

Chapter 4

Blockchain Smart Contracts

V. Sudha and D. Sathya

Contents

4.1 Introduction

In this computer world, digital transformation is a thoughtful and unavoidable one. The impact of this conversion is reflected both in the government and private sectors. Among these, the financial and business sectors have to face a lot of challenges to undergo this change. In the financial sector, the transaction between two parties has become a part of their life. A transaction normally occurs with the help of a few centralized authorities.

In the centralized system, all the transaction needs to be verified by a centralized authority. But many issues exist in executing this methodology. Among them, two important issues concerned with the financial sector are large storage space required for processing and the cost of committing a transaction. Blockchain, a blooming technology, has overcome this drawback by changing the execution model. Blockchain is a decentralized distributed ledger shared among the participating users. For instance, if two persons say person A and B need to communicate, then person A interacts directly with person B without any intermediate. Since in blockchain, everything is done in online mode, digital currencies are required to make financial transactions in online mode. Bitcoin is an instance of a digital currency which is used by blockchain technology. In blockchain, the already existing ledger cannot be modified; the new entries can only be appended.

Block is a collection of transactions. Each block has a gas limit. A transaction must have a gas limit to include itself within a block. The sum of the gas limits of each transaction within the block should not exceed the total gas limit of a block. Thus, there will be more than one block in a blockchain. Each block in the blockchain has only one parent and, in turn, each parent can have only one child. The header of the parent block stores the hash value of the transactions present in child block. Thus, when the number of transactions present in a block is either reduced or increased, the hash value gets updated. This refreshed value must be updated in the respective block. Thus, the transaction becomes immutable.

The Ethereum Virtual Machine (EVM) is the execution unit of the Ethereum network. The smart contract contains the code for all the agreements. EVM executes this program line by line. The initiation of a transaction is done by invoking the program in a smart contract. All the agreements to be executed are in the form of condition statements. When all the requirements are satisfied, the action followed by it takes place. When the transaction is successful, next, it must be added to a block. Miners are responsible for this action. More than one miner competes to add a transaction to the block. Among them, the miner solving the puzzle adds the transaction to the block and notifies the solution to others. They will verify the work and if it is correct, the transaction is added to the block. This job is known as Proof of Work (PoW). Thus, by increasing the size of the blockchain, the security of the transaction is increased.

Along with the above mentioned, a few other advantages are discussed in the latter part of this chapter. Though blockchain technology encompasses many advantages, it also has many disadvantages to its part. These are also addressed in this chapter.

The organization of this chapter is as follows. The initial part of the chapter discusses the working process of the smart contract. Followed by it, the technology related to a block addition in a blockchain is described. Next, the chapter describes the Solidity – the language used for writing the smart contract. The later part of the chapter discusses the pros and cons of this booming technology.

4.2 Smart Contracts

The transaction is an agreement between two parties. The agreement binding the two parties is known as the contract. The protocol used for the digital implementation of the contract is known as a smart contract. It enables the blockchain to execute a transaction without the involvement of a third party. Thus, the constraints are realized using smart contracts.

A smart contract was initiated by Nick Szabo in 1994. A smart contract can be created by anyone who is Turing combat. A smart contract once created remains lifelong. All the constraints are realized as self-executable contracts. Smart contracts reduce the cost of the transaction. The properties of a smart contract include [1]:

1. Autonomy – It implies that after the smart contract initiation, the deal initiator does not participate in the process.
2. Decentralization – Smart contract uses distributed network points rather than a centralized server.
3. Auto-sufficiency – It has a larger capacity for storage and resources for transactions.

4.3 Working Principle of Smart Contracts

Nowadays, most of the transactions performed are centralized, involving a lot of security issues and processing charges. Also, the transaction depends on the third party for its completion. Blockchain stores all the transactions happening in the network. A smart contract in the blockchain is responsible for imposing and verifying the constraints needed for the transaction.

A smart contract is responsible for the automatic execution of all the agreements required for a transaction. The definitions of the smart contract are classified into two categories: smart contract code and smart legal contract. Smart contract code is coded, verified and executed on a blockchain. The code substituting the legal contract is the smart legal contract.

Each smart contract consists of the following: executable code, an account balance and private storage. The instantaneous description of the smart contract consists of storage and account balance. Blockchain stores the state of the smart contract and updates it whenever it is invoked.

Each smart contract has an address of size 20 bytes. Once a smart contract is deployed on a blockchain, its address cannot be modified. To execute a transaction, send it to the designated smart contract address. Miners in the network execute the transaction until a consensus is reached. Later, after executing a transaction, update the account of the smart contract. There are three ways to update a smart contract. These include the creation of a new contract, send/receive messages to/from a smart contract and store/retrieve some amount in a smart contract account.

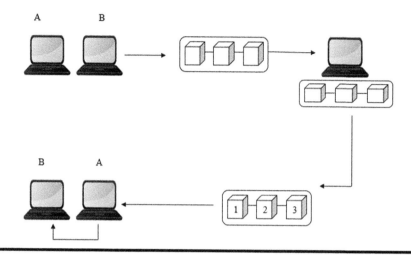

Figure 4.1   Working of smart contract.

Figure 4.1 shows the working of a smart contract. In this, node A wants to send something with B, hence the transactions are transferred into the network. Similar to this, all nodes in the network make transactions. These transactions are grouped into a block, and the block checking is done by the network nodes. The blocks are indexed and added to the blockchain.

4.4 Types of Smart Contracts

There are two types of smart contracts. They are deterministic and non-deterministic. A deterministic smart contract does not require any information from external sources, while a non-deterministic one requires knowledge from external sources.

In a smart contract, all the constraints are written as rules. When the condition gets satisfied, the action following it is executed.

4.4.1 Mining

Mining is a mechanism to secure the Bitcoin system in a decentralized manner. In Bitcoin mining, the miners confirm new transactions and record them in the global ledger. The block is mined every 10 minutes. The miners try to solve the cryptographic hash problems, and when miners find the solution, the transaction is confirmed. The Bitcoin is spent after the transaction is approved. For example, if we receive Bitcoin in a wallet, then the miners have to spend 10 minutes to confirm the transaction [2].

When a node is notified with a valid PoW, the candidate block is created. The candidate block is used to collect the new transactions in the transaction pool and remove the transaction of the previous block. Figure 4.2 depicts the work of a candidate block [2].

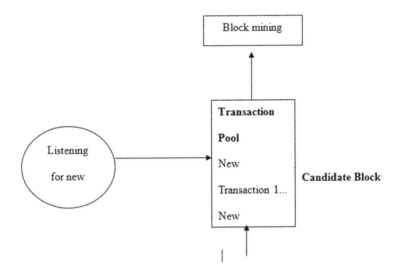

Figure 4.2   Candidate block.

4.5 Ethereum Virtual Machine

EVM is responsible for the line by line execution of the codes in the smart contract. EVM creates an abstraction between the code and the machine on which it is running.

Smart contract uses Solidity language that is similar to other high-level languages like Java and C++. The languages like Vyper, Bamboo, Serpent, Mutan are also used for writing a smart contract. Solidity is a high-level language that EVM cannot execute directly. This high-level language is converted to low-level language or opcode for execution [3].

The opcode is a set of instructions executing a specific task in EVM. There can be a maximum of 256 (162) opcodes. A byte is allocated for each opcode. The opcodes generally perform the following tasks [3]:

■ Stack-manipulating opcodes
■ Arithmetic/comparison/bitwise opcodes
■ Environmental opcodes
■ Memory-manipulating opcodes
■ Storage-manipulating opcodes
■ Program counter related opcode
■ Halting opcodes

The low-level programming languages use the stack for passing values to functions. The EVM uses the stack storage of 256-bit, which holds 1024 items. Due to the limitations in stack storage, opcode uses contract memory. The contract memory is not continual, i.e., the memory content is present until the contract execution. So, the contract memory is used only for retrieving data, whereas the data storage is expensive.

4.6 Byte Code

Byte codes store the opcodes efficiently. Byte code is made up of multiple opcodes. The opcode representation generally begins with '0x'. Thus, it makes use of hexadecimal format for its representation. Every transaction address begins with '0x' indicating that EVM takes any value in hexadecimal format.

```
"0x52" represents the opcode MSTORE and "0x55" describes
SSTORE, here "0x" is optional [12].
```

For example:

```
Push1 0x60 push1 0x40 MSTORE
```

The above opcode does the following tasks: (i) push 0x60 into the stack, (ii) push 0x40 into the stack and (iii) MSTORE allocates 0x60 of memory space and the pointer moves to 0x40 position.

EVM store data in three places:

1. PUSH represents storing the data in stack'
2. MSTORE represents storing the data in RAM;
3. SSTORE represents storing the data in the disk.

4.6.1 Deploying a Smart Contract

Create the transaction without 'to' address and copy some byte code as input. This initial byte code is essential for writing the first variables. Then, copy the runtime byte code [4]. The initial bytecode runs only once, whereas runtime byte code executes on every created contract call.

4.7 Processing of Smart Contracts

The blockchain where the smart contract can be processed are [5]:

1. Bitcoin – It can execute the Bitcoin transactions but limit document processing.
2. Sidechains – These provide more scope for processing smart contracts than Bitcoin.
3. NXT – It provides a public platform for blockchain where it has its code. The user cannot code their own.
4. Ethereum – It is also a public blockchain platform. It affords more scope for processing and coding, but the user has to pay for the computing power.

4.8 Solidity Language

Solidity is a high-level language whose syntax and processing are more or less similar to that of JavaScript. It executes a contract in the Ethereum environment.

4.8.1 Data Types

Solidity language supports the following basic data types. These data types are also called Value types, as the variables of these types are always passed as values.

1. Booleans
2. Integers
3. Address
4. String literals
5. Modifier
6. Array

The following gives a detailed explanation of these data types.

1. **Booleans**

   A Boolean variable can take either true or false as the possible values. The following list gives the operators that can be applied to a Boolean variable.
   a. ! (Logical not)
   b. && (Logical and)
   c. || (Logical or)
   d. == (equality)
   e. != (inequality)
   The operator && and || follows short circuit evaluation for evaluating the operands.

2. **Integers**

   The integers value type takes two forms, namely, int and unit. The keyword into represents the signed integers while unit denotes an unsigned integer. These forms take values ranging from 8 to 256 bits. The representation varies depending on the bit size it stores. For instance, the declaration uint8 v denotes that the variable v is capable of storing an 8-bit unsigned integer value.

   The following operations can be performed on an integer variable.
   a. *Comparison operators*
      <= (less than or equal to)
      < (less than)
      == (equal to)
      != (not equal to)
      >= (greater than or equal to)
      > (greater than)

All of the above comparison operators evaluate to a Boolean value, i.e., either true or false.

b. *Bit operators*

& (bitwise and)

| (bitwise or)

^ (bitwise xor)

~ (bitwise not)

c. *Arithmetic operators*

+, − (binary addition and subtraction)

+, − (unary addition and subtraction)

* (multiplication)

/(division)

% (modular division)

** (exponent)

≪ (left shift)

≫ (right shift)

3. **Address**

The variables of type address are capable of storing a 20-byte Ethereum address. There are two properties associated with this data type. They are balance and transfer. The balance property aids in retrieving the balance connected with a particular address. The transfer property helps in transferring some amount of ether to a particular account. Using the dot operator, these two properties are accessed. The following are the operators associated with this data type: <=, <, = =,! =, >= and >.

4. **String Literals**

String literals are enclosed either with single or double quotes. Unlike the C language, the string literal does not end up with the null character. Thus, the string literal 'remix' will occupy only 5 bytes of memory.

5. **Modifiers**

In a smart contract, modifiers ensure the integrity of the constraints specified before executing the code.

6. **Array**

An array is a fixed-size contiguous memory allocation by the user. It can be either statically or dynamically sized. A static array a of type T with size k is declared as

```
T[k] a.
```

A dynamic array d of type T is declared as

```
T [] a.
```

An array can be stored either in storage or memory. By default, the array index starts from the value 0. The keyword new is used for allocating space for an array in memory. For example, consider the following declaration where an array named a of size with type unit is allocated space in memory.

```
unit[] memory a = new unit[](10);
```

Enum

The Enum keyword creates a user-defined data type. Enum requires at least one member in the set. Enum data type can be explicitly converted to or from integers. Implicit conversions cannot be done.

Struct

Struct type creates user-defined data types that group's variable of the different data types. Consider the following example. In this, a structure named Detail is created.

```
pragma solidity ^0.4.0;
contract List {
struct Detail {
            string name;
            unit age;
            bool result;
        }
    }
```

An example program illustrating the above concepts is given as follows.

```
pragma solidity ^0.4.0;
contract Direction {
      unit axis;
      enum Path {Left, Right}
}
```

In the above source, the first line indicates the version of the solidity software. The pragma keyword intimates that the line following it is the instruction to the compiler. In this example, Direction is the name of the contract, the axis is the variable of type unsigned integer and Path represents an enum variable.

4.8.2 Functions

Functions are the executable codes within the smart contract. Functions in a smart contract can take arguments and return values. It can be invoked either internally or externally. Also, they can have different levels of visibility.

4.8.2.1 Syntax

```
function(parameter) {internal | external | public | private}
[pure | constant | view | payable] [(modifiers)] [return
(<return types>)]
```

The function parameter declaration is the same as the normal variable declaration. The syntax of the return values follows the same structure as that of the parameter declaration. A function can return more than one value. There are four types of functions namely, internal, external, public and private. By default, the function type is internal. The modifiers used in the function changes the flow of the program.

Other functions can call external functions, but cannot be called internal function. For instance, the add function in the following example cannot be accessed as add(); it can be accessed only through the keyword this: add().

Functions that are part of the contract interface are known as public functions. This function can be called either internally or through messages. Internal functions can be accessed only within the contract or the contracts derived from it, without using this keyword. The function that is accessed by the contract where it is defined is known as the private function. The contracts derived from it cannot access these functions.

In the following example, a function named add is defined with public visibility. It takes two arguments: x and y. It returns the sum of these values.

```
pragma solidity ^0.4.0;
contract Sample {
        unit sum;
        function add(unit _x, unit _y) public {
                sum = _x + _y;
        returns (sum);
        }
}
```

4.8.3 Events

Solidity events provide logging facilities allowing JavaScript to call back in the user interface. Events are the inheritable members of the smart contract. These logs are associated with the address of the smart contract. Hence, events exist until the corresponding block lives.

4.8.4 Mappings

Mappings map each key to some value. Mappings can be viewed as a hash table. Mappings follow the following syntax

```
mapping(_KeyType => _ValueType).
```

In the above syntax, _KeyType takes any data type except the following: Mappings, dynamically sized array, a contract, a enum and a struct. The _ValueType can any value even a mapping.

Example

```
mapping (account => unit) public value.
```

4.8.5 *Conversion between Elementary Types*

Both implicit and explicit type conversions are possible. Implicit type conversions are allowed only if there is no data loss. Explicit type conversion can be applied in cases where implicit type conversions are not possible. But when explicit conversions are applied, we should be very careful with the data loss and the value it takes. An example of explicit type conversion is given as follows:

```
int8 a;
unit b = unit(a).
```

In the above example, the variable a with type signed integer is typecast to the variable b of type b. Implicit conversion is not allowed between the data type signed and the unsigned integer.

4.8.6 *Type Deduction*

Sometimes the type of value a variable holds may not be known at the beginning. In such cases, the type of a variable can be deducted from the value assigned to it. In the following example, the type of the variable y int8 is inferred from the value x assigned to it.

```
int8 x;
var y = x;
```

4.8.7 *Reference Types*

Sometimes the size of the data cannot be fitted with 256 bits. In such a situation, we move on to complex data types. The coping process is the problem of using these data types. A variable can be stored either in memory (non-persistent storage) or storage (state-variable storage). The different locations can be accessed using the keywords memory and storage. A detail of these locations is given further. The function variables by default get stored in memory, while the state variables are cached in the storage.

Blockchain is a big database from where any of them can access the data while the modification is done only after getting the required permission. The integrity of the information must be ensured in the modification operation. The executed modification must be either complete or null. It should not land up in an intermediate state.

In Ethereum, the runtime environment for the smart contract is the EVM. EVM is like a black box where the contracts running inside cannot access its file systems. Ethereum consists of two types of accounts. They are contract and external accounts. Both of these accounts share the same address space. The public-private key pairs manage the external account while stored code controls the contract account.

When a transaction is created, anybody can execute it. When a person needs to execute a transaction, they must pay a certain amount called gas. The owner who creates the transaction specifies the amount of gas. Each time when a user executes a transaction, a certain amount of gas is decreased from their account. The amount of gas paid is specified as shown

```
gas_price *gas.
```

After the execution of a transaction, the remaining gas reverts to the user account. Also, an exception is raised when the account does not have the required gas [6].

Each account in the transaction has two types of memory associated with it. They are storage and memory. The storage that saves the value as a key-value pair is the persistent storage area. It maps a 256-bit word to another word of the same size. It is very costly to read and modify the content in storage. For each message call, fresh storage is allocated from the memory. Here, the read operation involves reading data with a size of 256 bits while the writing operation is restricted to the size of either 8 or 256 bits.

4.8.7.1 Costs for Smart Contracts

The attackers can create their contract and execute it to slow down the network. To prevent such attacks, the opcode is charged with base and dynamic gas cost per word. Every transaction initiates with 21,000 gas. Once the storage is set to zero, the 15,000 gas is refunded. If the contract is fully removed, then 24,000 gas is returned.

4.8.8 Message Call

A contract calls another contract or sends Ether to a non-contract through a message call.

4.8.9 Control Structures

Solidity language contains all the control structures that are in other programming languages. They are listed here for reference: if, else, while, do, for, break, continue and return.

The type conversion from Boolean to non-Boolean is not possible in Solidity language. For instance, the following expression is not allowed in Solidity language for the above reason:

```
if (1) {…}.
```

4.8.10 Contract Creation

A contract can be created from another contract using the new keyword. In the following example, a contract named Sample creates another contract Sample1 using the new keyword.

```
pragma solidity ^0.4.0;
contract Sample1 {
        unit diff;
        constructor (unit z) public payable {
                a =z;
        }
}
contract Sample {
        Sample1 s = new Sample1(5);//Here the contract Sample1
is invoked
        }
}
```

The default value for any numeric variables is 0, while false for the Boolean variables.

Blockchain is not a disruptive technology. It is a new foundation technology that changes the social and economic facts in the world.

4.8.11 Example

The following example illustrates most of the features in the Solidity language. It is based on the election system in our country. It is assumed that for each voting machine, a contract is created. Hence, the contract name Election represents a Ballot machine used in a booth.

In our country, as we all are aware of, each voter has some eligible age and identity number to cast a vote. In the following example, a voter is defined as a structure named Voter. The following are the parameters associated with a voter: age, sex, voter and vote value. The parameter age is used for performing eligibility tests for vote casting and variable vote describes whether the particular voter has voted or not. In this application, two types of weights are assigned. One for the persons belonging to the election commission and the other for the remaining. The variable votevalue in the Voter structure represents this. From the above description, it is inferred that when there is a tie between two parties, then the candidate for whom the election commission person votes becomes the winner.

Each party competing in the election will have a name associated with it. Finally, to announce the result, we need the total vote count of each party participating in the election. Thus, the party structure consists of two variables: pname and total votes. The following are the constraints verified while conducting the election. Initially, the eligibility of the user needs to be verified by checking their age. If they are eligible and have not already cast the vote, they are allowed for the voting. These constraints are verified by the functions of eligibilityToVote and castVote.

```
pragma solidity ^0.4.11;
contract Election {
//Voter structure represents the parameter associated
with a single voter.
        struct Voter {
                unit age;
                unit sex;
                bool vote;//gives the value whether the
                particular voter has voted or not
                unit votevalue;
        }
        struct Party
        {
                bytes32 pname;
                unit totalvotes;
        }
        address public electioncomission;
        mapping(address => Voter) public singlevoter;
        Party [] public applications;
        constructor(bytes32 [] memory partyNames) public {
                electioncomission = msg.sender;
                singlevoter[electioncomission].weight = 1;
                for (uint k=0; k < partyNames.length; k++) {
                        applications.push(Party({
                                pname: partyNames[k],
                                totalvotes: 0
                        }));
                }
        }
        function elgibilityToVote(address candidate)
        public {
                require(
                        !applications[candidate].vote
                );
                require(singlevoters[candiadate]. value ==
                0);
                singlevoter[voter].value = 1;
        }
        function assign(address to) public {
                Voter storage member = singlevoter[msg.
                sender];
                require(!member.vote, "voted already");
                require(to! = msg.member, "Voting is not
                possible.");
```

```
                 while(singlevoter[to].assign! = address(0))
                 {
                       to = singlevoter[to].assign;
                       require(to! = msg.sender, "Äction
                       repeated");
                 }
                 sender.vote = true;
                 sender.delegate = to;
                 Voter storage assign_ = singlevoter[to];
           }
           function castVote(unit applications) public {
                 Voter storage sender = singlevoter[msg.
                 sender];
                 require(sender.age <= 18, "Not eligible to
                 vote");
                 require(!sender.vote,"Completed voting");
                 sender.vote = true;
           }
           function winingParty() public view
                 returns (uint winingParty_)
           {
                 uint finalCount = 0;
                 for (uint 1 = 0; 1 < applications.length;
                 1++) {
                       if(applications[1].totalvotes >
                       finalVoteCount) {
                             finalVoteCount =
                             applications[1].totalvotes;
                             winningParty_= 1;
                       }
                 }
           }
           function winningCandidate () public view
                 returns (bytes32 winningCandidate_)
           {
                 winningCandidte_ =
                 applications[winingParty()].pname;
           }
     }
```

4.8.12 Executing a Solidity Program

In this digital world, we need something that regulates the administrative process. The process either depends on the centralized processing or on some human resource. Blockchain helps to overcome this constraint.

Since Ehtereum is the only platform that is proved to be Turing complete, most of the applications make use of this platform for blockchain development [7]. Each block is uniquely identified by the hash function.

4.9 Cryptocurrencies

Cryptocurrencies are digital currencies based on cryptographic techniques. Bitcoin is the most famous example of cryptocurrencies. Bitcoin, introduced in 2008, is the digital currency that is used to make the digital transaction between the sender and receiver. This enables us to transfer some amount between the sender and receiver without the involvement of the third party. Miners verify the validity of these transactions.

The single point of failure is avoided in blockchain by storing the database in a distributed manner.

4.10 Safety of Smart Contracts

We may think scalability as a very big issue in implementing a smart contract [8]. But it is not so. It is a well-known fact that all the conditions needed for the agreement are implemented as code by a smart contract. Hence, it is much important to secure it from vulnerable changes. To overcome the above problem, the smart contract codes can be made immutable.

The key areas that need improvement in certain fields of smart contracts [9] are

A. *Coding*
   The smart contract coding should be verified and optimally protected.
B. *Auditing*
   The smart contract has to be audited by any independent third party organization.
C. *Strong passwords*
   The passwords have to be kept secret to keep users safe and free from phishing attacks.

4.11 Applications of Smart Contracts

Some of the applications of Smart Contracts are discussed as follows.

4.11.1 Financial Services

The technology has not even left the financial sectors like banks. In a day, a bank branch receives thousands of applications for processing. The processing of these applications takes some number of days. Hence, they need technology that reduces these processing time and increases efficiency. Also, most of the processing is centralized. All the above-mentioned drawbacks are overcome by the application of blockchain and smart contracts. When centralized authorities are used for processing these documents, obviously a queue is formed causing a delay in the document. Also, the usage of the centralized database does not allow multiprocessing.

4.12 Advantages of Applying Smart Contracts in Financial Services

There are three areas where a smart contract is applied in financial services [10]. They are investment banking, retail banking and insurance. In investment banking, the number of days taken for processing is reduced; in retail banks and insurance, processing cost is reduced by the application of the smart contract.

4.12.1 Real Estate

To apply blockchain technology for the real estate business [11], the first step is to identify the actors. Usually, the actors in the business are the owners or the brokers who are responsible for selling the property. In this application, the landlord and tenants are considered as external owned accounts. Private keys are used for controlling this account. The code that is responsible for executing the given constraints forms the contract accounts. Miners are the persons who are responsible for verifying the transactions.

After deciding the actors and the accounts, the next step is to define the smart contract for the real estate application. Here, a smart contract is created between a landlord or the real estate owner and tenants. The created smart contract is responsible for verifying agreement policies, rent payment and contract termination. The flow of the smart contract process is as follows. Initially, the owner initiates the contract process by specifying the terms and conditions. The process starts when the tenant signs the contract. Followed by it, rent is transferred from the tenant account to the owner's account. This process continues until the owner terminates the contract. Thus, there are three important processes in applying smart contract to the real estate application. They are rent contract signature, rental payment and rent contract termination. Finally, in the implementation phase, the code necessary for the implementation of these process are realized.

4.12.2 Supply Chain

Usually, in the shipping industry, a product moves from one place to another and this journey is a long chain. This movement involves many geographical regions. A loss in any one of the regions may lead to great failure. Blockchain may give a solution to this problem by providing the path through which the product moves over [12]. In [13], a literature survey is done on agri-food supply chain management, which focuses on bibliometric and content analyses. Similarly, a literature review on resilience in agri-food supply chains is performed, and a novel framework has been built [14].

4.12.3 Telemedicine

The internet has not left even health care files. Most of the patient records are made online; securing and preserving the health care data also became an important concern. Since all the data present in these are very sensitive, it is important to provide secure access to these data. By applying blockchain technology [12], the patient will be able to control the data, but the ownership of the data lies with the doctor who has uploaded this data.

4.12.4 Radiation-Hardened Computing

Many systems are designed to work under very high radiations. When a device is exposed to high radiation, the performance of the device may get affected. This issue is resolved by applying the blockchain concept [12].

4.12.5 Automobiles

Nowadays, automated vehicles are used enormously for public safety. For example, if a person is about to crash, the automated vehicles have sensors to alarm about the crash and also find the faults. Also, we can find a personality involved in the fault. Based on this, the automobile insurance company uses smart contracts to charge the owner of the vehicle [5].

4.12.6 Copyrights

The blockchain allows protecting the individual ownership rights in a decentralized system. And this ensures to give the royalty to the concerned persons. The digital assets can also be saved in a decentralized server.

4.13 Advantages of Smart Contracts

There are a lot of advantages to using smart contracts for real-time applications, as discussed below [15].

4.13.1 Accuracy

The smart contract will record all the terms and conditions explicitly. The omission of recording the data will result in a transaction error. By the explicit recording of data, there is clear communication between the parties. At the same time, the manual recording is avoided.

4.13.2 Transparency

The term and conditions are fully visible for all parties. The concerned parties cannot deny after the establishment of smart contracts.

4.13.3 Speed

The transaction runs on software code and uses the internet. This provides a speedy process helpful for all types of businesses.

4.13.4 Security

The encryption standard used in the smart contract is the same as the standard used in cryptocurrencies. So it is highly secured.

4.13.5 Efficiency

The speed and accuracy of the contracts provide high efficiency. Higher efficiency leads to more transactions per unit period.

4.13.6 Storage

The records are stored explicitly for each transaction. When any data is lost, the data can be retrieved easily from these records.

4.14 Issues in Implementing Blockchain Smart Contracts

The following are some of the issues in the blockchain implementation [16].

4.14.1 Complexity

Blockchain is a new technology that is a combination of mathematics, cryptography and network. Because of this nature, understanding it is a little difficult. Also, the new terms used in the blockchain increase its complexity.

4.14.2 Human Error

The information stored in blockchain is very sensitive. Hence, the information to be stored in the blockchain must be done with great effort and carefulness. Otherwise, it may lead to severe consequences.

4.14.3 Interoperability

There are different types of blockchains such as private, public and consortium. Each of these blockchain networks has different rules and regulations to be satisfied. Hence, it is difficult to communicate with a blockchain from another. Thus, interoperability is very difficult to achieve in blockchain technology.

4.14.4 Authentication

It is known from the earlier discussion that each of the actors involved in the block-chain is managed by the private key. When these private keys are attacked and stolen, authentication of the user becomes the problem.

4.14.5 Scalability

It is known that each transaction added to the blockchain must pass the PoW. Thus, each transaction involves some default processing time. Hence, when the number of transactions needs to be processed is increased, the minimum time taken for processing may be a constraint.

4.15 Attacks on Smart Contracts

The attack that impacted a lot of blockchain smart contract is Decentralized Autonomous Organization (DAO) attack [17]. The developer and investor can learn about the following three attacks when they learn fully about the DAO attack:

1. Reentrancy attack
2. Underflow attack
3. Cross-function Race Condition attack

The attacks and their effects are explained below.

4.15.1 Reentrancy Attacks

The attacker endlessly calls the targets to withdraw function which is called a reentrancy attack. Figure 4.3 gives the flow of the reentrancy attack. When a contract fails to update its state before sending the funds, the attacker calls the withdraw function endlessly until it drains the target funds.

4.15.2 Underflow Attacks

The attacker credits 1 Wei to the target contract. The 1 Wei withdrawn from the target leads to zero balance. Since the attacker's fallback function is triggered, a withdrawal is called again. The balance of the target becomes –1. The attacker's balance is updated to 2256 once the balance becomes zero. The target account is fully withdrawn and made empty [18].

The newer version is updated by all the nodes in the network. Keeping the older versions may lead to pitfalls in the contract. The protocols have to be updated to a newer version. The mismatch of versions may create a data difference problem, confusion and errors.

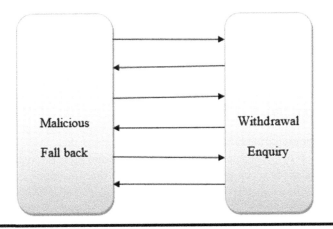

Figure 4.3   Reentrancy attack.

The underflow error [19] is when a number is decremented below its minimum value, it is called an underflow error.

For example: This is opposite to the overflow error, suppose unit 8 is assigned to 0. The decrementing the value by 1 leads to –1 which is below the minimum value.

4.15.3 Cross-Function Race Condition Attacks

The cross-function race condition attack shown in Figure 4.4 occurs when multiple functions call and share the same contract state. For example, if the attacker calls the transfer function and external withdrawal balance function at the same time.

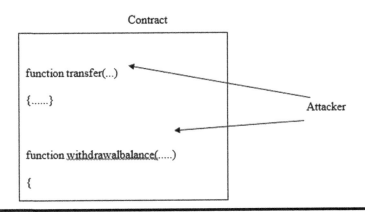

Figure 4.4   Cross-function race condition attack.

4.15.4 The Overflow Error

When a number gets incremented above its maximum value, it is called overflow error [19].

For example: If we take an unsigned variable whose size is 8 bits, then it can have a value from 0 to 255. The solidity language can accept up to 256-bit numbers. Incrementing 1 to this unit will lead to an overflow error that solidity cannot accept.

4.15.5 Deprecated and Historical Attacks [20]

Updating the protocol version in all the nodes avoids these types of historical attacks

i. *Call Depth Attack*
   Deprecated or Call Depth attack is the attack caused when the gas is consumed fully before reaching the call depth limit of 1024.
ii. *Constantinople Reentrancy Attack*
   Constantinople protocol up-gradation is delayed due to the security vulnerability caused by EIP 1283. This issue leads to a new re-entrancy attack. The attackers by knowing the previous withdrawal patterns, attack the control flow of the code and consume gas.

4.15.6 Other Attacks and Vulnerabilities

The SWCR (Smart contract Weakness Classification Registry) has a list on up to date vulnerabilities, and attacks with real-world examples. The test cases are also explained in the list. Studying the list and upgrading it with the latest attacks is good for developers and users.

References

[1] https://hackernoon.com/advantages-and-disadvantages-of-smart-contracts-in-financial-blockchain-systems-3a443145ae1c.
[2] https://dev.to/damcosset/blockchain-what-is-mining-2eod.
[3] https://medium.com/mycrypto/the-ethereum-virtual-machine-how-does-it-work-9abac2b7c9e.
[4] https://medium.com/@blockchain101/solidity-bytecode-and-opcode-basics-672e9b1a88c2.
[5] https://blockgeeks.com/guides/smart-contracts/.
[6] https://solidity.readthedocs.io/en/v0.4.21/introduction-to-smart-contracts.html#blockchain-basics.
[7] Maher Alharby and Aad van Moorsel, "Blockchain-based smart contracts: A systematic mapping study", International Conference on Cloud Computing, Big Data and Blockchain, pp. 125–140, 2018.

[8] Sukrit Kalra, Seep Goel, Mohan Dhawan, and Subodh Sharma, "Zeus: Analyzing Safety of Smart Contracts," In: Network and Distributed Systems Security (NDSS) Symposium, 2018.

[9] https://medium.com/contract-vault/staying-safe-with-smart-contracts-a0177ef174f3.

[10] Smart contracts in financial services: Getting from hype to reality – Capgemini Consulting.

[11] Ioannis Karamitsos, Maria Papadaki, and Nedaa Baker Al Barghuthi, "Design of the blockchain smart contract: A use case for real estate," Journal of Information Security, vol. 9, pp. 177–190, 2018.

[12] Reinforcing the links of the Blockchain, IEEE future directions Blockchain initiative white paper.

[13] Jianli Luo, Chen Ji, Chunxiao Qiu, and Fu Jia, "Agri-food supply chain management: bibliometric and content analyses," Sustainability, vol. 10, p. 1573, 2018.

[14] Jamie Stone and Shahin Rahimifard, "Resilience in agri-food supply chains: a critical analysis of the literature and synthesis of a novel framework," Supply Chain Management, vol. 23, no. 3, pp. 207-238, https://doi.org/10.1108/SCM-06-2017-0201.

[15] https://medium.com/@ChainTrade/10-advantages-of-using-smart-contracts-bc29c508691a.

[16] Divyakant Meva, "Issues and Challenges with Blockchain: A Survey," International Journal of Computer Sciences and Engineering, Vol. 6, Issue. 12, pp.488–491.

[17] https://hackernoon.com/smart-contract-attacks-part-1-3-attacks-we-should-all-learn-from-the-dao-909ae4483f0a.

[18] https://medium.com/haloblock/unit-underflows-and-overflows-ethereum-solidity-vulnerability-39a39355c422.

[19] https://blockgeeks.com/guides/underflow-attacks-smart-contracts/.

[20] https://consensys.github.io/smart-contract-best-practices/known_attacks/.

Chapter 5

Blockchain in Supply Chain Management

Vinay Reddy Mallidi, V. Madhu Viswanatham
and P. Ashok Kumar

Contents

5.1 Introduction

Supply chain management is a crucial process in today's business. A supply chain consists of an appended network of people, resources and organizations that are into the manufacture or sale of products. It consists of several entities in a chain where the products shift hands to reach the consumer from the place where it is manufactured. Supply chain is a vast concept. All the commodities of daily use undergo multiple transactions across various business processes to reach consumers.

In the existing supply chain, a lot of information is hidden. Supply chain is very complex with numerous business processes and a large number of transactions taking place on a daily basis. The longer the supply chain, the greater is the chance for fraud to happen due to loss of accountability and negligence.

There is a chance for discrepancies to occur in the supply chain such as introducing counterfeit products in place of the original ones, etc. All the businesses around the world are built on "TRUST" and trust is at stake due to such activities [1].

Consumers are looking out for the companies that provide them transparency about the product that they use or consume.

Blockchain technology can be deployed over the supply chain to maintain a sharable and tamper-proof record of the product transactions at each business level. This helps in building trust among the consumers as they are provided with all answers to their queries about the products such as:

- Where it was manufactured?
- Did the product reach safely without being altered – is it the same as when it was manufactured or is anything compromised?
- What is the genuine composition of the purchased product?

All these queries are answered by the blockchain through its novel features of transparency and immutability. Once a record has been updated on the blockchain, it is permanent and cannot be changed.

Using Internet of Things (IoT) and blockchain together it is possible to implement blockchain technology in supply chain management which would bring a revolutionary change as the transparency increases providing the user with the in and out details of the product.

For instance:

Blockchain provides both the manufacturer as well as the consumers' traceability and provenance of the product thereby establishing trust by projecting the details such as:

- The authenticity of product – Genuine/Fake
- Whether the product meets with the compliance conditions through each business process

The objective of this chapter is to explain how blockchain technology enhances the supply chain management of several commodities through transparency and immutability.

5.2 Background

Every industry across the globe is on the verge of digitizing their supply chain and integrating the blockchain technology into it. The security and cost-effectiveness of the digital supply chain can be improved greatly using blockchain [2]. One of the main features of blockchain is that it maintains a distributed ledger of transactions. If any change is to be made in the data of distributed ledger, approval must be there from the majority of the peers in the network. In real business transactions, this process involves two parts: a public ledger entry about the transactions and private messages between the parties about identities. By combining both the parts, the transaction can bypass the trusted third party and the transaction can be done rapidly at a very low cost [3].

Blockchain is a disruptive technology that excludes the need for any intermediator in the transaction between entities. The use cases of blockchain are endless. It can be implemented in any industry as it is a distributed ledger where the transactions are shared among all the peers in the network in a way it can be viewed but cannot be tampered. Provenance and traceability can be provided using blockchain technology [4]. Smart contracts can be employed by means of which payments can be done without the need for third parties in a secure way and also saving costs and time [5].

The advent of Bitcoin and other cryptocurrencies has shown that transactions are possible without a third party [6]. The security can be provided by having a decentralized peer network with a public ledger. In a similar fashion, the blockchain technology can be used to protect personal data. But in this case – the transactions are not purely financial – but are used to carry information such as storing, querying and sharing data. Blockchain is an important resource in trusted computing [7].

A blockchain may be used as a public ledger including an ordered and time-stamped record of transactions. A participant can give consent to be monitored, and one or more members of the monitored system can perform one or more authorized transactions in accordance with authorization data [8].

Blockchain in supply chain management is at its early stages of development. Supply chain provenance can be achieved more efficiently using IoT and blockchain technology [9]. Blockchain has numerous use cases to consider in order to maintain immutability and provide provenance at the same time. Smart contracts are to be written to handle the use cases that vary with the blockchain paradigm, purpose and complexity of the business-inter-organizational, intra-organizational, technical and external barriers [10].

5.3 Main Focus of the Chapter

The chapter discusses the use cases of blockchain technology for the supply chain of several commodities like food, pharmaceuticals and auto motives. The author also explains the types of blockchain networks that can be developed for supply chain management, the efficient consensus model to deploy blockchain technology for transactions over a supply chain and the technology that can be used to bring that consensus model into force.

5.4 Features of Blockchain and How It Benefits the Supply Chain

- Blockchain provides distributed and decentralized data ledger as opposed to a centralized database in case of existing centralized database for supply chains.
- Smart contracts can be written in a blockchain to which the business processes involved in the supply chain must concur to. This eliminates the need for any third party to validate the transactions.
- In the existing supply chains, the transaction records are prone to tampering but in a blockchain, each block is related to its preceding block using a cryptographic algorithm that makes the records immutable. This provides security to the data and enhances reliability by eliminating errors.
- In the existing supply chain, a lot of detail is opaque and the user knows very minimal information about the product. Blockchain provides transparency to the supply chain so that all the participants are provided with genuine information.
- Blockchain greatly improves the process to track and trace the products. As all the transactions are transparent and distributed – the time to track can be reduced to seconds while it takes about a few days in the current supply chain to trace the information about the roots of a product such as the raw materials and chemicals involved to produce the commodity and so on [11].

5.5 Blockchain in the Food Supply Chain

Food is an essential part of our daily lives. It gets processed at a faraway location – in a farm – then it is processed using a few chemicals – distributor buys it from the farm and sells it to super markets/restaurants where it is prepared and consumed by the people.

A number of people are prone to illness everyday across the world. Food is a daily commodity that might cause illness. All the individuals of the current generation are very health conscious. They desire to know the in-and-out detail about the product. They need transparency about the food, the materials used to make and process it and how it finally reaches them.

Blockchain can be used in building the trust of the consumer in the supply chain [12]. It is an alternative to alleviate the trust in the food industry by providing transparency and accountability. See Figure 5.1.

The use cases are discussed next.

5.5.1 Use Case 1: Traceability of Food

In the general scenario, it takes from days to weeks to track the food in order to know where it has been processed or in which farm the food is produced.

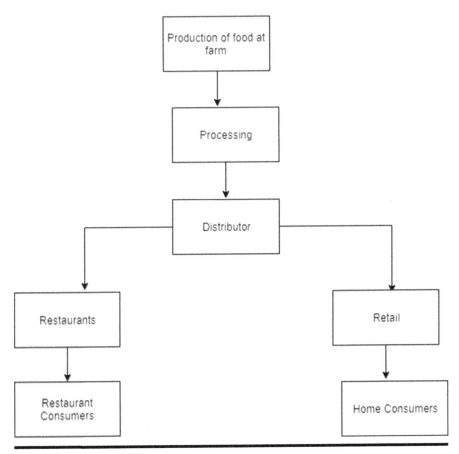

Figure 5.1 Food supply chain.

Using a blockchain, the food can be tracked within a short span. Our world has a huge population. Many people suffer from food-borne illnesses. In the current scenario, it is difficult to trace back to the root cause as to why and where the problem has occurred or at which level of supply chain did this take place.

Blockchain is extremely helpful in this situation due to its feature of 'track and trace'.

The issue can be identified quickly and the adulterated food can be thrown out of the supply chains.

For example: If consumers who had taken food at a particular restaurant fall ill, the food is tested to find if it is due to the vegetables. If it is due to the way food is processed, the restaurant can track the identification number of the package and mark the concerned person along the blockchain so that any other individual who bought the product from that entity is prevented from the danger of food-borne illness. For a solution of this sort, two things are extremely important. A unique

ID must be provided to each entity in the supply chain and a specific serial number must be linked with each package being shipped.

5.5.2 Use Case 2: Verifying the Authenticity of Food Products through Labeling

In the general setting, the details of food products such as the date of production and the chemicals used can be tampered in a centralized system thereby leading to a breach of trust.

Using blockchain, the package of food products is labeled and its details are available on the distributed ledger. All the details of the food product, such as the soil in which it is produced, chemicals used to process it and its production date, are all available in the ledger. This provides transparency to the data on a global network which cannot be tampered with in the future. This improves the trust of a consumer on the products that they consume on a daily basis.

5.5.2.1 Industrial Example

Walmart in association with IBM has been working on blockchain for food traceability since 2016. The aim is to implement a distributed ledger system to work in real time for keeping track of food products across the supply chain from farm to the Walmart stores [13]. This is an effort to improve the traceability of food products and gain the trust of consumers for the company by providing them with every detail of the products that they consume.

Called IBM Food Trust – this tool is used to maintain and run the blockchain network. It works on IBM Cloud and it is developed using Hyperledger Fabric. This blockchain considers the two use cases mentioned above. The outcomes are achieved through transparency and provenance of products in the blockchain networks.

The following are achieved through this blockchain:

- **Safety of Food:** Products are traced in seconds to prevent consumption of contaminated/faulty food and prevent illness which is food-borne.
- **Sustainability:** All the details and certifications of the products are digitized in order to optimize the management of information and provide authenticity.

This blockchain helps to identify any inefficiencies in the supply chain and take necessary measures to:

- Track food products
- Identify the root cause of food-borne illness in a short time span and take necessary measures to maintain a check on the contaminated food product
- Gain the trust of consumers and satisfy them

5.5.3 Use Case 3: Checking the Compliance of Food Conditions

Any food product be it a fruit, vegetable or meat retains its essence only if care is taken to comply with its conditions such as the temperature at which it must be stored, humidity and the number of days within which it must be supplied. So IoT and blockchain can be used to work in harmony to achieve this use case. All the food packages are provided with unique IDs and microchips. The microchips are used to keep a track of the compliance conditions and add the details on the blockchain. This enables us to track if the compliance is met at each level of supply chain or if something was breached.

In addition, smart contracts can also be written on the blockchain to create all alter between the consecutive parties when a compliance condition is not met.

5.6 Blockchain in Pharmaceutical Supply Chain

Medicines are used to treated people suffering from health ailments. They must be handled with utmost care through the transactions in the supply chain. The blockchain technology is being prospected to be helpful for the use cases of pharma industry in the real world [14].

Consumers today are very conscious of their life style of which health care is a crucial part. They even want details about the composition of the medicine and also by what means it has reached them.

Blockchain provides transparency and accountability to pharmaceutical supply with permanent transactions that cannot be tampered. See Figure 5.2.

The use cases are discussed next.

5.6.1 Use Case 1: Ratifying the Originality of the Drugs That Are Returned

The medicines are often returned from the wholesalers to the manufacturer when there is an unsold stock in order to manage the inventory. There is a need to verify the originality of the drugs prior to receiving them back. First, each product must be assigned an ID. Then the best approach is to be sorted.

It is impossible to maintain a centralized database to verify the originality of the drugs where all drug details can be stored and distributors verify the originality of drugs by connecting to it.

The best approach is to implement a blockchain where the IDs of the packages are recorded on the distributed ledger by drug manufacturers. All the other entities in the supply chain – customers, distributors and pharmacies – can ratify the originality of drugs by means of blockchain connections.

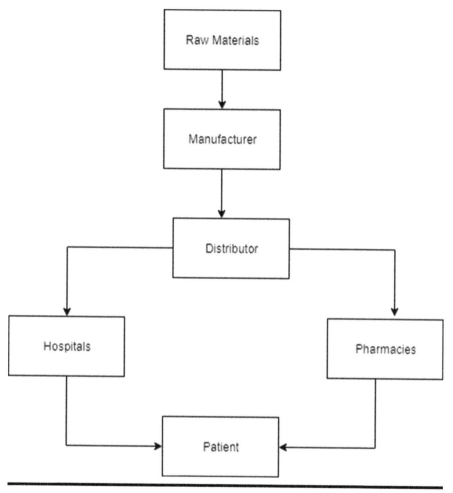

Figure 5.2　Pharmaceutical supply chain.

5.6.1.1 Industrial Example

SAP Blockchain PoC App has been launched for this use case by Merck and SAP [15]. It functions as follows:

- Unique IDs are generated for each drug package by advanced track and trace for pharmaceuticals.
- Each manufacturer registers its package on the application with four details: item ID, serial ID, batch number and date of expiry.
- The distributor can deduce these four information fields simply by scanning the barcode of the package.
- Each barcode is unique and shared between the manufacturer and distributor.

5.6.2 Use Case 2: Interception of Sham Drugs

The features of traceability and provenance of blockchain technology are an asset in dealing with this use case of the supply chain.

Drug manufacturing companies that ship and deliver their products have a tough time to track their products. This in a way allows sham drugs to be introduced into the supply chain. This is a serious issue as counterfeit drugs affect the health of the consumer as well as the revenues of the drug manufacturing company.

This problem can be countered by implementing a blockchain on which all the transactions of the drugs in the supply chain are recorded. The drugs can be tracked across the cycle by all the parties in the supply chain.

Blockchain transactions can be viewed by all the parties in the network but they cannot be tampered with due to the PoC encryption. Therefore, it would impossible for sham drugs to be introduced into the supply chain.

5.6.2.1 Industrial Example

Novartis is currently working on the blockchain network for the institution between European Union and European pharmaceutical industry, which is tentatively called Innovative Medical Initiative Blockchain Enabled Healthcare Programme [16]. The league of participants in this blockchain network consists of small-and-medium-sized enterprises, universities, laboratories, hospitals and other relevant entities [17]. This network is being worked on to deal with a number of use cases in the supply chain like detecting fake drugs, handling patient information and checking with the compliance of drugs and their governance [18].

5.6.3 Use Case 3: Compliance of the Drug Conditions in the Supply Chain

The logistic companies must keep an eye on handling drugs and their guidelines of transportation and storage. Medicines have certain conditions to be taken care of else they are void. These conditions are humidity, quality of air, temperature range, etc.

These environmental conditions have a severe impact on the effect to be produced by drugs – especially vaccines and ointments. Blockchain along with smart IoT provides a way to include compliance and governance across the chain – from manufacturer to the consumer.

5.6.3.1 Example

A few medicine instructions are written that they must be stored in a cold and dry place at about 15°C. When the medicine reaches the consumer's hand after its traversal through the supply chain –What is the proof that the criteria were met at each and every stage of its transport?

Blockchain provides help in this case. Each product can be associated with a microchip which maintains a record of the medicine at every stage of the supply chain and stores it on a distributed ledger.

In addition, smart contracts can be included by means of which the next level entity in the supply chain is alerted when the compliance conditions are not met.

5.6.3.2 Industrial Example

Novartis is in the final stages of implementing a blockchain related to this use case where blockchain and IoT are being used to track temperatures of the drugs during their traversal across the supply chain.

5.7 Blockchain in the Automotive Supply Chain

Bikes, cars, lorries and other vehicles have become extremely important in today's lifestyle. Automotive vehicles are actually the ones that provide transportation and make the supply chain exist – as the commodities are transported and brought to the doorstep through this medium.

To use the features of a vehicle to its full potential, all parts must be genuine and as per the company's prototype. So, the consumer must be aware of the genuineness of the parts and also how the vehicle has reached him. Hence, the supply chain of automotive vehicles is extremely important as each vehicle is composed of several parts from different manufacturers all put together to manufacture a vehicle. Through blockchain features, transparency and accountability records are stored permanently to provide proof at every business process involved across the supply chain.

In addition, several other issues of automobiles such as overspeeding can be in check using blockchain. Using IoT and blockchain together, the speed ranges of a specific vehicle can be recorded on the blockchain and smart contracts can be implemented for the same to alert the consumer in case compliance in speed is not met. See Figure 5.3.

5.7.1 Use Case 1: Validating the Labels of All the Spare Parts of the Vehicle

A vehicle is an ensemble of various parts, each manufactured by a different manufacturer. All the parts from different companies are placed as per the vehicle design of the manufacturing company and sent to other business processes of the supply chain. So, a blockchain needs to be implemented keeping the spare parts of the vehicle in mind.

Adding all the details of every part, manufacturer, composition of the part provided and manufacturing date, to the distributed ledger of the blockchain provides every participant on the blockchain to view the data in an untampered form. In the currently existing automobile supply chain, there is a chance that the genuine parts

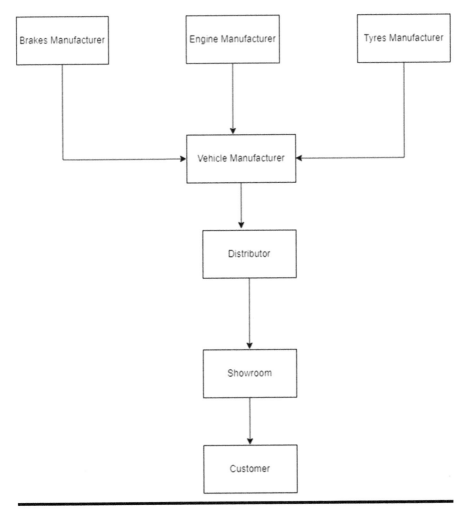

Figure 5.3 Automotive supply chain.

of the vehicles can be modified and the centralized database can be altered making the entire supply chain inefficient. So deploying a blockchain for automotive supply chain improves its efficiency and enhances the reliability of the consumer.

5.7.2 Use Case 2: Indicating a Consumer about the Need to Replace the Parts of Their Vehicle

Each part of a vehicle is unique and is worn out after a specific period of time. The consumer might not be aware of the period for which the specific part can be used. So by using blockchain technology, smart contracts can be initiated if a specific condition is not met to alert the consumer to change the specific part before utilizing his vehicle.

5.7.3 Use Case 3: Tracking and Tracing Spare Parts

In the same manner as mentioned for food and pharmaceutical supply chains, the spare parts of the vehicles can be traced from the respective manufacturers through other business processes across the supply chain due to the track and trace features of blockchain.

5.7.3.1 Example

Mercedes has become a member of the Hyperledger consortium in order to bring advancement to this revolutionary technology. Porsche has already performed several tests of blockchain technology on several business processes in association with a startup called XAIN [19].

5.8 Types of Blockchains and the Suitability to Supply Chains

Basically, there are four types of blockchains as discussed below.

5.8.1 Permissioned or Private Blockchain

Permissioned blockchains have restricted access. They are mainly useful in multinational companies and business organizations so that they can perform their business operations securely only by providing access to the crucial ones so that the transactions can be stored permanently and the information can be transferred securely. The ecosystem of these blockchains is small and restricted. Additionally, only a few participants are provided with access to validate the transactions or initiate smart contracts. Governance is a key function of any business organization which can be made efficient through a permissioned blockchain.

5.8.2 Permission-Less or Public Blockchain

This is the blockchain model used for financial transactions such as Bitcoin and Ethereum [20]. Every individual has their own identity and interacts with others in the network by performing transactions. All the new transactions are automatically updated on the ledger. Verification of the transactions can be performed by various mining protocols. In a public blockchain, anybody in allowed to be a participant in the network. It provides a distributed and decentralized ledger so that the transactions can be audited by anyone in the network. This helps in easy detection of fraud, which is very important especially during monetary transactions [21].

Now there are two main situations to be considered in order to deploy blockchain technology for a supply chain:

■ Bring transparency to the consumers – Permissioned Blockchain (Public)
■ Provide accountability for transactions between the business processes involved in the supply chain – Permissioned Blockchain (Private)

5.8.3 Public Permissioned Blockchain

This type of blockchain is used when the user is to be provided complete transparency about the product under use. There are only a fixed number of participants and the supply chain ends with the consumer. The distributed data ledger is immutable but new data can be added to it. So at each business process, new data is added to the ledger.

5.8.3.1 Example

The raw material processor provides details of the fertilizers used and composition of the product and updates these to the ledger. The packaging person updates the ledger with compliance condition of the product. The distributor updates the ledger with his own identity, and so on. The consumer at the receiving end is provided in and out with the complete information of the product through distributed ledger through public permissioned blockchain.

5.8.4 Private Permissioned Blockchain

Sometimes a business might not want to provide transparency to the consumer. They need a few transaction details limited to themselves such as accounting details and transactions done on a regular basis. A manufacturer may hire a local company to do a few processes that are to be performed by him. These are regular transactions and are to be kept private. So, public view is restricted in this type of blockchain. A permanent record of transactions is maintained on the ledger and the transactions are validated on updation.

5.9 Consensus Methods for Blockchains in Supply Chain Management

Blockchain is a distributed ledger system. All business processes involved in the network must concur with regard to the information of the distributed ledger. For this reason, a consensus model must be developed for each blockchain. It makes sure that the succeeding block in the chain is valid. The consensus models completely avoid the need of a central entity to validate the transactions.

The consensus models that are currently in use are discussed below.

5.9.1 Proof of Work (PoW)

This consensus model provided immutability to the ledger data and provides transparency to the participants in the network. A strong cryptographic puzzle is used to validate and bind all the blocks of data together to achieve this status of security and reliability [22].

5.9.2 Proof of Stake (PoS)

In PoS, instead of a cryptographic puzzle any participant in the network is chosen to validate the block. A validator may be selected randomly on the value of their stake. POS uses less energy in comparison to PoW and hence it is more efficient.

5.9.3 Proof of Authority (PoA)

PoA is an altered form of PoS. The identity of the validator performs the role of stake in this consensus method. Each participant in the network is provided with a unique identity. PoA enables fast transactions through its mechanism of consensus. In PoA, the risk if any is restricted only to the central node which has the authority.

PoA is the consensus model that functions at its best when blockchain is deployed over supply chains. The reputation of the validator is at stake in this consensus model. So, blockchains with PoA have validators who are selected on a random basis as trustworthy entities.

5.10 The Process Involved to Develop Blockchains for Supply Chains

We have discussed the use cases of blockchains for recording of transactions and the technicalities of the blockchain.

Now we discuss how the front end is created and the connection is established with the blockchain to record the invoices successfully.

The key requirements are:

- Client Dapp
- Ethereum Network
- Blockchain (either Ropsten/Rinkeby testnet)

5.10.1 Client Dapp

Decentralized Apps are abbreviated as Dapps. It is the application that forms front end to interact with the blockchain. JavaScript is a key programming language that can be used to serve the purpose of interaction with the backed blockchain.

Dapps are different from the traditional applications that store data on centralized databases. This makes these apps unique in their own way.

For a supply chain, Dapp is designed to record transactions for several business processes such as:

■ Supplier
■ Manufacturer
■ Distributor
■ Wholesaler
■ Seller
■ Consumer

Multiple transactions take place between each business process, and data are also updated by user at each business process. All these transactions happening between multiple users across various business processes and the data they update are reflected on the blocks and are immutable and transparent [23].

The business process flow must be designed for the supply chain to enable every business process user to update the data from their end.

An administrator application could be designed to add new users to the network of a particular organization. Each user in the network is provided with Ethers to facilitate the mining process.

He is the person who adds new users to the supply chain and initiates a transaction by creating batches. He is the controller of creating users and assigning them with their specific roles and also looks into the transaction for each batch and every level.

The following data could be recorded to the blockchain:

■ Sign up of new user to the supply network
■ Initiation of new batch for transaction of a particular product
■ Invoice related to a particular transaction uploaded by every business user

Every process that happens in the supply network is transparent but immutable. It makes the process of managing simpler and more effective to record transactions in comparison to the existing ERP systems.

The business process diagram shown in Figure 5.4 clearly indicates what happens at each business level. Given the details at each business process, they are auto validated via smart contracts without the need of any third party and the same is mined to the blocks of a chain. Integrating IoT with the product in the blockchain and recording the conditions such as temperature, moisture, etc., using microchips would also be of even greater use to enhance the trust upon the product for the consumer.

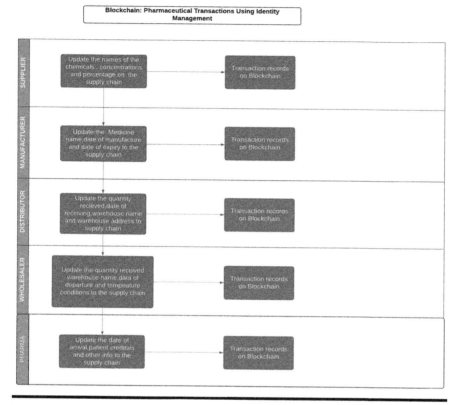

Figure 5.4   Business process flow for supply chain of pharmaceuticals.

The user logins and the authority are given the privilege to accept or reject the transaction recording to blockchain. The data of the user who approves the transaction, i.e., the user who has the authority over that particular transaction are also recorded to the block. This is called PoA where the transaction recording on the blockchain is validated by a specific user.

5.10.2 Ethereum Network

Local Ethereum Network can be deployed by using **Docker** and **Geth** on a server.

Docker is used to deploy the nodes of Ethereum network. A simple Ethereum network can be implemented using:

- ▪ 1 Authority Node – to handle requests from the client end Dapp and forward the request to the mining nodes
- ▪ 2 Mining Nodes – to perform the computational work to add the data to the blocks

A local Ethereum network is private and permissioned [24].

Alternatively, open source testnets are available on the Internet which can be used to mine your records and add them to the blocks. Using open source tools such as Etherscan you can check the status of your transaction which is mined on the blocks in a public blockchain.

Open-source testnets such as **Rinkeby** and **Ropsten** are public and permissioned.

5.10.3 Blockchains

The transaction mined by your Ethereum network is added to a block that is chained to the previously mined blocks using Hash values. A particular block can be retrieved using its block ID or transaction hash to verify it, but it is practically impossible to alter the data of a block in any form as the chain is agile and it's very complex to intercept the chain and tamper the block in the existence of several other blocks.

Blockchain has its pillars in Ethereum nodes and smart contracts. Without these utilities, blockchain serves no purpose.

For this, it is extremely important to choose wisely:

■ The consensus algorithm required to perform mining
■ Smart contracts for the logics involved
■ Ethereum nodes depending on the complexity involved.

Figure 5.5 depicts how the data on a block looks.

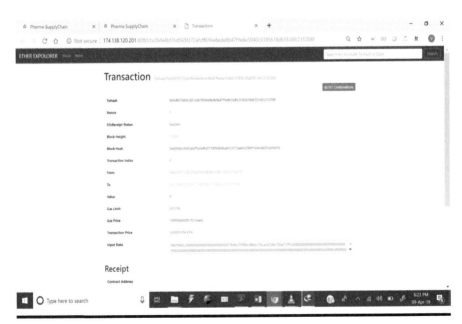

Figure 5.5   Transaction record on a block.

- **Transaction Hash** is a unique hash value for each transaction done.
- **Nonce** is an arbitrary value for every block which prevents replay attacks
- **Status** is whether the transaction is successful or not.
- **Block Height** is the number of a specific block in the chain.
- **Block Hash** is a unique hash value assigned to the block.
- **From** is the wallet address of the user by whom the transaction is performed.
- **To** is the address of the complete batch of transaction.
- **Gas Limit** is a representation of the maximum computational work that can be put upon to mine the transaction.
- **Gas Price** is the actual gas that is consumed to mine the transaction to the block.
- **Transaction Price** is the ethers consumed for the transaction between two entities.
- **Input Data** is the representation of invoice data as hash.
- **Confirmations** indicate the new blocks that were added to the chain following the block mined with our transactions.

5.10.4 Smart Contracts

Smart Contracts are the essential components of blockchain. They are like rules and regulations to be followed by the blockchain to record the transactions. Smart contracts vary with the application for which the blockchain is used. Smart Contracts are *"IF-THIS-THEN-THAT"* cases written in programming languages such as SOLIDITY, GoLang. The purpose of smart contracts is to eliminate the third party validator and automate the validation process within the supply chain. Logic for the transaction/invoice recording is written and deployed at the Genesis Block of the blockchain.

The logics are written to record new users and their roles as defined by admin, record the information updated by user at every business process and flow in the blockchain. Now, whenever a new transaction is added to the blockchain, the smart contracts are called to validate the logic. If the defined logic is satisfied, then only that particular information is added to the blockchain. Truffle is a framework used to compile and deploy the smart contracts over the supply chain. The smart contracts once deployed onto the blockchain cannot be altered in any form.

5.11 Tools Required to Deploy a Simple Commercial Blockchain: Supply Chain Management

5.11.1 Metamask

Metamask is a browser extension used to handle user wallets. Whenever a transaction is to be recorded on the blocks, the particular user performing the transaction should be active in Metamask. Whenever a new user is added to the network or

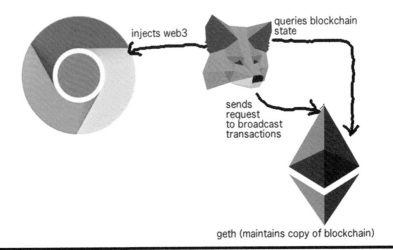

Figure 5.6 Metamask functionality.

data is submitted by the end user application, the particular transaction must be approved/rejected.

To put it in technical terms, PoA is a consensus algorithm that is put into practice through Metamask. Every user having sufficient ethers and gas has the authority to enable the mining of transactions into the block irrespective of their stature.

The purpose of Metamask (see Figure 5.6) is to:

- Inject the browser with web3JS
- Query the state of Ethereum blockchain
- Send requests in order to record the transactions

5.11.2 Web3JS

Web3JS is a collection of libraries used to call the Ethereum nodes using HHTP or IPC connection calls.

Purpose of Web3JS: Sometimes a function in a smart contract is to be called for the computational work to take place. So when it is to be called, a node in the Ethereum network is to be queried to convey:

- Smart contract's address
- The address of the function to be called
- The variables which are to be used by the function

Ethereum nodes communicate via JSON-RPC which cannot be intercepted by humans. So it masks the queries to the users and enables their communication via JavaScript. See Figure 5.7.

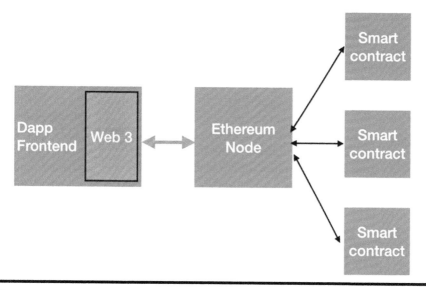

Figure 5.7   Web3JS application for enabling communication between user interface and Ethereum network.

5.11.3 Solidity

Solidity is the language in which smart contracts are written. Smart contracts are like the rules and regulations to be followed while computing the transactions to a block. Solidity is the widely used programming language for smart contracts. They are general "IF-THIS-THEN-THAT" that validate the transactions automatically without the need of any third party to serve the purpose.

5.11.4 Truffle

Truffle is an open-source framework used to compile and deploy the smart contracts onto the Ethereum blockchain at a specific address of the Genisis block. Commands such as truffle-compile, truffle-migrate and truffle-deploy are used to compile, migrate and deploy the smart contracts to the blockchain.

5.12 Future Research Directions

The concept of blockchain came into the limelight only after the burgeon of cryptocurrency transactions and their value. Every sphere of business started to investigate what features blockchain has and how the concept of blockchain can be applied to existing technologies to make them efficient. Currently, blockchain is widely being used in financial institutions such as banks [25]. It is still on the verge of implementation or testing in other fields such as supply chain, e-commerce, real estate, health care, transportation and many more.

The use cases of blockchain for each of these fields can be studied. It would be a valuable resource to develop novel applications using these cases and deploying apps to make the functioning of the respective fields efficient by providing transparency and improving manageability.

Though blockchain makes the entire process cost efficient – all the currently existing networks must be redone in most cases to deploy in to utilize its full potential. Research can be performed as how this can be achieved through minimal costs. The other fields and spheres of life where application of blockchain is productive and enhances trust must also be worked on as technology maintains reliability is always valued.

5.13 Conclusion

Blockchain is currently a trending technology across the world. All the companies are in the process of replacing the existing technology with blockchain. Blockchain provides transparency and immutability to the stored data. This paves way for several applications such as track-and-trace and verifying the authenticity in one go. Supply chain is a huge network where millions of transactions take place on a daily basis. All the features of blockchain are apt and essential for supply chains as it benefits each business process associated with the supply chain by ensuring "trust" and improving it in comparison to the existing centralized system.

References

[1] K. Korpela, U. Kuusiholma, O. Taipale, and J. Hallikas, "A framework for exploring digital business ecosystems," In: 2013 46th Hawaii International conference on System Sciences (HICSS), pp. 3838–3847, 2013.

[2] P. Wells and M. Seitz, "Business models and closed-loop supply chains: A typology," *Supply Chain Management: An International Journal*, vol. 10, no. 4, pp. 249–251, 2005.

[3] K. Korpela, J. Hallikas, and T. Dahlberg, "Digital supply chain transformation toward blockchain integration," In: *Proceedings of the 50th Hawaii International Conference on System Sciences,* January 2017.

[4] F. Tian, "A supply chain traceability system for food safety based on HACCP, blockchain & Internet of things," In: *International Conference on Service Systems and Service Management,* pp. 1–6, June 2017.

[5] M. Peck, "Blockchains: how they work," *IEEE Spectrum*, vol. 54, no. 10, pp. 26–35, 2017, https://spectrum.ieee.org/computing/networks/blockchains-how-theywork-and-why-theyll-change-the-world.

[6] A. Nordrum, "Wall Street firms to move trillions to blockchain in 2018", IEEE Spectrum, October 2017, https://spectrum.ieee.org/telecom/internet/wall-street-firms-to-movetrillions-to-blockchains-in-2018.

[7] G. Zyskind and O. Nathan, "Decentralizing privacy: Using blockchain to protect personal data," In: IEEE Security and Privacy Workshops (SPW), pp. 180–184, May 2015.

[8] J. Buurman, *Supply chain logistics management*, 2002. McGraw-Hill.

[9] H. M. Kim and M. Laskowski, "Toward an ontology-driven blockchain design for supply-chain provenance," *Intelligent Systems in Accounting, Finance and Management*, vol. 25, no. 1, pp. 18–27, 2018.

[10] S. Saberi, M. Kouhizadeh, J. Sarkis, and L. Shen, "Blockchain technology and its relationships to sustainable supply chain management," *International Journal of Production Research*, vol. 57, no. 7, pp. 2117–2135, 2019.

[11] IBM Press Release, BlockChain at Interconnect 2017 conference, March 21, 2017 https://www.ibm.com/blogs/blockchain/2017/03/guideeverything-blockchain-ibm-interconnect-2017/.

[12] F. Tian, "An agri-food supply chain traceability system for China based on RFID & blockchain technology," In: *13th International Conference on Service Systems and Service Management (ICSSSM)*, pp. 1–6, June 2016.

[13] Stanley Aaron. Ready to rumble: IBM launches food trust blockchain for commercial use. Retrieved from https://www.forbes.com/sites/astanley/2018/10/08/ready-to-rumble-ibm-launches-food-trust-blockchain-for-commercial-use/#3c103f347439.

[14] B. Alangot and K. Achuthan, "Trace and track: Enhanced pharma supply chain infrastructure to prevent fraud," In: International Conference on Ubiquitous Communications and Network Computing, Springer, Cham, pp. 189–195, August 2017.

[15] Lisa Penski. "Blockchain Co-Innovation in the Pharmaceutical Industry," Retrieved from https://blogs.sap.com/2018/04/17/blockchain-co-innovaion-in-the-pharmaceutical-industry.

[16] K. A. Clauson, E. A. Breeden, C. Davidson, and T. K. Mackey, Leveraging blockchain technology to enhance supply chain management in healthcare. *Blockchain in Healthcare Today*, 2018.

[17] B. Clegg and B. Tan, "Using QFD for e-business planning and analysis in a micro-sized enterprise," *International Journal of Quality & Reliability Management*, vol. 24, pp. 813–828, 2007.

[18] Morris Nicky, "Novartis explores blockchain's potential for pharmaceuticals," Retrieved from https://www.ledgerinsights.com/novartis-pharma-blockchain/.

[19] K. Lewis, "Blockchain: four use cases transforming business," IBM Internet of Things blog, May 2017 https://www.ibm.com/blogs/internetof-things/iot-blockchain-use-cases/.

[20] Nakamoto Satoshi, *Bitcoin: A peer-to-peer electronic cash system*. 2018, HN Publishing.

[21] D. Norman, "An experimental application of the delphi method to the use of experts," *Management Science*, vol. 9, no. 3, pp. 458–467, 1963.

[22] C. DeCusatis, M. Zimmermann, and A. Sager, "Identity-based network security for commercial blockchain services," In: IEEE 8th Annual Computing and Communication Workshop and Conference, pp. 474–477, January 2018.

[23] Yves-Alexandre de Montjoye, C'esar A Hidalgo, Michel Verleysen, and Vincent D Blondel. "Unique in the crowd: The privacy bounds of human mobility," *Scientific Reports*, vol. 3, 2013.

[24] A. Flores and K. Gannon, "BlockChain on AWS: Disrupting the norm," paper GPSD301, AWS Re:Invent 2016 (November 29, 2016), https://www.slideshare.net/AmazonWebServices/aws-reinvent-2016-blockchain-on-aws-disrupting-the-norm-gpst301.

[25] J. Lang, "Three uses for blockchain in banking," October 23, 2017, https://www.ibm.com/blogs/blockchain/2017/10/three-uses-forblockchain-in-banking/.

Chapter 6

Securing the Internet of Things Using Blockchain

S.A. Bragadeesh, S.M. Narendran and
A. Umamakeswari

Contents

6.1 Introduction

In the present data-driven world, the advancements in technology have a drastic impact on our day-to-day lives. Given the pervasiveness of devices, it is possible to access information from anywhere, anytime. Internet of Things (IoT) creates a network of embedded devices that have access to the Internet and communicate with each other to seamlessly enable data transfer across the network. IoT has found its roots across multiple domains, some of which include Smart cities, Smart grids, business, social media, Industries such as manufacturing, automobiles, aviation and many more. The data from IoT has attracted huge attention and generates business value for organizations. Even though lots of effort has been put into realization of solutions using IoT as a platform, one of the major bottlenecks for successful adoption is the security and privacy of the system. IoT is having an exponential increase of value in research and business, but it still suffers from problems of security. Traditional security and privacy methods can't be used for IoT, primarily because of its localized topology, resource-constraints, large number of devices [1].

Security and privacy are two of several key concerns. It is crucial to ensure the security and privacy of data, systems and devices for data-sensitive applications. In most of the scenarios, a threat is more often than not a security measure which has not been properly implemented. It is necessary to have a proper knowledge about working of the system and the risks associated with them. Security requirements should be addressed right from the design phase of the system. This will help in ensuring that the system is secure and safe.

In recent years, one technology that has promised so much and often touted as the next big revolution is the emergence of blockchain (BC). BC is essentially a fully distributed ledger that is immutable, has transactions that are permanently recorded and a decentralized structure. Even though in the beginning, BC was mainly used as the underlying technology of Bitcoins, it has been extensively studied for adoption across other applications as well. The major benefit of BC is the removal of an explicit third party for establishing trust between two or more unknown individuals/organizations in order to transact among them [2]. This essentially removes all the threats that focus on a centralized infrastructure that is used for storage, computation and processing. There are several forms of cryptocurrencies currently available in the market, which are used by various organizations to achieve their own purposes. BC is considered to resolve the safety and privacy issues in the IoT. Cryptography used behind Bitcoin transactions would guarantee the secrecy in keeping the user information. IoT devices will be embedded with digital identities and digital signatures where these devices can get a specific ID. It is possible to use BC technology to create a secure environment for the system.

It can be observed that there is some common ground on which both IoT and BC can coexist and some fundamental architectural similarities like distributed entities, data exchanges between devices/nodes among others. One major difference is that the amount of computing and power resources available in IoT devices is significantly lower compared to devices on which BC transactions are performed. The major contribution of this work is to identify the similarities, explore the advantages that result when these two technologies are combined and propose a conceptual framework in which BC is used for securing the IoT.

The contents of this chapter are organized into the following sections: Section 6.2 gives a brief overview of the BC technology, Section 6.3 discusses the benefits of BC, Section 6.4 highlights the key challenges and requirements of IoT security and Section 6.5 discusses the threats in IoT and BC; in Section 6.6, a conceptual framework is proposed. Section 6.7 gives an idea of when to use BC as a solution for IoT applications; Section 6.8 presents the various challenges involved in the adoption of BC for securing the IoT. Finally, Section 6.9 provides the concluding remarks and some future directions

6.2 Overview of BC Technology

BC, the underlying technology of cryptocurrency Bitcoin [3], is capable of ensuring security and privacy of peer-to-peer (P2P) networks with topologies that are similar to IoT. BCs are blocks of data that are appended by timestamps, and these blocks of data are linked by the use of hash functions based on cryptographic primitives that results in a chain structure – hence, named BC [4].

6.2.1 Basic Operational Principles

The basic requisite for BC is establishing a P2P network in which all the member nodes have a role to play. Asymmetric cryptography is applied in BC in which separate keys are used for encryption and decryption of data usually referred to as private and public keys. Each node has a public and private key pair. The public key is required to encrypt the data sent by other nodes, and the private key is used by the individual node to decrypt and access the data. Essentially, it can be summarized that the private key is used for transaction approval, and the public key is a unique ID (address). Only the user with an appropriate private key can decrypt the messages that are encrypted with the public key.

The data are usually updated when a transaction occurs. The node that performs the transaction will append its digital sign and then a message is broadcasted to all the nodes within single hop. The addition of signature is done to ensure authentication (only with the specific private key data can be encrypted) and integrity (decryption is not done if there is an error during transmission). The neighbors that receive the data verify its validity and then retransmit it to its one-hop neighbors. All such verified and valid transactions are grouped into a block and a timestamp is associated with it. This process is usually performed by dedicated nodes known as miners. A consensus algorithm is used to elect the miners and validate the data that is added to the block. The miners then broadcast this block across the network which is verified by all the members. The members verify the validity of transactions in the block and also the hash values of the previous block upon which the block gets added. If the verification fails, the block is discarded.

6.2.2 Smart Contracts

The above-mentioned process can be automated by creating Smart Contracts (Blockchain 2.0) [5, 6]. Smart contracts are a reliable decentralized self-contained piece of code capable of autonomous execution when predefined conditions are satisfied. It is designed to ensure that every transaction has been executed correctly and that the data are stored safely. Smart contracts can be

- Used to create trust between parties, which is important when building a new network
- Used to secure the network and make sure that data is safe
- Used to verify that there are no fraudulent activities and that the data are not compromised
- Programmed to execute automatically if necessary
- Programmed to perform transactions in real time
- Programmed to execute on a specific set of conditions that allows for a decentralized system where all participants have full control over their own data
- Used as a platform for creating and executing decentralized applications

Smart contracts have a major role in optimizing the performance of BC. Special rules and guidelines are to be followed for the creation of Smart contracts. With respect to IoT, platforms such as Ethereum and Hyperledger that runs on smart contracts can be used for building sample applications and learning BC.

6.2.3 BC Devices

The devices in the BC network perform two major roles: Users and Miners. Users perform transactions and broadcast it to the immediate hop peers. Before transmitting it, the user encrypts the data using their own private key and adds their timestamp. The neighbors receive the transaction, check for authenticity by decrypting using the public key. If the transaction is verified successfully, then it adds to its block and transmits the data. When the cascaded data are received by all the users, the miners then create the block, add the timestamp, generate the cryptographic hash and broadcast it to the users. The users verify the hash, and if the hash matches, the block is added to their memory else it gets discarded. When smart contracts are used, the miners essentially act as the authenticators and all data transactions happen based on the guidelines of smart contract.

6.2.4 Consensus Algorithms

BC consists of multiple devices that perform transactions among them. The transactions performed should be consistent, verifiable and all devices must agree upon them. This is necessary to establish trust among all the devices and achieve decentralization. This agreement process is tedious, and one of the most common problem encountered is the Byzantine Generals problem [7]. This problem can be overcome by the use of consensus algorithms that are used by miners to validate and verify transactions before they are added to blocks of individual devices. Consensus is a necessary requirement and basis of BC infrastructure. There are multiple consensus algorithms available, each with its own advantages and limitations [8].

The choice of consensus algorithms is crucial for addressing the scalability, computational complexity, time complexity, average cost incurred for block addition, fault tolerance, throughput, energy and resource utilization of IoT applications. Consensus mechanism is helpful for detecting malicious activity and mitigation of possible threats. Only when the consensus is agreed upon, the block gets added to the chain else the data block is discarded. Specially designed hardware that is optimized for implementing consensus protocols can help in achieving desired performance for IoT applications.

6.2.5 Types of BCs

There are different types of BCs depending on how the data is managed, user actions permitted and availability of data [9]. The major classification types are as follows.

6.2.5.1 Authentication – Based on Who Can Access the BC

6.2.5.1.1 Public and Private BCs

In the case of Public BCs, no third-party approval is required for joining the network, and the new user can be either a member or a miner. Miners also known as validators are given special economic incentives. They are strictly decentralized, where all devices can participate in the network activities such addition of blocks and accessing the contents. The addition of data blocks requires computation-intensive consensus methods to avoid any possible security threats.

In private BCs, the owner usually restricts the access of network. All the members are either part of a single organization or trusted known parties.

6.2.5.2 Authorization – Based on What a Device Can Do

6.2.5.2.1   Permissioned and Permission Less BCs

In case of permission less BCs, the node can view/add data whenever new transactions are to be added or verifed. Often permission-less BCs can also be referred to as private BCs. Permissioned BCs require explicit permissions (tokens/smart contracts) to view/add data.

6.2.5.3 Federated BCs

Also known as consortium BCs that can be a private and permissioned structure. Multiple organizations are involved, and transparency is the major requirement. It is essentially a distributed database that is synchronized, reliable and auditable. Computationally it is less expensive for publishing new blocks. One major drawback is it is not truly decentralized.

6.3 Benefits of BC

Major benefits of BC are:

- Integrity
- Transparency
- Robustness
- Immutability
- Decentralization
- No single point of failure
- Auditability
- P2P communication
- Fault tolerance
- System wide transaction verifiability
- Scalability
- Cost reduction
- Improved performance for task automation
- Preservation the order of transaction
- Data protection
- Data traceability and tracking

It can be observed that BCs are computationally costly and require higher bandwidth overhead and delays, which may not be directly suitable for IoT devices. The solution is to scale down the computational complexity and delays of BC to a level where it can be easily implemented in any device without compromising the basic services offered by BC.

6.4 IoT Security Challenges and Requirements

IoT security involves securing the devices that are connected and also the network that acts as the backbone of the system. Since IoT involves connecting devices to the Internet, this leads to possibility of opening them up to serious vulnerabilities if proper protection is not ensured. Numerous attacks such as Stuxnet, Mirai, German Steel Plant attack have demonstrated that if an attacker gets access to a single device in the network, it is possible to gain access to critical infrastructure components, access control and network policies. By gaining such access, the attacker then possibly mounts a Virus/Botnet/Trojan that can infiltrate the entire network and cause serious damage [10–12]. As pointed out earlier, traditional security solutions can't be used as is for IoT applications majorly because of resource limitations, scalability and processing overhead.

6.4.1 Challenges and Requirements

- IoT usually depends on cloud infrastructure in which the end devices collect the data and send it to the cloud via gateways. The major problem here is the possibility of occurrence of failures that affects the entire network operation. Such cloud-based systems are prone to attacks such as distributed denial of service, eavesdropping, sinkhole among others.
- Security has not been considered a priority during the design phase of the devices.

Manufacturers and product designers are keeners to reduce the time to market rather than focusing on establishing security right from the design. This is mainly because incurs additional costs tend to slow down the development time and sometimes affect the intended functionality of the device.

- The use of default/hardcoded passwords is a major cause for breach of security – even when passwords are changed periodically, they are not sufficiently strong hence easy to break
- IoT devices have limited resources that makes implementation of strong security measures a challenging task
- Once the devices are deployed, they are left in the field until the end of their lifetime and more often than not, they don't receive any software/security updates
- Integration of legacy devices with IoT requires additional efforts during which the security is not always focused on
- Lack of common standards for IoT security that can be used across multiple domains – Proprietary frameworks & solutions leads to interoperability and security issues
- Lack of skilled workforce for ensuring system-wide security

The security requirements differ for each IoT application – there is no solution that can fit the requirements of all applications

- Heterogeneity of devices – IoT devices are diverse and different protocols are used
- Scalability – Number of devices that get added to the network may increase with time
- Fundamental security requirement is compliance of CIA triad – Confidentiality, Integrity, Authenticity
- Ensure availability of devices – The security measures implemented shouldn't affect the device normal operations
- Privacy of user's sensitive data has to ensured
- Scalability of IoT applications has to addressed
- IoT protocol stack uses different protocols at different layers – the interoperability among the various protocols is a key issue

Security is a shared issue that involves all the stakeholders from manufacturers to end users. Service providers and manufacturers should add encryption and authorization as a default requirement during the system design itself. Even the end users should follow their own precautions which include periodic change of passwords which are strong, installing the updates and patches whenever they are available. BC has to complement existing security infrastructures such as network firewalls, intrusion detection and prevention systems, encryption techniques, Adaptive security appliance in order to achieve end-to-end system security.

6.5 Threats

Any deviation from normal operating procedure may possibly be caused by a threat or attack. It is important to have knowledge about the various possible threats before designing the security architecture. It has to be remembered that security is an evolving and continuous process, in which the strategies and policies need to be frequently updated in order to ensure safety and reliability of the system. The threats can be grouped into major classes based on their targeted action – manipulation, authentication, access control, integrity, confidentiality, privacy, service based, identity based [13]. Table 6.1 identifies the various possible threats in IoT and BC.

6.6 A Conceptual Framework of Secure IoT Using BC

IoT architectures are generally organized into hierarchical levels in which the data processing, storage, computation, available power for devices are different at different levels. Such structure reduces the burden on devices with specific functions

Table 6.1   Classification of Threats in IoT and BC and Their Effects

Threat/Attacks	Type	Effect
Tampering Modification attack False data injection Man-in-the-middle Overlay attack	Manipulation	Modification of stored data, affects data integrity Data consistency will be lost Data may not reach the intended destination as any intermediary node that is compromised drop the data packets
Spoofing	Authentication	Leak of critical user data
Repudiation	Confidentiality	Duplicate transactions
Botnets Ransomware Dictionary Jamming Side channel attacks Flooding	Access control	Stealing data to launch a wide scale attack Users have to pay huge amounts to regain their access to devices Loss of securely stored data The network bandwidth is fully utilized preventing any communication and faster energy depletion
Eavesdropping	Privacy	Leak of sensitive data
Distributed denial of service (DDoS) Collusion Double spending Physical damage	Service based	Prevent user from accessing the data or device The device is not available to use any further
Replay Impersonation Sybil attack Key attack	Identity based	Multiple nodes are compromised

assigned for each level of devices. As we can see from Figure 6.1, the layers in IoT are as follows.

Device layer: Usually consists of sensing and actuating devices, users, machines that have limited processing capabilities. Their general role is collection of data from the physical world and forwarding it to the next level for further

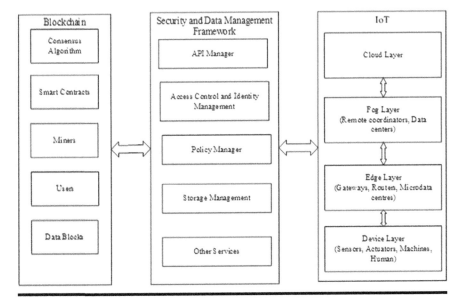

Figure 6.1 Framework for securing IoT using blockchain.

processing. They are the lowest price segment in IoT chain but account for the highest average number of units. Basic communication protocols are used in which the security is provided such as bit-level error detection and correction, basic encryption and hashing capabilities.

Edge layer: This layer consists of devices with higher storage, processing, communication and power resources. They are usually data aggregators/data preprocessors and perform preliminary operation on the data collected by the devices in the device layer. Devices in this layer are usually gateways, routers, micro data centers and single-board computers. They perform the coordination and management of device layer nodes. These devices are provided with stronger cryptographic capabilities and can operate on encrypted data if required.

Fog layer: Devices in layers 1 and 2 are generally located in the environment from where data are collected. The devices in Fog layer are located at a remote location usually to compliment the cloud infrastructure to service the requests from devices at the lower layers. They have a wider scope in the context of knowledge about the application and perform actions on data received from the edge devices. There is often a notion that Fog and Edge are the same. It is partially true. In some applications, there is no need for an explicit fog layer as the edge layer itself directly communicates with the cloud layer. Fog layer is usually present in applications to enable real-time processing, reduce the impact of cloud downtimes, network outages and end-to-end delay of request to response time. Third-party service providers, use of application-specific management protocols, strong network security and robustness are major features of fog layer.

Cloud layer: This layer consists of highly specialized and sophisticated infrastructure that is generally assumed to have no limitation in terms of resource requirements. Server arrays, distributed grids, clusters, large storage facility, high performance, high bandwidth communication capabilities are some of the attractive features of the cloud layer. Specialized softwares that are capable of performing complex analytical operations on data are available in the cloud layer. Cloud layer is responsible for storing history of transactions and perform complex intensive computation on data. Application-level security, Data visualization, Data analytics, Storage, resource management are some of the benefits of cloud layer.

Recent technologies, like Software-Defined Networking (SDN), Network Function Virtualization (NFV), have actually improved the performance of IoT architecture described above. SDN and NFV when used at the Fog layer can help in leveraging the full potential of underlying infrastructure in order to achieve real-time performance, reduce latency, improve resource utilization and complement the cloud infrastructure.

Now that we have discussed about the architectural elements in IoT, let's see how we can adapt BC into this architecture. The fundamental challenge is to adopt BC without compromising the objectives of IoT application. In Section 2, the various components of BC such as users and miner devices, smart contracts, data blocks and consensus mechanism were described. In order to facilitate the adoption of BC into IoT, a conceptual security and data management framework is proposed. The objective of this framework is to generalize the functions that are required in order to achieve IoT security using BC. The various components of the framework are API Manager, Access control and Identity management, Policy manager, Storage management and other general services. Let us look into these in detail.

API Manager: Application Programming Interface (API) is well-defined software modules that help in achieving portability, interoperability, ease of communication and hassle-free deployment. Since IoT involves multiple communication protocols, Heterogeneous devices and devices from different vendors, a well-defined API would help in establishing uniformity among them. In order to adopt BC for securing IoT, APIs play a major role. APIs can help us achieve decentralization, distributed consensus, uniform transaction executions and implementation of cryptographic functions such as signature and hashing. API manager facilitates regulation of APIs, detects any misbehavior and ensures time-bound execution and structured data transactions.

Access Control and Identity Management: Pseudo-anonymity is essential to preserve the actual identities of the devices and users in the network. This is the primary means for ensuring privacy of users. In the case of public BCs, the network can be accessed by any person. So, in order to protect the network from threats, proper access control policies have to be framed. The devices and users are usually referenced with help of addresses and these addresses are protected by cryptographic hashes. Even when the addresses are captured, the attacker should not be able to link it back to the physical identity of a user. In the case of private BCs, the network consists of closely trusted parties hence the possibility of privacy leakage is significantly less. The access permissions for miners and users when defined clearly help in proper definition of APIs.

Policy Manager: Application-level policies have to be framed in order to create smart contracts that can facilitate autonomous operation. These policies have to be carefully defined in order to ensure consistency, security and achieve faster consensus among devices. There is also a need for updating these policies based on the threats and malicious activity encountered by the devices in the network.

Storage Management: The limitations of storage in IoT devices require dedicated efforts to enable the devices act on incoming data, store and retrieve them. One possible solution is dividing the group of devices into subblocks, discussed in detail in the hybrid architecture. When the devices are grouped into subblocks, it is sufficient that the data that are relevant and necessary among the devices in that particular block alone are stored and processed. A dedicated device with higher resource capabilities can perform the management role in order to communicate and enable transactions between other subblocks. A certain degree of centralization is observed here but the overall requirement of decentralization without burdening the IoT devices is achieved through this mechanism. Dedicated hardware units that are used for performing consensus can be used to manage all the subblocks and ensure P2P operation.

Other Services: The basic security services such as Confidentiality, Integrity and authentication are fundamental requirements and it goes without saying that they have to be ensured in the proposed framework. Other services include updating the software whenever new updates are available, creation of log files for recording malicious activity & possible threat scenarios. The integration with other security services such as Network firewalls, Intrusion detection and prevention mechanisms is necessary for ensuring end-to-end security. Certain IoT applications require additional services such as traceability, payment services, grant access when needed and accommodate any future requirements that may arise.

One possible strategy to effectively adopt BC for resource-constrained IoT devices is to scale down the network into sub-BCs [14] which can then be coordinated with other subblocks in order to achieve decentralization, distributed consensus, P2P communication. In order to create sub-BCs, there are few guidelines that have to be followed. They are

■ Each sub-BCs should accommodate IoT devices in the range of few hundreds
■ The IoT devices in each sub-blocks should be grouped according to their location proximity and frequency of communication
■ The size of blocks and time interval of block generation should be set to guarantee decentralization and distribution of Mining power
■ The maximum permissible block size is 1MB
■ The time interval for block generation should be as minimum as possible

The interconnector framework used to connect the subblocks is Byzantine Fault Tolerant and guarantees transactions between subblocks. This is done in order to achieve high transaction throughput, low latency rates, and ensure normal operations of the application. The transaction flow is as follows:

1. Each subblock handles its own transactions among themselves and when consensus is achieved the transactions are formed into blocks.
2. When two subblocks need to execute transaction between them it is facilitated through the interconnector framework. The authenticity and transaction accuracy is ensured by the interconnector framework and if the transaction is verified, the block is transferred to the corresponding subblock's pool of transactions which also contains incomplete transactions.
3. When the subblock receives the new block from the interconnector framework it adds the newly verified block after completion of subblock's consensus process.

The proposed hybrid architecture as shown in Figure 6.2 makes use of a permissioned BC in which only nodes that are predefined participate in the consensus procedure. This is done to ensure that the IoT devices are less susceptible to major attacks. When dedicated hardware is used for mining process, it could act as an

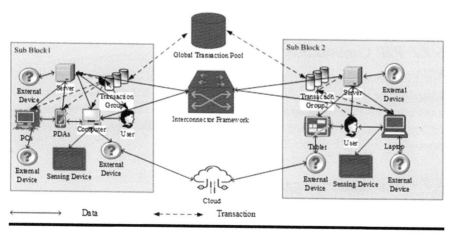

Figure 6.2 Hybrid secure IoT architecture using sub-blockchains.

IoT device using minimal mining power and control the subblock. The complexity of the consensus helps us to avoid the occurrence of attacks that target capturing of device or cloning of device. Though the consensus in subblocks is relatively less complex, high rate of block generation vulnerabilities can be mitigated.

The proposed Hybrid architecture could easily fit into the hierarchical IoT structure but requires proper design and planning. The major areas of focus when considering such an architecture are minimization of resource consumption – power, memory and computation, reduce latency, improve security and privacy.

6.7 When Should We Use BC for IoT Applications?

Even though many of IoT's security requirements can be fulfilled with help of BC, there are cases in which BC can't be the best solution. Conventional solutions based on Cloud support, traditional centralized security solutions or Directed Acyclic Graph based distributed ledgers may prove sufficient. Hence, in order to delve into further details of how to use BC for IoT security, the stakeholders involved should consider the following as prerequisites for an IoT application.

6.7.1 Decentralization

BC can be used as a solution to IoT applications that require decentralization. In certain IoT applications, there exists a centralized system in which all the stakeholders, companies, supply agencies, financial institutions share a mutual trust. Under such scenarios, BC is not required. BC essentially provides a platform for establishing trust between two interested parties but don't share a mutual trust. BC can effectively perform verifiable transactions, thus avoiding the need for intermediaries and the long redundant process of excessive documentations and agreements there by reducing both time and cost.

6.7.2 P2P Communication

Few IoT applications don't require P2P communication. The end devices usually communicate with a group head or gateway, and the decision-making, management operations are done by the head devices. In such cases, Edge computing or Fog computing based solutions provide better security. BC works well for applications which require P2P communications.

6.7.3 Transaction Logging

Certain IoT applications collect data in fixed time intervals and the data gets stored sequentially with the timestamp. Traditional databases are more than effective for such applications since the security is easily guaranteed. Also, when the possibility of attacks is rare, then sticking to the traditional infrastructures is a wise choice.

6.7.4 Payment System

IoT applications like supply chain, transportation and logistics, smart grids involve payments and financial transactions for services between unknown parties. Use of conventional payment systems involves additional transaction charges, need for banks and some cases brokers. BC can help in reducing the cost and perform such economic transactions.

6.7.5 Robust Infrastructure Support

IoT applications that make use of cloud-based distributed systems usually have robust and secure infrastructure support. If there are trust issues between the stake holders and service providers, only then BC is a viable choice. In the absence of trust issues, the use of proprietary and well-managed infrastructure will usually be enough for effective operations.

6.7.6 Use of Big Data Techniques

Few IoT applications may have mechanisms for data and transaction logging for auditing purposes or for ensuring traceability. Later, Big Data techniques shall be applied to the logged data at the cloud layer. Application in which the data are collected at intervals and these intervals are sufficiently large, it is effective to use IoT nodes to log data locally and then process it in batches as a single transaction.

Two possible scenarios in which BC can be used for securing IoT include the following.

Scenario 1: When an organization integrates all its connected devices to process data, which, in turn, is connected to the BC network. In this scenario, BC enables completion of transactions, exchange of data and creates a permanent verifiable record of all transactions which can be available for audit.

Scenario 2: In this scenario, smart contracts are created which automate the entire process and ensure fairness and seamless trust establishment.

To summarize, IoT applications don't necessarily require BC when there is

■ No requirement to keep multiple copies of ledger
■ No need to maintain redundant copies of ledgers that are distributed in multiple computers
■ The entities in IoT trust each other
■ A trusted third party service provider is present to manage the data
■ All the participating devices are inside a restricted and managed network

Recently, many solutions have been proposed that integrate BC and IoT. In [15], a lightweight BC-based solution for IoT security has been proposed. The proposed model Efficient Lightweight Integrated BC is deployed in a smart home environment in which three different levels of network are used. Efforts have been made to reduce the overhead of integrating BC by optimizing the consensus algorithm, using modified cryptographic techniques and managing throughput in a distributed manner. Other notable works include use of BC for developing a collaborative IDS [16] in which a distributed anomaly detection for IoT devices with limited resources is proposed. Trust-based anomaly detection model is proposed which is tested on a hardware testbed. The test results show that the proposed model produces significant outputs. Similar approaches for Intrusion detection systems are presented in [17] and [18]. As explained earlier, BC can definitely be used as a solution for securing IoT.

6.8 Challenges in Adopting BC-Based Security Solutions for IoT

As with collaboration of any two paradigms, the effectiveness of BC to solve IoT's security issues brings out its own set of challenges. Since BC solutions are still in nascent stages [19], it is always wise to evaluate the possible downsides of combining the two technologies to have a clear picture of what should be done. The challenges that need to be addressed to propose an effective BC-based IoT security solutions are

Volume of Data – While designing the architecture that supports BC, the amount of traffic generated by IoT applications is to be considered. Since there is huge number of devices even minimal transactions among them in order to verify may lead to enormous flow of data.

Asymmetric Cryptography – Public Key Infrastructures are necessary for providing security in BC-based systems. In resource-constrained IoT devices, the execution times may be slow, require additional memory and energy consumption would be high. Hence, all these factors must be considered while choosing the cryptographic algorithms.

Timestamping – Messages and transactions require timestamping and digital signature which has to be performed in a synchronous manner. This is the key requirement for achieving complete decentralization. Separate servers are usually maintained for this purpose. The placement of such servers is the key challenge since it has to be easily accessible and also secure.

Consensus Mechanisms – Arriving at a common consensus is the key for proper functioning in BC. The choice of consensus mechanism greatly impacts the scalability, energy consumption and throughput.

Anonymity – Since all the users share a common public key, it is possible for attackers to observe transactions, generate user patterns and identify the user. This may lead to loss of user privacy.

Identity Management – Device which is used to certify identity can also be used to block them. Privacy, Identity and Access management are three main security requirements and care should be taken to ensure them.

Ensuring CIA – In centralized IoT networks, the Confidentiality, Integrity and Authentication (CIA) is usually performed by servers that have higher security, and hence it is relatively difficult to break the system as long as there is trust between the devices. BCs are essentially decentralized hence providing the same level of security to all resource-constrained devices is a huge challenge.

Throughput and Latency – Owing to the volume of data that the IoT network creates the number of transactions increases drastically. Hence, the number of transactions processed per unit time is one of the critical factors for ensuring real-time operation of IoT devices. The processing of BC transactions requires a significant time period. In order to avoid double-spending problem and allow for the inherent verification process of transactions latency, time windows have to be explicitly defined. This is one area that needs extensive research to meet out the demands of IoT applications.

Bandwidth Utilization and Energy Efficiency – When the network grows so does the size, complexity and bandwidth associated with processing the transactions. Compression techniques have to be used to reduce the size of BC, and use of sub-chains among group of nodes is also a valid approach. Decision of what data gets stored in each node, whether to store data or not, can be done by using a hierarchical structure in which powerful nodes at different levels maintain the other nodes that have limited resources. The bandwidth of IoT communication channel plays a major role in determining the size of the blocks and transactions. The effect of energy consumed by IoT devices for multiple small transactions and few large transactions with bulk payloads have to be extensively examined.

Rate of Adoption – BC facilitates the creation of pseudo-anonymity in which devices and users are identified by addresses but there is no way to clearly link them. This may affect the adoption of BC-based solutions for Government projects since it requires clear identity management. Also, there is a possibility of different government policies in different countries which makes it further difficult. The security of BC increases with the number of users, hence in order to agree upon a consensus, the processing power of miners should be high to handle the large volume of transactions.

Enforcing Autonomous Smart Contracts – As pointed out earlier, smart contracts help in autonomous operation of BC and achieving consensus faster. Still efforts have to be made to legalize the development and execution of smart contracts.

Infrastructure Requirements – The elements of BC such as mining hardware, Decentralized storage, communication protocols, network administration and address management are required to enable efficient working. Use of dedicated hardware designed with the goal of optimized performance specific to BC is currently the focus of industry and technology corporations.

6.9 Conclusion and Future Directions

IoT and BC are two technologies that have the ability to revolutionize our world. IoT has seen widespread adoption across multiple domains. Extensive research and monetary and technical workforce investments are being done by industries, academic institutions and technology enthusiasts in order to bring out solutions that can help them with solutions to everyday problems and make life easier. Even though BCs were primarily designed for financial transactions, their capabilities have created an interest for their adoption to other domains as well. The benefits of BC that make it an attractive choice for securing IoT are decentralization, distributed processing, scalability, traceability, data integrity and privacy among others. The major contributions of this work are a brief overview of BC technology is provided, the various security requirements and challenges in IoT are identified and a conceptual framework for securing IoT using BCs is proposed. The development of solutions in both IoT and BC is still an ongoing research and keeps evolving. We have analyzed the possible requirements for IoT security and proposed a framework that can address those requirements. It is our sincere belief that security is a learning process and there is never one permanent magic solution that could solve all issues. The combination of existing security mechanisms like Intrusion detection and prevention systems, firewalls, secure operating systems, device authorization and authentication services along with BC infrastructure can provide a well-rounded security infrastructure for IoT.

The future scope of this work is to develop a security solution that could be added to any IoT platform as a standard package and can be customized to fit the specific application requirements. The downside of using BCs is that the amount of processing and storage is required in individual devices that perform transactions. The consensus algorithms used in BCs require additional network bandwidth that incurs additional overhead which has to be properly studied and quantified. BCs can't be used to secure all IoT applications, hence the knowledge about tradeoff between security, performance and resource utilization is mandatory. Also, the decision about implementing BC on which layer in the IoT hierarchy and how to scale down the BCs structure for it to be accommodated in the IoT devices with limited resources has to be carefully examined.

References

[1] H. Aldowah, S. U. Rehman, and I. Umar, "Security in Internet of Things: Issues, Challenges and Solutions," *Recent Trends in Data Science and Soft Computing*, vol. 843, 2019, Springer International Publishing, Cham.

[2] T. M. Fernández-Caramés and P. Fraga-Lamas, "A review on the use of blockchain for the Internet of Things," *IEEE Access*, vol. 6, pp. 32979–33001, 2018.

[3] S. Nakamoto, "Bitcoin: A peer-to-peer electronic cash system," *Journal for General Philosophy of Science*, vol. 1, pp. 1–9, 2008.

[4] A. Rosic, *"What is blockchain technology? A step-by-step guide for beginners,"* vol. 1, pp. 1–33, 2018.

[5] K. Christidis and M. Devetsikiotis, "Blockchains and smart contracts for the Internet of Things," *IEEE Access*, vol. 4. pp. 2292–2303, 2016.

[6] N. Fotiou and G. C. Polyzos, "Smart contracts for the Internet of Things: Opportunities and challenges," In: 2018 European Conference on Networks and Communications, pp. 256–260, 2018.

[7] L. Lamport, R. Shostak, and M. Pease, "The byzantine generals problem," *ACM Trans. Program. Lang. Syst.*, vol. 4, no. 3, pp. 382–401, 1982.

[8] V. Saini, "ConsensusPedia: An Encyclopedia of 30 Consensus Algorithms: A complete list of all consensus algorithms," *Medium.* 2018.

[9] M. S. Ali, M. Vecchio, M. Pincheira, K. Dolui, F. Antonelli, and M. H. Rehmani, "Applications of blockchains in the Internet of Things: A comprehensive survey," *IEEE Communications Surveys and Tutorials*, vol. 21, no. 2., pp. 1676–1717, 2019.

[10] F. I. Khan and S. Hameed, "Understanding security requirements and challenges in Internet of Things (IoTs): A review," *Journal of Computer Networks and Communcations*, vol. 2019, pp 1–14, 2018.

[11] Rouse. M, "What is IoT security (Internet of Things security)? - Definition from WhatIs.com," IoT security (Internet of Things security), 2015. [Online]. Available: https://internetofthingsagenda.techtarget.com/definition/IoT-security-Internet-of-Things-security. [Accessed: 21-Oct-2019].

[12] M. A. Ferrag, M. Derdour, M. Mukherjee, A. Derhab, L. Maglaras, and H. Janicke, "Blockchain technologies for the Internet of Things: Research issues and challenges," *IEEE Internet Things Journal*, vol. 6, pp. 2188–2204, 2018.

[13] A. Dorri, S. S. Kanhere, R. Jurdak, and P. Gauravaram, "Blockchain for IoT security and privacy: The case study of a smart home," In: *IEEE International Conference on Pervasive Computing and Communications Work,* pp. 618–623, October 2017.

[14] G. Sagirlar, B. Carminati, E. Ferrari, J. D. Sheehan, and E. Ragnoli, "Hybrid-IoT: Hybrid blockchain architecture for Internet of Things-PoW sub-blockchains," In *Proceedings - IEEE 2018 International Congress on Cybermatics: 2018 IEEE Conferences on Internet of Things, Green Computing and Communications, Cyber, Physical and Social Computing, Smart Data, Blockchain, Computer and Information Technology,* 2018, pp. 1007–1016.

[15] S. N. Mohanty *et al.*, "An efficient Lightweight integrated Blockchain (ELIB) model for IoT security and privacy," *Future Generation Computing System*, vol. 102, pp. 1027–1037, Jan. 2020.

[16] T. Golomb, Y. Mirsky, and Y. Elovici, "CIoTA: Collaborative anomaly detection via blockchain," 2018.

[17] M. Signorini, M. Pontecorvi, W. Kanoun, and R. Di Pietro, "BAD: Blockchain anomaly detection," 2018.

[18] S. Kim, B. Kim, and H. J. Kim, "Intrusion detection and mitigation system using blockchain analysis for bitcoin exchange," In: *Proceedings of the 2018 International Conference on Cloud Computing and Internet of Things*, pp. 40–44, 2018.

[19] Bragadeesh SA and Umamakeswari A, "Role of blockchain in the Internet-of-Things (Iot)," *International Journal of Engineering Technology*, vol. 7, no. 2.24, p. 109, Apr. 2018.

Chapter 7

Blockchain Identity Management

K. Sneha, M.R. Manu, B. Balamurugan and S. Sreeji

Contents

7.1 Introduction

Electronic information of an individual in a specific identity system is called a digital identity. Digital identity has become a prominent key for every transaction that occurs online. These identities can be used for authentication and authorization. An identity management (IDM) system enables the authorized individuals or organizations to access the right resources for a legitimate purpose. Traditional IDM systems such as passports or driving license are difficult to process and unreliable as they can be easily forged.

Most online transactions require individuals to reveal their personal information before they can proceed to access the services. Before every financial transaction on platforms like Amazon Pay, PayPal, etc., users have to provide their login details which include both financial and personal details. Thus, on each transaction, this information gets stored on numerous Internet databases. In a centralized IDM, the same credentials can be used by each service provider. A Certificate Authority issues certificates to users. Each user can use same certificate before accessing the services. An example is Single sign on (SSO) model, which requires a user to login only once and be authenticated automatically by all other service providers. Centralized models of IDM currently face challenges due to the increasing number of data breaches that lead to identity fraud and loss of privacy [1]. These recurring events highlight a lack of control that end users have with the digital identities they collected.

A centralized IDM is typically more secure since it provides unified IDM. It can simplify an organization's security systems by making access controls easier to manage and maintain. With a centralized authentication system, users can access all their documents and assets through a single set of login credentials. Figure 7.1 shows the various application areas of digital identity.

Centralized system will also result in a single point of failure (SPOF). Hackers need to breach only one set of credential to access everything that verified users can access. An alternative to the centralized IDM system is to have identities distributed across different systems.

7.1.1 An Overview of Credit and Identity Data (Equifax)

A data breach is a security incident where a lot of private information is exposed due to **malicious attack** or negligence or system error. The data exposed include names, addresses, telephone numbers, email addresses birth dates and more. There may be highly sensitive information like account numbers, driver license numbers, passwords, credit or debit card numbers, PINs, user names, etc. Breaches of data incidents will involve a large number of compromised records of large enterprises and public institutions. The global average of the number of records lost or stolen per breach is 24,615. IBM classified a larger class of data breaches called mega

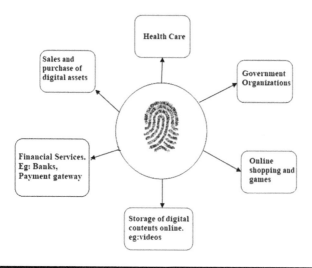

Figure 7.1   Application areas of digital identity.

breaches. A mega breach will involve more than 1 million compromised records. Password hacks are the reason for 81% of breach [2]. Otherwise, a company can unknowingly set off the leak of sensitive information. These types of incidents are known as accidental data breaches and can be caused by things like failure to follow password guidelines, etc. A Google report found that lot of credentials was stolen through third parties and phishing attacks.

Equifax data breach: Credit reporting agency Equifax collected information on over 800 million individual consumers and more than 88 million businesses worldwide. In 2017, they announced that a cybersecurity attack affected approximately 143 million US consumers. Hackers used a US website application vulnerability to gain access to certain files [3]. Those stolen credentials can be used for illegal activity for years. Some other examples of data breaches include:

Facebook: In 2018, Facebook reported an attack on its network, which had exposed the information of nearly 50 million users with 14 million having user names and recent Facebook searches accessed. The attackers utilized a feature in Facebook's code to gain access to user accounts and take control of them.

US Office of Personnel Management: They collected personnel information for US federal workers. A cyberattack was reported in 2015 in which the data of about 4 million current and former employees were compromised. As per IBM and Ponemon Institute report, 48% of all data breaches are by malicious cyberattack. The studies on alternate approaches to centralized IDM are being held to widen the integrity and acceptance of digital identity [4]. Centralization is a major problem when it comes to deal with privacy of users. Internet became increasingly privatized, and more and more small or big companies started to gain control over online identities.

In 2018, the personal details of over 220,000 organ donors had been leaked through government official databases in Malaysia. Their personal details, identity card numbers, addresses and mobile phone numbers were leaked and can be used for illegal activities.

In April 2019, Docker Hub, the official repository of container images has announced that hackers had access to a portion of its database for a short period of time. The hackers managed to take away the data of approximately 1.9 lakh users. Hackers have gained access to Docker Hub usernames, hashed passwords, GitHub, and Bitbucket tokens that are used for auto-building Docker container images. Another risk is that the hackers can bypass the two-factor authentication on GitHub code repository using the stolen access tokens and keys.

7.1.2 Blockchain's Relation with IDM

Blockchain creates a platform that protects an individual's identity from theft and reduces unlawful activities. This technology can help industries to handle the issues of authentication and reconciliation. It provides freedom for individuals to create their own encrypted digital identities that will replace multiple usernames and passwords while offering more inclusive security features. Blockchain technology distributes a ledger among all members of the network [5]. Blockchain authentication can eliminate data from being altered maliciously. On every transaction or addition of block of data to the chain, a majority of members of the network must verify the validity of new block. Thus, integrity of the ledgers is assured. Public key encryptions like RSA encryption can be used to securely send the credentials. The recipient then verifies this against an entry in the immutable blockchain. This result is a remarkable, safe and reliable way to handle the verification of identity.

The self-sovereign blockchain-based IDM systems eliminate unnecessary centralized identity providers by creating the blockchain identity on the blockchain platform. In that platform, all users and service providers follow the identity consensus and can verify identities instead of blindly believing some third-party identity providers [6]. In blockchain, users have the knowledge of what data is collected about them and how they get processed. By the open nature of blockchain, any modification of the protocol requires the consensus of the participating nodes. Thereby, ideal security and transparency are provided for all the users. With the combination of secure end-to-end encryption and open nature of the blocks, the privacy concerns arising are reduced.

The reasons behind why blockchain technology is used for these types of systems are as follows.

- Integrity of data: The blockchain system lets the network participants to accept and verify (consensus) each transaction and record it cryptographically on the blockchain. Thereby integrity is ensured in each step of the process and is distributed too, i.e., not entrusted to any single member. Each block must refer to the previous block to be a valid one. Any of the member cannot hide a transaction, and that makes the transaction more trackable.
- Security: Use of cryptography ensure security in the system.
- Distribution of power: This system uses peer-to-peer networks to distribute power so there is no single point to control the power. A single individual cannot shut down the whole system.
- Privacy: As individuals themselves are maintaining their data privacy is guaranteed.

7.2 IDM – Overview

Authentication is a process of determining whether someone is who he is proclaimed to be. This concept is the key feature of any reliable online system that handles sensitive data or transactions. A perfect authentication process should be user friendly, reliable and able to protect user's privacy and verify data credentials. Users who subscribe to multiple online services will have to store passwords in all the servers they use for authentication and hence authentication data are replicated and stored in multiple servers [4]. These recurrent actions of signing in or authenticating data may lead to flaws in the authentication system. These vulnerabilities will further lead to data breaches and identify theft. Thus, IDM is a broad field that creates, maintains and revokes online user accounts and users identity. IDM should simplify the user access to his online process. Some of the IDM schemes follow.

7.2.1 Centralized IDM

The user credentials are issued, authenticated and managed by a single entity. This server-based IDM model has some drawbacks. It is difficult for the service providers to manage and authenticate users. Passwords and personal identity information are traditionally stored in a centralized server that makes it easier for hackers to hack, misuse or manipulate the data. Therefore, strong mechanisms have to be employed, by using multiple factor authentication for access and stronger encryption, which finally complicates the whole system. Sensitive identity records can be revoked or misused by the third-party identity provider. After all the users were hinged into a single authority who has the authority to deny their identity or even confirm a false identity. See Figure 7.2.

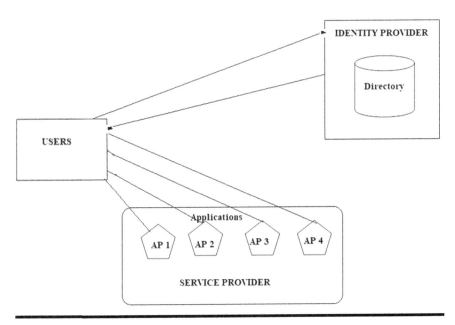

Figure 7.2   Centralized identity management.

7.2.2 Federated IDM

In federated IDM systems, organizations allow users to use the same identity on different online services. This comes in the form of SSO on Facebook login, Google ID, etc. This forces an agreement between several providers, an identity at one provider is recognized by other providers and there should be contractual agreements on data ownership. In a federated IDM scheme, user's credentials are stored only with the user's identity provider. While accessing service, the user does not need to provide credentials to the service provider. The service provider trusts the identity provider and validates the user's credentials. Hence, the user needs to provide credentials only to the identity provider, which is the user's trusted domain.

Identity providers have access to the information stored by subscribers for authentication purpose and this presents a privacy issue. It is difficult for users to make sure the proper Service Level Agreement rules are enforced since there is a lack of transparency that allows the users to monitor their own information. This can be seen in recent Facebook and Cambridge Data Analytica dispute over alleged harvesting and use of personal data.

Federated IDM systems can provide authentication and authorization capabilities across organizational and system boundaries. User account is managed independently by identity provider and no enterprise directory integration is required. This lower the security risk as credential are not replicated but propagated on demand. This approach is relatively more complex to implement and requires proper agreement and trusted relationship between online services. See Figure 7.3.

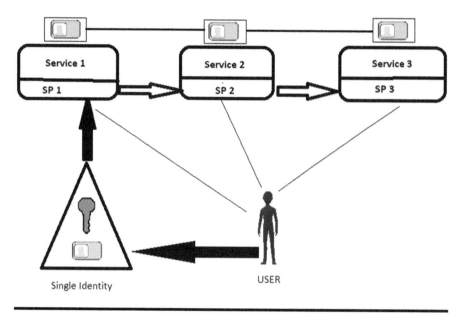

Figure 7.3   Federated identity.

7.2.3 User-Centric Identity

User-Centric IDM gives an individual administrative control over his identity across multiple authorities while no federation is required. For users to manage an unavoidably growing number of passwords and credentials by remembering or other traditional methods is totally impractical. So this method allows users to store identifiers and credentials from different service providers in a single tamper-resistant hardware device which may be a smart card or some other portable personal device.

This approach opens up large possibilities for improving the user experience and strengthening the trust and authentication between users and service providers. Before the device can be used for authentication purposes, the user must authenticate to the device with a PIN or any other method. See Figure 7.4.

7.2.4 Self-Sovereign ID

In self-sovereign ID (SSI), users are the authority and they can decide how to share an identity and with whom it to be shared. Thus, user autonomy is achieved. It can be implemented by a decentralized identity system that allows the recording and exchange of identity and building trust among participating entities. Blockchain digital IDM applications allow users to control their data, secure it and legalize it. The capability to manage Personal Identity Information will be the highlight of using blockchain applications for financial services, travel, gaming and all other

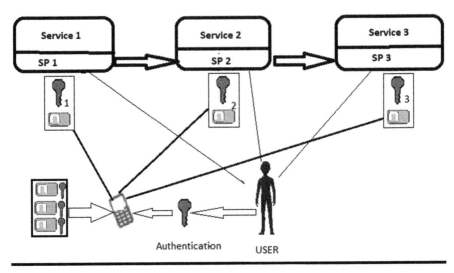

Figure 7.4 **User-centric identity management.**

areas of digital world in a single sign-on and secure data environment. Some features of self-sovereign identity are:

■ Accessibility: Users should have direct access to their own identity and all related data. All data are visible and accessible without third parties.
■ Persistence of data: Identities once stored should be kept intact until the user himself changes it.

7.3 Blockchain for IDM

Blockchain technology eliminates the intermediaries and allows users to manage identity on their own. It helps in designing a platform to protect individual's identities from thefts and breaches. Moreover, it allows users to create self-sovereign and encrypted digital identities, replacing the need to memorize multiple usernames and passwords. An IDM platform with blockchain technology is efficient in following characteristics. It is decentralized, so no central authority can control the data. With the cryptographic consensus algorithm, data are secured. Immutability of the records and smart contract improves trust in the network.

7.3.1 Approach

A blockchain is a linear form of a distributed ledger that includes immutable blocks of data, each block contains a list of transactions and a reference to its previous block. Strong cryptographic techniques are employed to maintain integrity between each block and its previous one. Blockchain uses a distributed ledger technology (DLT), where many people can write entries into a record of data, and a group of users can control the updation and modification of records. Thus, blockchain is a distributed database of records, or a public ledger of all transactions that have been executed and shared among the participating users in a peer-to-peer networks [7].

DLT means the ledgers are stored not in a central location but in decentralized locations. Each entity participating in the transaction has the complete copy of the ledger, which includes all the transactions. These ledger copies can reconcile themselves in a specific interval and keep them updated. Thus, the whole system is completely autonomous. A ledger is simply a group of blocks. Data are permanently stored in the network in files called blocks. A block is a container of some or all of the most recent transactions which occurred in a specific period of time. A block consists of block header and block body. The header of a block has three metadata. First, there is a hash reference to a previous block and a hashed list of all transactions that took place since the last created block, which connects this block to the previous block in the blockchain. The second set of metadata is timestamp relative to the time when the block is created, which helps in the mining of data. The third metadata is the Merkle tree root, a data structure used to represent all the transactions in the block. The block body includes a record of all transactions. See Figure 7.5.

Hashing is used in blockchain technology to connect blocks, by including a hash value of the previous block to the current block. This guarantees that the confirmed transactions in the ledger cannot be tampered with. Any change to the contents of a block invalidates the hash of that block, which, in turn, invalidates the hash of the next block and so on. The blocks are stored in a multi-level data structure called the

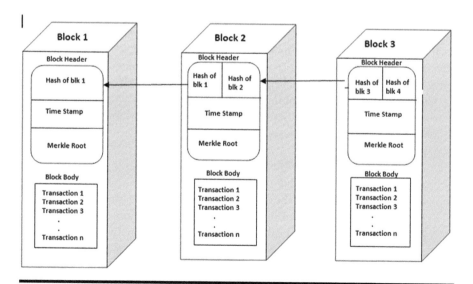

Figure 7.5 Blocks in a blockchain.

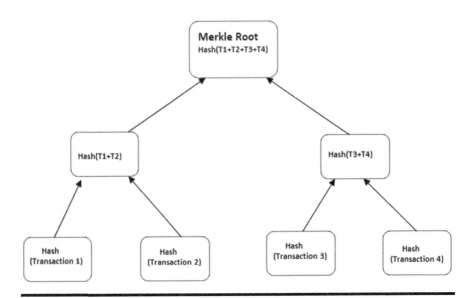

Figure 7.6 Merkle tree.

merkle tree. This structure is the reason for easy mining. The merkle tree is a type of binary tree, where the bottom of the tree contains the transactions in hashed form, the intermediate tree nodes contain the hash of the two child nodes that made it. On top there it is a hashed tree-node called the Merkle root. See Figure 7.6.

In the leaf node of the tree, there are hashes of four transactions T1, T2, T3, T4. The intermediate nodes combine the hash of its child node, i.e., hash (T1+T2). Finally, the root node contains the hash of all the leaf node, which, in turn, is the hash of list of all transactions took place in that block. The advantage of implementing merkle tree data structures is that any node in the network can check the previous transactions easily, and hence it is guaranteed that the block tamper is free.

Consensus: For the functioning of a blockchain, it needs acceptance and verification by all the users in the network called a consensus. Mainly there are four consensus algorithms that can be applied.

1. **Proof of Work (PoW):** The PoW consensus algorithm is the most widely used algorithm in blockchain. It was used in Bitcoin which works by finding a nonce value such that when hashed with Merkle hash, the new hash value should be smaller than the current target value. When a nonce is found, the miner can create the block and forward it through the network. Other users in the network can verify the PoW by computing the hash of the block and checking whether it is less than the current target value.

2. **Proof of Stake (PoS):** In the case of bitcoin using PoS algorithm, the peer that generates a block will be accepted by a network only if it produces a proof

that it has access to a certain amount of coins. Thus, only those who can provide the PoS can participate in the process of maintaining the blockchain. Since computation is low, this technique saves computational energy.

3. **Practical Byzantine Fault Tolerance:** This consensus algorithm was developed to tolerate Byzantine faults like the unexpected behavior of the node, joining and quitting the network in a distributed system. This algorithm presents a state machine replication algorithm to tolerate Byzantine faults. It also uses an efficient authentication scheme based on message authentication codes.

4. **Delegated Proof of Stake:** In this consensus algorithm, the user can choose the peers to validate a block. So by lesser nodes validating the block, the transaction can be confirmed quickly.

7.3.2 Data Storage and Protection

Depending on the participants of consensus, there are three types of blockchains: public, private and consortium blockchains.

■ **Public Blockchains:** Public blockchains or permission-less blockchains can be accessed by all and anyone can participate as a node in the decision-making process. In public blockchain, nodes can reach consensus without central authority and thus it is decentralized. All users have a copy of the ledger on their local nodes and use a distributed consensus mechanism to reach decision. Any changes in the ledger will be updated in all copies. Bitcoin is an example of a public blockchain. Details of each transaction will be updated on every copy of the block.

■ **Private Blockchains:** Private blockchains are open only to a consortium or group of individuals or organizations that have decided to share the ledger. Only the owner of the blockchain has the right to make any changes to it. For example, blockstack which supports the financial institutions with back office operation on private blockchain

■ **Consortium Blockchains:** This blockchain is basically a hybrid of public and private blockchains. In this not all nodes will participate in consensus but a group of preselected nodes. It has many advantages like efficiency, privacy of transactions and faster in execution.

7.3.2.1 Adding a New Block to the Blockchain

The basic working of IDMs using blockchain technology are as follows [8]:

■ Whenever the user uploads the identity documents, that makes a transaction and all details of transaction are collected in a new block.

■ That new block is then broadcasted to all the peers in the network.

- All the network peers will validate the transaction and the block will be added to chain and user will successfully upload the document to his account.
- Each successful transaction will have Transaction ID and Document ID whenever the document is uploaded, and the document will be digitally signed which ensures that unauthorized person cannot tamper the document, thereby it provides authenticity for the document and transaction.
- After successful completion, that transaction will be recorded on public ledger which will be visible across the network.
- Whenever any department or organization requests for the access of any particular document of user, that will also be considered as one new transaction and will be stored on a block and that block will be broadcasted to all the network peers and after approval of all network peers this block will be added to the chain.
- Once the block is added to the chain, the intended user (department or organization) can access the requested document.
- The approval or rejection of the document done by the user will be stored in new block and the new block will be broadcasted to all network peers.
- On approval by all the network peers, this block will be added to the same blockchain transaction.
- The newly added block will also have a hash of the previous block, so if someone tries to tamper the specific block in the block of chains they have to correctly recompute the hash value of all the blocks in the chain. Which is computationally difficult, and thereby makes the transaction more secure. See Figure 7.7.

Protection: Blockchain offers evident improvements in terms of security and data integrity from traditional IDM systems. User can decide and track which all third parties have access to their identity, thereby privacy is employed effectively. The main security features of blockchain are:

- Cryptography: Many cryptographic functions are used like hashing, digital signature, etc.
- Consensus: Algorithms that decided the validity of transactions.
- Timestamp: Based on the time of block creation.
- Distributed ledger: Transactions are grouped together and stored in blocks and hash is calculated.

Blockchain implementation gives a unique identification for each block and each transaction. That identification is a large random number (Hash) derived from the private or public key. Each transaction has its own hash. Hash codes can detect tampering of data [9]. Hashing in blockchain also helps to establish a link between blocks. This assures that any confirmed transactions in the ledger cannot be tampered by an intruder. Any change to the contents of a block invalidates the hash of that block, which leads to the invalidation of hash of the next block.

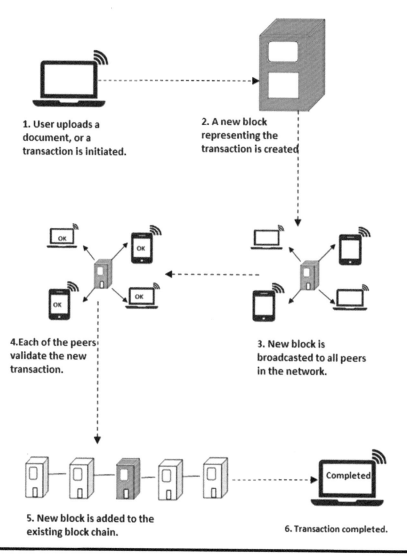

Figure 7.7 Adding a new block to a blockchain.

Since a block includes hash of previous block and current block, the current block's hash value is decided by the factors, its timestamp, hash of previous block, merkle root and transactions in that block. If someone attempts to tamper a block or make changes in transaction, he should recompute the hash of that block. But the new hash value will not match with the next block. An efficient intruder can even change the hash value of the next block too, but it will lead to a mismatch in upcoming blocks. It is practically impossible to recompute the hash value for all the blocks in a blockchain, as it will include thousands of blocks and the computational cost is incomparable.

Asymmetric cryptography: DLT technology employs asymmetric cryptography using private and public keys to sign transactions. Only the owner of a private key can generate a transaction address, which can then be validated by the network using the associated public key. This approach provides a way to authenticate somebody and all transactions are made only by the legitimate user, hence owner-controlled management of personal data is achieved.

Time stamping and consensus: The completion of a transaction is dependent on the consensus made between network nodes. For an intruder to reach consensus with majority of peers in a network, they should recompute the hash and details of at least 51% of peers in the network which is difficult.

7.3.3 *Transparency and User Access*

The main benefits of using blockchain technology are (see Figure 7.8):

- Transparency: Decentralized architecture employs transparency in the functioning of a blockchain.
- Immutability: On confirmation of a transaction data cannot be altered.
- Consistency: Data will be available as long as the blockchain exist.
- No third parties: Implementation of consensus and distributed nature removes intermediaries from the system.
- Speed and reduced cost: Transactions are much faster and less expensive.
- Security: Cryptographic techniques and consensus provide more stronger security system.
- Unique ID: While registering on blockchain, the IDM system user will be provided with a unique ID. The unique ID includes all personally identifiable information which is encrypted. These details are stored on the user's device supported by interplanetary file system (IPFS) [10]. Users can share the unique ID with any service provider to authenticate themselves through the IDM system.
- Consensus: User's personal information will not be stored in a blockchain IDM system. The smart contract between user and system allows a user-controlled disclosure of personal data. Data stored in a blockchain are immutable and secure. Transactions are proceeded only with the consent of more than 50% participants of the network.
- Decentralized: Centralized servers are not used to store user's personal information. All the documents are stored on user's device and can be accessed

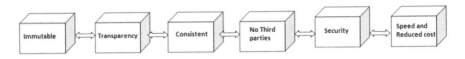

Figure 7.8 Benefits of blockchain technology.

by IPFS which is securing that http. Decentralized implementation removes the faults or data loss occurred by SPOF fault, and thereby availability is enhanced. SPOF means if that node fails, the whole system will stop working.

■ No geographic boundary: Users can access data from any platform and any place.
■ User access: Now a days many applications built on blockchain technology are available for IDM. These apps are useful for users in verification and authentication of their identity in real time.

Step 1: Installation of Mobile App

A user can download the mobile app from play store to establish their identity. After installation, user can create a profile. After profile creation, the user will get a unique ID [11]. That ID helps organizations to access the user's identity.

Step 2: Uploading the documents

The user can then upload the government-issued identity documents on the app. The documents are saved in the IPFS having hashed addresses stored in the blockchain. The app will extract personal information from these documents. The user will have the complete authority of their data. Thereby users can decide on what information to be shared with organizations [12].

Step 3: Smart contracts for calculating trust score of a person

Smart contracts have the logic which can generate a trust score for a user from the information they provide in creating a self-sovereign identity.

Step 4: Third-party companies requesting access

If a company wants to access details of a person for authentication, a notification will be sent to the individual who is the owner of the identity. Once the user allows the companies to access their details, third parties can also use the information for authentication. Moreover, users can trace the purpose that their identity is being used.

Blockchain does not store any user's data or information. It only stores the transactions between identity holders and organizations. For example, if a bank verifies the person's identity through an app, then that transaction will be added on the blockchain and approval of the transaction by the majority of peers, data will be visible to all the connected nodes.

7.4 DLT-Based IDM

Some of the distributed ledger-based IDM systems are as follows.

7.4.1 Civic

Civic is a blockchain-enabled system for the protection of identity of users who access untrusted sites apps. By using the Civic platform as a buffer, users can access the websites without a login and password. All identity information entered on Civic is completely encrypted; so the identities are intact from threats. Thus, Civic App supports organizations by making identity verification easier and reduces the expenditure [13, 14].

User can download the civic app in their smartphone and use like a digital ID card. Civic Identity Partners, such as any government agency, can add authenticated identity information to the app and moreover it can act as a trusted authentication authority. This app does not store the data on a centralized server. Users can access their accounts through biometric verification which provides an extra level of security [15].

When a user needs to submit proof of identity for a new bank account, for example, the bank can verify the person's identity much faster because the app would stand in place of the current KYC process. The user would scan a QR code from the bank for submitting a request. For the approval of the request, the bank receives verification and the transaction is recorded on the blockchain. Civic can function as a warning system for identity theft. Users will receive notifications when their identity information is being compromised or used.

7.4.2 uPort

uPort developed by ConsenSys is a secure system for self-sovereign identity, built on Ethereum. uPort presents an identity system, which allows the user to be in complete control of their identity and personal information. uPort identities are benefited by individuals, devices, entities, or institutions. The uPort technology consists of three main components: smart contracts, developer libraries and a mobile app. The mobile app stores the user keys. Ethereum smart contracts form the basement of the IDM. It also contains technique to recover identity even if mobile device is lost. The developer libraries support integration of uPort with third-party app developers [16, 17].

For the creation of a new identity, a uPort mobile application creates a new asymmetric key pair and sends a transaction to Ethereum. Then, a new proxy is created, the address of the proxy comprises the unique uPort identifier (uPortID) of a user. A user is free to create multiple uPortIDs that are unlinkable. The private key that controls a uPortID is stored only on the user's mobile device. In case of theft or loss of user's mobile, users must nominate the uPortIDs of group of trusted persons who can participate in voting to replace the public. The controller replaces the lost public key with the new public key. Thus, a user can maintain a consistent uPortID even after the loss of keys.

Finally, uPort scheme supports secure mapping of user identity to a particular uPortID. The uPort registry is a smart contract that enables mapping of identity and uPortID. Any entity can query the registry, but only the owner of a specific uPortID can modify the corresponding data. The data are stored on IPFS: a distributed file system where a file can be retrieved using hashing.

7.4.3 Sovrin

An SSI is an identity owned and controlled by an individual or organization. Without the owner's knowledge no one else can access it. Sovrin enables a user to generate as many identifiers as they'd like by keeping separate identities for privacy purposes [18]. These identifiers as they'd like are managed by the user or an admin service, in a decentralized way. Sovrin has a distributed data structure which includes the user identifier, cryptographic public key and other data for transaction. The primary part is the Sovrin ledger. These ledgers hold the transactions in a distributed and replicated among the nodes [19]. The consensus algorithm used is Byzantine fault-tolerant protocol named Plenum. The main attraction of Sovrin is less expensive consensus, i.e., protocol used in this is less expensive than a proof of work. Therefore, the system becomes cost effective and, in turn, increased throughput is provided.

Users access Sovrin through a mobile app and control software provides platform for interactions with other on the network. Agents are nodes that are addressable. Agents also provide storage of user credentials in encrypted form and backup service for data is also there. Key recovery facility is also provided with the help of a group of trustees in sovereign.

7.4.4 ShoCard

ShoCard is a secure IDM services with multifactor authentication through blockchain [20, 21]. Users can securely log into online services and devices without a user ID and password. A ShoCard is a digital identity that protects consumer privacy, it is basically a tiny file that only you can manipulate. A ShoCard ID can be created through the App. While creating ShoCard ID, user can scan their identity document and sign it [22]. Later a private and public key for sealing the documents will be generated by the app. The documents will be encrypted, hashed and sent to the blockchain and it cannot be tampered.

ShoCard is user-friendly similar to one showing his driving license. It is secure and even bank can use it for authentication [23, 24]. The user's identity is encrypted and hashed and can be accessed when needed. Users can give banks temporary access to the private side of this blockchain record for identity verification. Once it is completed, the bank will create its own record that can be referred in future for authentication.

ShoCard has a central server that intermediates the verification of identity information between a user and organization [9, 25]. Once a ShoCard ID is created, the user can then interact with identity providers to gather certificates. The identity provider first verifies that the user knows both the cryptographic key and data hashed, for issuing the certificates. ShoCard server offers the storage for encrypted certificates. In the validation phase, the user should first provide the certificate reference and cryptographic key with the service provider. After retrieving the certificates from the ShoCard servers, the service provider checks the signature of certificates and key and identity data provided by user matches with hashed data. Thus, multi-level authentication is achieved in ShoCard [26, 27].

7.4.5 Authenteq

Authenteq is an automated identity verification system that provides privacy for the user. It helps users to verify their identity and create their own sovereign digital identity [28, 29]. These identities are stored in a blockchain in encrypted form. Any personal user information is owned and controlled by the user himself and is not accessible by anyone. With an Authenteq ID, users can verify their identity to third parties with the claims verification API [13]. Authenteq can be used with type of online services like online shopping, online betting, financial service, etc.

7.5 Conclusion and Future Work

The blockchain is highly developed and praised technology for its decentralized infrastructure and peer-to-peer in nature which is highly recommended for IDM. Impacts of using blockchain for IDM are: Blockchain is highly cost effective and time efficient. The cost involved in verifying identities is lowered for organization and user. All nodes connected to the network can trace the transactions in the blockchain. All transactions are authenticated and verified. It ensures the privacy of the transactions for the users connected to the blockchain. Apart from storing the data on a single centralized server, decentralization is achieved by the distribution of information on every node in the network, thereby SPOF errors are avoided.

The main challenges faced by blockchains are scalability and lack of privacy. With the increase in number of transactions, the size of blockchain grows uncontrolled. Due to the restricted size of blocks, number of transactions processed by a block is restricted to seven transactions. But larger blocks will reduce the speed of transactions. To solve the bulky blockchain problem, a novel scheme was proposed by Bruce et al. In this scheme, old transaction blocks are removed by the network and a database named account tree is used to balance the remaining transactions. So nodes do not need to store all transactions to validate a transaction. Eyal et al. [4], Bitcoin-NG, proposed a key block for leader election and microblock to store transactions. Another challenge is the lack of privacy. Solution proposed for this is to increase the anonymity of blockchain. Zero knowledge proof is an example technique used. For a blockchain IDM system to work in the real world, there should be a governance model and a trust framework. These will facilitate the sharing of identities with more trust. This will be the highlighting area in the near future. This will enable the enterprises with a much more secure environment.

References

[1] Dunphy Paul and Petitcolas Fabien A. P., A first look at identity management schemes on the blockchain. IEEE Security and Privacy Magazine special issue on "Blockchain Security and Privacy," 2018.

[2] Zheng, Zibin et al., Blockchain challenges and opportunities: A survey. International Journal of Web and Grid Services, Vol. 14, No. 4, 2016.

[3] Nagaraju S. and Parthiban L., SecAuthn: Provably secure multifactor authentication for the cloud computing systems. Indian Journal of Science and Technology, Vol 9, No. 9, 2016.

[4] Eyal I., Gencer A.E., Sirer E.G. and Van Renesse R. "Bitcoin-NG: a scalable blockchain protocol". Proceedings of 13th USENIX Symposium on Networked Systems Design and Implementation (NSDI 16), Santa Clara, CA, (2016), pp.45–59.

[5] Tschorsch F. and Scheuermann B., Bitcoin and beyond: A technical survey on decentralized digital currencies. IEEE Communications Surveys Tutorials, Vol. 18, No. 3, pp. 2084–2123, 2016.

[6] Ahn Gail-Joon, Ko Moo Nam, and Mohamed Shehab, "Portable user-centric identity-management". IFIP International Information Security Conference (2008), pp.573–587.

[7] Lim Shu Yun, Fotsing Pascal Tankam et al. Blockchain technology the identity management and authentication service disruptor: A survey. International Journal on Advanced Science Engineering Information Technology, Vol.8, No. 4-2, 2018.

[8] Gandhi Mardavkumar, Survey on identity management using blockchain technology. International Journals of Advanced Research in Computer Science and Software Engineering, Vol. 7, No 12, December 2017.

[9] Zheng Z., Xie S., Dai H., Chen X., and Wang H., "An overview of blockchain technology: Architecture, consensus, and future trends". Proceedings of the 2017 IEEE BigData Congress, Honolulu, Hawaii, pp. 557–564.

[10] Shayan Eskandari, David Barrera, Elizabeth Stobert, and Jeremy Clark, "A First Look at the Usability of Bitcoin Key Management". Presented at the NDSS Workshop on Usable Security 2015 (USEC 2015), San Diego, California, 2015.

[11] Christidis K. and Devetsikiotis M. Blockchains and smart contracts for the internet of things. IEEE Access, Vol. 4, pp.2292–2303, 2016.

[12] Bentov I., Lee C., Mizrahi A. and Rosenfeld M. Proof of activity: Extending Bitcoin's proof of work via proof of stake. ACM SIGMETRICS Performance Evaluation Review, Vol. 42, No. 3, pp. 34–37, 2014.

[13] Kraft D., Difficulty control for blockchain-based consensus systems. Peer-to-Peer Networking and Applications, Vol. 9, No. 2, pp.397–413, 2016.

[14] Eyal I. and Sirer E.G. "Majority is not enough: Bitcoin mining is vulnerable". Proceedings of International Conference on Financial Cryptography and Data Security, Berlin, Heidelberg, pp.436–454, 2014.

[15] Omohundro S., Cryptocurrencies, smart contracts, and artificial intelligence. AI Matters, Vol. 1, No. 2, pp.19–21, 2014.

[16] Crosby Michael et al, Blockchain technology: Beyond bitcoin. Applied Innovation, vol. 2, pp. 6–10, 2016.

[17] Jaag C., Bach C., et al., Blockchain Technology and Cryptocurrencies: Opportunities for Postal Financial Services, Technical Report, 2016.

[18] Alpár Gergely and Jacobs Bart, "Credential design in attribute-based identity management". 3rd TILTing Perspectives Conference on Bridging Distances in Technology and Regulation, (2013), pp. 189–204.

[19] Butkus Pranas et al. "A user centric identity management for Internet of things". 2014 International Conference on IT Convergence and Security (ICITCS) (2014), pp. 1–4.

[20] Bakre Akshay, Patil Nikita, and Gupta Sakshum, Implementing decentralized digital identity using blockchain. International Journal of Engineering Technology Science and Research, Vol. 4, No. 10, October 2017.

[21] Azaria, A., Ekblaw, A., Vieira, T., Lippman, A., "Medrec: Using blockchain for medical data access and permission management". Open and Big Data (OBD), International Conference, pp. 25–30. IEEE (2016)

[22] Chen, J., Liu, Y., and Chai, Y., "An identity management framework for internet of things". 2015 IEEE 12th International Conference on e-Business Engineering (ICEBE), pp. 360–364, (2015).

[23] Ali Muneeb, Nelson Jude, Shea Ryan, and Freedman Michael J., "Blockstack: A global naming and storage system secured by blockchains". 2016 USENIX Annual Technical Conference (USENIX ATC 16), Denver, CO, pp. 181–194, 2016.

[24] Nakamoto Satoshi, Bitcoin: A Peer-to-Peer Electronic Cash System, 2008. Springer, Cham.

[25] Gervais Arthuretal, "On the security and performance of proof of work block-chains". Proceedings of the 2016 ACM SIGSAC Conference on Computer and Communications Security (2016), pp. 3–16.

[26] Kosba Ahmed et al., "Hawk: The blockchain model of cryptography and privacy-preserving smart contracts". 2016 IEEE Symposium on Security and Privacy (SP) (2016), pp. 839–858.

[27] Mann Christopher and Daniel Loebenberger, Two-factor authentication for the Bitcoinprotocol. International Journal of Information Security, vol. 16, no. 2, pp.213– 226, 2017.

[28] Dennis R. and Owen G. "Rep on the block: A next generation reputation system based on the blockchain," 2015 10th International Conference for Internet Technology and Secured Transactions (ICITST) (2015), pp.131–138.

[29] Hardjono T. and Smith N. "Cloud-based commissioning of constrained devices using permissioned blockchains". Proceedings of the 2nd ACM International Workshop on IoT Privacy, Trust, and Security, ACM (2016), pp. 29–36.

Chapter 8

Next-Generation Logistics: A Novel Approach of Blockchain Technology

Kavita Saini

Contents

8.1 Introduction

The use of Information Technology (IT) is considered prerequisite for the effective control of today's complex logistics management. Nowadays, almost all the data and operations are being handled through IT only. In this chapter, there will be discussion about handling the logistics securely using the blockchain technology. Handling logistics using the blockchain technology has some specific reason, as it is one of the complex activities for any organization [1]. In this chapter, we are discussing how blockchain technology is helpful in handling such complex logistics or supply chain beautifully [2]. The chapter will elaborate the various functions that can be taken care through blockchain-based application [3, 4]. These are various activities that take place under logistics such as:

- Transaction processing
- Supply chain management
- Order tracking and delivery coordination
- Data collection
- Data analysis and many more

The importance of IT for effective *logistics* is widely acknowledged [5, 6]. Multiple participants in *logistics* during the shipment and distribution of goods face a lot of challenges where there is a scope of utilizing blockchain feature. The aim of this study is to provide a solution of *logistics* challenges by utilizing features of blockchain technology.

8.2 Problem Statement

Demand amplification is a well-known phenomenon in logistics. According to the researchers, demand amplifications affect the feedback and decision making in the logistics [7, 8]. It also affects the cycle of excessive inventory, poor decision making, poor prediction and product backlog if not tracked properly. Traditional logistics management of even computerized logistics management is also not able to update and track all transactions made by one or other. Accidently, any data may change or even may be deleted. To avoid all these problems, blockchain technology is emerged with logistics which helps in maintaining distributed ledger and immutable records [2].

There are various problems involved in current logistics system:

- Logistics is complex in nature and multi-party intervention makes it difficult to manage
- Fraud is a significant issue in logistics
- Cheating in supply chains is a significant issue
- Logistics chain is very large and difficult to manage
- Multiple people and products are involved which lead to unmanageable chain and give them opportunities or holes to do fraud

8.3 Objective of the Proposed System

- Helps in detecting and preventing frauds at all levels
- Improves transparency, traceability and tractability of people and products
- Facilitates to keep immutable records
- Updating and validating records are possible through consensus among participants
- All participants have similar power to participate in logistics process
- Products are digitized on blockchain which makes products traceable back to its origin as the information will be shared and stored on distributed ledger
- Records are immutable in nature and help in making changes, which is almost impossible without consensus of the majority of participants in logistics

8.4 Literature Survey

Marko Hölbl et al. (2018) explored Electronic Healthcare Records which is a Blockchain-based patient centric to healthcare systems. Researchers summarized that the system increases the accuracy of electronic data of patients. It is defined that blockchain-based healthcare systems can support drug prescriptions, logistics and can reduce risk of leakage of critical health data.

Asad Ali et al. (2019) outline the benefits of blockchain technology in healthcare industry. Researchers mentioned that this technology has changed the traditional healthcare model by introducing effective diagnosis. It is also mentioned by the researchers that healthcare using blockchain helps in securing data sharing among various entities [9].

Axin Wu et al. (2019) discuss the attribute-based encryption where blockchain technology is used to guarantee the integrity and non-repudiation of data. When a secret key is abused, the source can be audited where it shows the proposed system is efficient and secured [10].

8.4.1 Drug and Pharmaceutical Industry

The blockchain has a complex functionality where digital records combine to form blocks, and such blocks make a chain cryptographically and chronologically connecting the network with each other through sophisticated mathematical algorithms [8, 11]. Each block has a unique set of records with a connection to the previous one [4]. Any new block is added to the end of the blockchain only [3, 12].

8.4.2 Blockchain into the Picture

Blockchain is a distributed digital ledger that has all the transaction stored in chronological order. Initially, this technology was used for cryptocurrency Bitcoin,

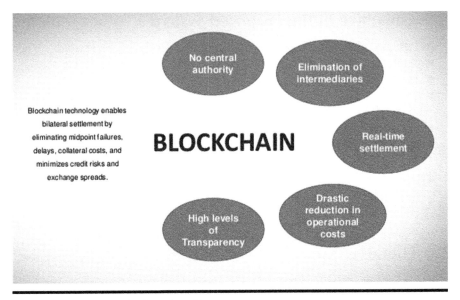

Figure 8.1 Blockchain functionality.

however, because of its versatility, now this technology is being used for various business functions [12, 13]. Supply chain management as one of the main functions of business can utilize features of blockchain which has proven it to be beneficial and include decentralization, distributed ledger, database stored in chronological order, immutability, accessibility, security and transparency, auditability and traceability and quick response time [14, 15].

These features have made blockchain a versatile technology which is highly customizable, and thus, it finds application in almost all the business niches [16]. However, here we will be concentrating on logistics.

Figure 8.1 depicts the functionality of blockchain.

8.5 Logistics and Blockchain

Blockchain technology is considered to be a game changer for decentralizing infrastructure and building a trust layer for business logic. With multiple participants, *logistics* has a significant role in business development and performance [17, 18]. Blockchain technology is a unique technique to help create trust, transparency and accountability among all participants in supply chain management in terms of trace provenance and necessary traceability for particular goods by signing the chain along the way.

As a system of trust, blockchain provides necessary methods of cooperation and consensus for the global economic system. Supply chain logistics can benefit from blockchain technology.

As an optimized system of a shared database, blockchain includes information on the products, people or events that can be inspected and accessed by many entities. To improve supply chain management, blockchain technology is quite helpful as it uses the distributed ledger. This distributed ledger will not be helpful in reducing errors; rather, it will be helpful in avoiding product delays, eliminating fraudulent activities, improving management and increasing consumer and supplier trust.

8.6 Proposed Model: Blockchain Technology's Impact on Logistics

Logistics is an essential part for running a business. The entire process as shown in Figure 8.2 of logistics has too many intermediaries and most of the system still relies on paper or on traditional software, and from these applications products tracing and tracking are a tedious job.

Everybody in the entire chain has to deal with a third party rather than dealing with each other. To deal with manufacturers, suppliers, clients, providers and other entity, blockchain might come to a solution provider.

Logistics through blockchain depicted in Figure 8.2 allows security and transparency for all types of transactions [19]. The main tasks related to logistics are order management, transaction processing, online payment, supply chain management, order tracking, delivery coordination, etc.

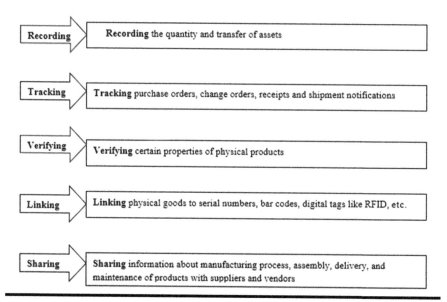

Figure 8.2 Managing logistics using blockchain.

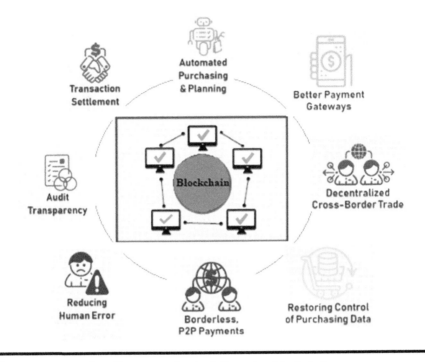

Figure 8.3   Functionality: managing logistics using blockchain.

In blockchain, data are recorded in a public ledger, including information of every transaction ever completed. This ensures the elimination of the double spend problem with the help of public-key cryptography where each agent is assigned a private key [4, 20]. Blockchain is a distributed database solution that maintains a continuously growing list of data records that are confirmed by the nodes (people concerned) participating in it. The data are stored in such a way where they are completely shielded from deletion, altering and any modification [21].

Blockchain could reduce transaction's cost, reshape the economy to form a unified process and also improve the transaction time.

8.7 Features of Blockchain-Based Logistics

After studying blockchain's role in logistics, we can say that it will transform the logistics industry [4, 22]. It's not only about the supply chain management; rather blockchain is helpful in almost all the business verticals for making the process more transparent and agent-free [1, 18, 23]. The idea behind using this technology is to streamline the process. See Figure 8.4.

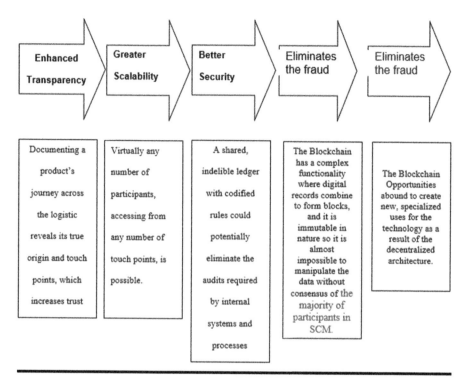

Figure 8.4   Features of blockchain-based logistics.

8.8 Blockchain for Preventing Fraud in Logistics

The blockchain has a complex functionality where digital records combine to form blocks, and it is immutable in nature; so it is almost impossible to manipulate the data without consensus of the majority of participants in logistics [24]. A shared, indelible ledger with codified rules could potentially eliminate the audits required by internal systems and processes [3, 25]. This technology helps in tracing the origin and ownership of any product due to shared and distributed ledger in blockchain and so help in preventing the fraud.

References

[1] P. Jiang, "Socialmanufacturing paradigm: Concepts, architecture and key enabled technologies", Adv. Manuf., pp. 13–50, 2019.
[2] P. Gallo, U. Q. Nguyen, G. Barone, and P. van Hien, "DeCyMo: Decentralized cyber-physical system for monitoring and controlling industries and homes", In: 2018 IEEE 4th International Forum on Research and Technology for Society and Industry, pp. 1–4, 2018.

[3] Kavita Saini, "A future's dominant technology blockchain: Digital transformation", In: IEEE International Conference on Computing, Power and Communication Technologies 2018 (GUCON 2018), Galgotias University, Greater Noida, 28–29 Sept, 2018.

[4] Kavita Saini, Vaibhav Agarwal, et al., "E2EE for data security for hybrid cloud services: A novel approach", In: IEEE International Conference on Advances in Computing, Communication Control and Networking (IEEE ICACCCN 2018), Galgotias College of Engineering & Technology, Greater Noida, 12-13 October, 2018

[5] https://www.belfricsbt.com/2018/05/03/how-can-blockchain-eliminate-fraud-in-financial-transactions/.

[6] R. N. Bolton, J. R. McColl-Kennedy, L. Cheung, A. Gallan, C. Orsingher, L. Witell, and M. Zaki, "Customer experience challenges: bringing together digital, physical and social realms", J. Serv. Manag., vol. 29, no. 5, pp. 776–808, 2018.

[7] https://www.engineerbabu.com/blog/how-is-blockchain-disrupting-the-supply-chain-industry/.

[8] https://www.blockchain-council.org/blockchain/blockchain-technology-for-supply-chain-management/.

[9] F. Longo, "Advanced data management on Distributed Ledgers: design and implementation of a Telegram BOT as a front end for a IOTA cryptocurrency wallet", Jul. 2018.

[10] C. Jaag, C. Bach et al., Blockchain technology and cryptocurrencies: Opportunities for postal financial services, Technical Report, 2016.

[11] D. Kraft, "Difficulty control for blockchain-based consensus systems", Peer-to-Peer Netw. Appl., vol. 9, no. 2, pp. 397–413, 2016.

[12] I. Bentov, C. Lee, A. Mizrahi, and M. Rosenfeld, "Proof of activity: Extending Bitcoin's proof of work via proof of stake", ACM SIGMETRICS Performance Eval. Rev., vol. 42, no. 3, pp. 34–37, 2014.

[13] S. Omohundro, "Cryptocurrencies, smart contracts, and artificial intelligence", AI Matters, vol. 1, no. 2, pp.19–21, 2014.

[14] Peck, Morgen, et al. "Reinforcing the links of the Blockchain." IEEE Future Directions Blockchain Initiative White Paper (2017): 1–16. paper.

[15] A. Wu, Y. Zhang, X. Zheng, R. Guo, Q. Zhao, D. Zheng, "Efficient and privacy preserving traceable attribute-based encryption in Blockchain", Ann. Telecommun., vol. 14, pp. 401–411, 2019.

[16] K. Christidis and M. Devetsikiotis, "Blockchains and smart contracts for the Internet of things" IEEE Access, vol. 4, pp. 2292–2303, 2016.

[17] Ioannis Karamitsos, Maria Papadaki, and Nedaa Baker Al Barghuthi, "Design of the blockchain smart contract: A use case for real estate", J. Inf. Security, vol. 9, pp. 177–190, 2018

[18] https://medium.com/applicature/how-to-apply-blockchain-to-supply-chain-management-8cc673c66c4c.

[19] Jianli Luo, Chen Ji, Chunxiao Qiu, and Fu Jia, "Agri-food supply chain management: Bibliometric and content analyses", Sustainability, vol. 10, p. 1573, 2018.

[20] https://www.supplychain247.com/article/why_blockchain_is_a_game_changer_for_the_supply_chain.

[21] https://blockchainlibrary.org/2018/01/most-cited-supply-chain-and-blockchain-publications/.

[22] https://www.ibm.com/blogs/blockchain/2017/07/blockchain-for-fraud-prevention-industry-use-cases/.

[23] A. Siyal, A. Junejo, M. Zawish, K. Ahmed, A. Khalil, G. Soursou, "Applications of blockchain technology in medicine and healthcare: Challenges and future perspectives", Cryptography, vol. 3, no. 1, p. 3, 2019.

[24] Divyakant Meva, "Issues and challenges with blockchain: A survey", vol. 6, no. 12, pp. 488–491, 2018.

[25] https://www.forbes.com/sites/stevebanker/2018/02/22/the-growing-maturity-of-blockchain-for-supply-chain-management/#4c675cc011da.

Chapter 9

A Blockchain Technology for Asset Management in Multinational Operations

Neethu Narayanan, K.P. Arjun and Kavita Saini

Contents

9.1 Introduction of Computing

Blockchain is the inclining innovation of Bitcoin which is garnering critical attention and ventures from various money-related foundations in the business. Given the innovation's capability to both disturb and advance procedures and frameworks, numerous organizations have committed assets to guarantee and incorporate blockchain into their organizations. This may show how riches and resources the board firms are ready to invest for innovation to saddle the benefits of blockchain just as essential key inspirations to recognize this innovation. In future, this will remark the nearby term-sensible applications for blockchain and how to collaborate with the blockchain improvement.

  Blockchain innovation was developed in January 2009 as the fundamental innovation of Bitcoin. While Bitcoin made tad commotion in the cash, a resource of this budgetary world, blockchain innovation, picked up rise as an interesting issue of talk other than anything else. As financing from funding firms kept on increasing for what was considered for the future age business, blockchain innovation developed in 2014 to incorporate 'keen agreements'. The new obstinate blockchains highlight essential restrictive rationale, enabling legally binding situations and terms to be coded. For instance, a stage to be done that could be executed to discharge a discharged measure of installment to member A once member B conveyed to a particular resource.

9.2 Smart Contracts

A smart contract is a deliberate code running on the leader of a blockchain containing a lot of data under which the assets to that savvy agreement consent to contact with one another. In the event when the pre-characterized rules are met, the understanding is consequently implemented. The brilliant agreement code issues [1, 2], checks and clears the antagonism or affectivity of an understanding or exchange. It is the most straightforward type of decentralized mechanization [3].

It is an instrument including computerized resources and at least two individuals, where a few or the entirety of the gatherings put resources into the savvy contract and the advantages naturally get reproduced and conveyed among those gatherings as per a contingent equation that is dependent on specific information, which is not known at the hour of agreement inception.

The term brilliant agreement [4] is somewhat genuine since a keen agreement is neither savvy nor is it to be mistaken for a lawful agreement.

■ It can likewise be as dynamic as the individuals coding considering all accessible data at the hour of coding.
■ While brilliant agreements can become lawful agreements if certain conditions are fulfilled, they ought not be blended and mistook for lawful agreements acknowledged by courts as well as law implementation agencies. Be that as it may, it might most likely observe a blend of legitimate and savvy agreements developed throughout the following few years as the innovation turns out to be increasingly compact and rises, and lawful conditions are embraced.

9.2.1 Slashing Transaction Costs of Coordination and Enforcement

Shrewd contracts fundamentally decline exchange costs [5]. The precise standard exchange rules consequently lessen the exchange expenses of:

■ Reaching an understanding
■ Formalization
■ Enforcement

A shrewd agreement can involve the connections between individuals, establishments and the advantages they claim. The exchange understanding of the shrewd agreement characterizes the conditions—rights and commitments—to which the gatherings of a convention [6] or brilliant agreement assent. This exchange rule set is overseen in advanced structure, in PC lucid formalization. These rights and commitments, built up in the shrewd agreement, would now be able to be naturally executed by a PC or a system of PCs when the gatherings have gone to an understanding and met the states of the requirement.

The idea of a brilliant agreement isn't a lot of new or old which can be seen at any place in this innovation. In any case, blockchain is by all accounts the reason for shrewd agreement usage. The most essential type of a brilliant agreement is a candy machine. The principles of an exchange are fed into a machine. An item is selected by squeezing a numerical value identified with that item, coins are put, and the machine goes about as a savvy contract [7] seeing whether the coin inserted is sufficient for cash. On the off chance that indeed the machine is told to launch the item, and on the off chance that you inserted an excess of cash, it will likewise discharge the change. On the off chance that you didn't put enough cash or if the machine came up short on the cash, you will recover your cash.

9.2.2 Characteristics of a Smart Contract

Figure 9.1 shows the working of brilliant agreement by utilizing blockchain. Savvy contracts [8] are fit for hacking execution continuously and can bring enormous cost investment funds. So as to get foundation data, a keen agreement needs guidelines prophets, who feed the savvy contract with outside data.

Smart contracts are:

- Self-checking
- Self-executing
- Tamper-safe

Smart contracts can:

- Turn legitimate commitments into mechanized procedures
- Guarantee a higher level of security
- Lower dependence on confided in mediators
- Reduce exchange costs

9.2.3 Blockchain Asset Management

A blockchain is an appropriated record of all things considered and related directions for a specific property. This common record—a dispersed record or database [9]—is noticeable by all watchers with allowed consent to the record. A blockchain analyzes a consistently advancing arrangement of exchange information hinders that

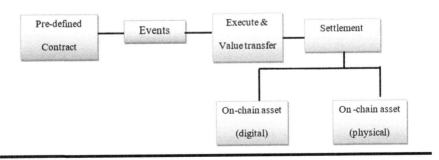

Figure 9.1 Smart contract.

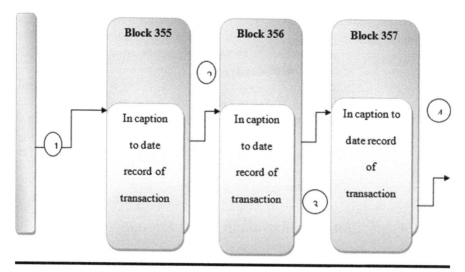

Figure 9.2 Asset management using blockchain.

are checked by individuals from the system, usually alluded to as 'diggers'. Figure 9.2 shows the blockchain innovation in resource management.

Each square contains a lot of exchanges between at least two individuals (e.g., party A pays party B in return for an advantage) and is added to the current chain of squares, making a total history of exchanges [10]. With every additional square, the whole circulated record is screened and settled upon by all members that incorporate the hubs. All hubs are luckily checking the exchange foundation, bringing about a blockchain of permanent information.

9.2.4 Challenges to the Adoption of Blockchain in Asset Management

Overview of blockchain innovation and its application to money-related administration firms is still in its infancy, and numerous businesses and resources are inexperienced with regard to how blockchain implements functions or what benefits it may have later on [11]. There are many negative hurlers who guarantee that blockchain innovation is 'searching for a business issue to tackle', and we concur that business cases should drive innovation arrangements, not the opposite.

The outline beneath depends on 2016 EY investigation and shows that versatility is relied upon to be an obstacle to industry-wide appropriation for some associations. Until this point, blockchain has seen constrained organization in circumstances requiring enormous volumes of information, and the straight idea of the innovation raises doubt about its capacity to deal with such a volume. Likewise, firms face item multifaceted nature confinements, as introductory rollouts of complex items can be hard to change later on the disseminated record.

This shocks no one when flow establishments can deal with billions of exchanges with a high level of unwavering quality and security [12]. Bitcoin blockchains, for instance, can just accomplish 7 exchanges for each second contrasted with Visa's VisaNet, which as of now accomplishes 50,000+ exchanges every second.

There are additionally critical questions identified with the administrative and legal obstacles that exist with regard to money and resources, for example, the custodial prerequisites if resources are hung on a blockchain arrangement anytime. Different boundaries across the board reception incorporate information protection and the significant expense of supplanting heritage frameworks. Figure 9.3 shows resources for the wide selection in different levels.

Blockchain record that advantage as the game plan of record.

9.2.5 Applications of Blockchain to Wealth and Asset Management

Blockchain innovation, otherwise called disseminated records, contains various useful use cases inside the money and resources' life cycle [13]. Distributed records are profoundly compactable; when done, they can be utilized to expel contact from the customer on making process, streamline the board of model portfolios, speed the evacuating and focuses of exchanges and straightforwardness consistence challenges related with hostile to illegal tax avoidance (AML) and realize your colleague or client [14]. The result is conclusion of repetitive capacities, wiped out operational expenses and expanded opportunities to advance the customer experience. While blockchain innovation is probably not going to move over current frameworks, it might be utilized to reproduce guidelines crosswise over them or empower new firms for new markets and items.

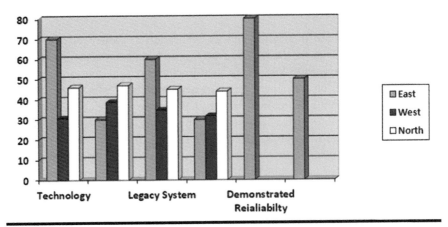

Figure 9.3   Asset management broad adoption.

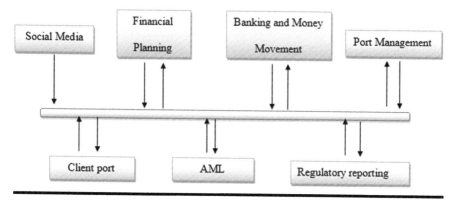

Figure 9.4   Blockchain with asset management.

By extending, these ideas can spread to wide assortment of utilizations, for example, rollovers, trusts, bequests, protection and other distributional exchanges where resources are moved between gatherings or agreements are actualized. A dispersed record [15] rouses the accuracy and makes sense of an exchange in current time. The customer experience is advanced and the procedure streams out, and expenses are deducted. Figure 9.4 shows blockchain with resources.

9.2.5.1 Use Case 1: Client Onboarding and Profiling

9.2.5.1.1   Key Drivers of Revolutionizing Client Onboarding for Wealth Managers

Blockchain presents the plausibility of changing customer onboarding for riches administrators. In this day and age, potential customers must give evidence of distinguishing proof, residency and conjugal status, wellsprings of riches, occupation, business premiums and political ties [16]. Experiencing this procedure can take days or weeks to gather and confirm the information. Difficulties looked through the present situation are:

- Strict onboarding prerequisites
- Proof of recognizable proof
- Residency
- Marital status
- Sources of riches
- Occupation
- Business interests
- Political ties
- Complying with various announcing necessities
- Information security methodology

- Ongoing observing of profiles
- Automated clearinghouse (ACH) and robotized client record move (ACAT) [17] frameworks take different days and include manual procedures utilizing various frameworks and databases

9.2.5.1.2 Main Approaches of Handling the Event Holders

- Profile put away on a blockchain/conveyed record
- Trusted gatherings are allowed access to all or part of the profile dependent on cryptography
- New connections would be started by profile proprietor
- The framework innately empowers a review trail for following changes to the chain. Subsequently, forms requiring certainty checking, for example, AML, are disentangled
- Integrate blockchain innovations into onboarding and ACH and ACAT frameworks and procedures

9.2.5.1.3 Benefits That Operate on the Function of Client Onboarding

Client onboarding can encourage many key elements of onboarding such as:

- Client and hazard profiling
- Financial arranging
- Anti-illegal tax avoidance checks and cash development
- Upgrade or perhaps supplant conventional frameworks, for example, ACH and ACAT
- Enables close quick moves of benefits between money-related foundations with validated provenance of followed changes

9.2.5.2 Use Case 2: Trade Order Generation and Model Management

9.2.5.2.1 Key Drivers of Operational Challenges for Wealth Managers

The open engineering multiplication of venture contributions and the accessibility of outsider [18] speculation models in independently overseen records have introduced various operational difficulties for riches directors. Disseminated record innovation would enable portfolio chiefs to, in a split second, impart portfolio changes to all customers 'bought in' to the model, just as empower continuous perspectives on individual record execution, float outside of resistances and incomes. Likewise, shrewd agreements would take into consideration the administration of expenses paid by the patrons basically taking an installment each time the model is utilized or downloaded. Difficulties of get the benefit from the board regarding exchange and model administration [19] include:

- A riches and resource chief utilizing various stages and information structures causes challenges in conveying, observing and refreshing outsider models.
- Firms must help repetitive model administration frameworks.
- Managers are frequently required to email models to program supporters or utilize restrictive gateways.

9.2.5.2.2 Approach of Maintaining and Creating the Asset Models

Speculation chiefs would make and keep up a model—like how they do it today.

- Models could be transmitted through a blockchain to different bought in merchants.
- Individual records can be contributed by the model.
- Customization for limitations and other record level imperatives can be put away and applied.

9.2.5.2.3 Benefits That Operate on Trade Generations of Asset Management

- Will permit other record exchanges and exchanges to be shared all the more effectively.
- Can give close continuous execution, portfolio hazard and float information, enabling supervisors to watch all the more effectively and have more noteworthy bits of knowledge.
- Can diminish the measure of compromise required by moving from the current isolated ace record to a safe, dispersed one.
- Reduces the requirement of certain middle people liable for settling and executing exchanges.

9.2.5.3 *Distributed Infrastructure*

Innovation permits the circulation of believed worth exchange and execution [20], permitting the disintermediation of delegates: the system turns into the mediator. Figure 9.5 presents disseminated foundations.

9.2.5.3.1 A Practical Approach to Blockchain

Blockchain is a troublesome subject to comprehend, and deciding a decent business procedure [21] for utilizing it is considerably harder. While numerous technologists can get a handle on the idea and the fundamental calculations, numerous business chiefs are uncertain of how it can profit their business in an important manner or where it can upset current models. To achieve this, EY prescribes breaking technique improvement into three key stages: first, distinguish the open doors for the

Allow move from master ledgers

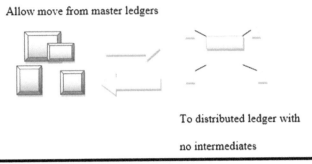

To distributed ledger with

no intermediates

Figure 9.5   Distributed infrastructures.

innovation; at that point, center around creating imaginative answers for benefit from the chances; and, at last, work with your innovation accomplices to effectively actualize the arrangements. There are a bunch of firms discovering some early victories and the ones that are making progress are adopting a system-centered strategy.

We prescribe that as firms inspect the chances, they look inside first, as it is a lot simpler to create and pick up reception inside your very own firm. As small interior courses of action gain footing, firms should hope to extend the arrangement inside—crosswise over useful gatherings and afterward crosswise over lines of business—to exhibit viability and increase backing and energy. At long last, when interior help is acquired, business cases and advancement for adjusting existing income-producing plans of action ought to be inspected [22].

With such a large number of potential blockchain openings, setting up a compelling structure to recognize genuine business worth is basic need. As noted in the past segment, there are use cases that can be grown rapidly to drive results. Firms should concentrate on those utilization cases that have the best open door with negligible hazard and utilize a system to appropriately allot time and assets. Notwithstanding making blockchain explicit use cases, blockchain ought to be viewed as an empowering innovation to the difficulties of the same old thing activities. To this point, firms ought to expect blockchain disruptive to develop where operational overhead, information and resources issues exist or where potential income-producing openings are driven by straightforwardness and convenience.

A base ought to contain the open-door appraisal technique; following are the segments:

■ The foundation of a structure for recognizing the territories of chance and dangers and characterizing pertinent use cases for examination
■ A group structure that incorporates key partners, just as select topic specialists in the regions of concern (e.g., activities, item the board, innovation, technique)
■ An interchanges plan for mingling discoveries and basic leadership
■ A prioritization network or structure for distinguishing key use cases for the execution guide

9.2.5.3.2 Sample Opportunity Framework Approach

The following sensible advance is to concentrate on creating arrangements—first from a more minor perspective inside, yet bit by bit increase to bigger, increasingly significant interior and customer confronting arrangements. A few firms have received this methodology through a development technique [23]. This procedure is normally characterized as the procedure for surveying the open doors recently distinguished in your investigation, deciding the effects to current plans of action and methodologies and making answers for make the most of those chances and effects.

In a few cases, firms have executed an advancement procedure through an 'advancement lab', where groups can concentrate on assessing the chances and creating evidences of ideas and working models to investigate the potential outcomes of blockchain. While some of these advancement labs start as individual, independent gatherings, many are created with the possibility that the yield will be coordinated into the association's business lines in the long run. Most firms presently understand that working in a vacuum can defer usage or perhaps bring about huge improve to coordinate new arrangements into existing frameworks and business forms. The best firms characterize the structures for advancement in advance and afterward work inside the prioritization set before to build up the arrangements.

It is additionally conceivable that the innovation arrangement will not have to be created in-house. There are as of now many blockchain innovation suppliers, and more are growing all the time. When the ideas have been point by point during the advancement stage, the subsequent stage includes adjusting the answer for your innovation technique and abilities. Numerous organizations—even probably the biggest players in the business and resources space—are working together to actualize blockchain arrangements; the biggest consortiums in the space today (Hyperledger) incorporate numerous organizations that would typically assemble arrangements in-house individually.

9.2.5.3.3 Using Blockchain to Reenvision Asset Management

The equipment and programming deal with the benefits that have become an unpredictable procedure inside conveyed conditions. The customers frequently search out outsider apparatuses and give administrations to achieve better control of their IT condition and build the stock consistence act in their foundations. Combined with the components of multiplication of IT information stores and framework plans/process streams, makes the most straightforward approach to characterize 'following an advantage' complex, access to error, and with long time in review basic data required by administration conveyance entertainers. The brain of sheltered and secure information sitting in a profoundly disallowed vault is presently changing to cloud-based applications with most anticipating conglomeration and discernment of comparative metadata to bring commented trust in information. Here yet it shows robotization-improved systems have tended to interior, back-office capacities, however once in a while do they give direct advantage to customers.

The blockchain based framework aims to change a significant number of the inheritance processes [24], undertakings, and manual moves made by different help conveyance entertainers all through the procedure. The framework will change conflicting and esteemed information with a 'hinder' of data that educate as a definitive and unchanging arrangement of record truth, accessible in close to continuous for all nonexistent acting to use for progressing directions and exchanges. Banding together with extra providers and customers is same as essential to guarantee the framework is worked to customer needs and desires.

The impact of new conveyance process include: developing or implementing the business system envisioned for blockchain innovation, all gatherings involved in an exchange on any key information component would have the option to counteract debates, approach the single truth of status in close proximity to continue and ease, if not deny, programming consistency exposures and even reviews. The receptive, mid-esteem administration by means of organization and investigation are moving endlessly to high-esteem, robotized administrations that incorporate all the significant gatherings executing on information with proactive checks in another procedure that dispenses with any excess, approvals, compromises, and consistence documentation. As shown in Figure 9.6, the innovation and procedure for overseeing value-based restores applies to equipment, programming, and having a place contracts through blockchain innovation, yielding a totally different arrangement-of-commitment way to deal with all assistance conveyance activities and customers, aside from the lifecycle of these equipment and programming resources.

9.2.5.3.4 Key Decisions in Architecting the Blockchain Solution

- ◼ Identify the portion of the business procedure with the difficult to focus around information quality in the benefit's lifecycle.

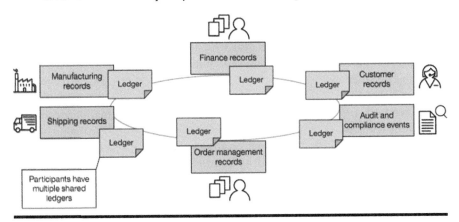

Figure 9.6   Basic applications of key blockchain concepts for asset management services.

- Identify the personas in question and their particular issues to address
- Identify the business worth acknowledged by the arrangement

Before settling on some key engineering choices, we need to do some examination:

- What are the specialized alternatives accessible to explain this?
- Who are the partners and in what capacity will they profit by this?
- What are the partners' jobs and obligations inside their associations?
- What is the normal information important to all foundations or associations/partners?
- What are the information sources/yields, and which applications produce as well as devour them?
- We confirmed that applying blockchain innovation will yield noteworthy long haul benefits.

Accordingly, the key design choices are as follows:

Blockchain record that advantage as the game plan of record: The blockchain will go about as a solitary wellspring of truth for an IBM-fabricated [25] sellable resource, for example, a server, naturally following each change to its lifecycle, so it is auditable, dependable and straightforward.

Improve permission: The associations that members, for example, guaranteeing fabricating, coordinations, fund, and the client will be called as and permissioned onto the blockchain organization.

Information model sharing: A particular information model arrangement that is of normal enthusiasm to the taking an interest associations will be kept up on the blockchain.

Brilliant contracts improvement: Business decides that the relationship administers between personas, exchanges and occasions influencing the benefit will be overseen on the blockchain. For instance, a shipper won't have the option to have a sequential number crisscross, however a beneficiary can.

Confirmation of presence: Proof got for exchanges and occasions, for example, a 'plant request' or 'bill of replenishing' will be carefully hashed and recorded.

Interface to customer: The blockchain will issue to outer exchanges and occasions, for example, "resource transported" or "resource introduced" by means of a customer interface.

9.3 Asset Management Using Blockchain's Distributed Ledger

The board of directors on a blockchain system resolves the problems of contest goals and effectively utilizes the time required to comprehend information inequalities. It additionally implies that they can occur in a timelier way. Each phase from resource production and serialization through to establishment can be followed with applicable proof kept in the blockchain record. Composed errands around the database and trade of information between assets can be surrendered over to the trusted, straightforward nature of blockchain. Shrewd agreements will further upgrade the simplicity of move of advantages by endorsing conditions which must happen for exchanges to occur, and making the correspondence of such conditions being arrived at undeniable. The expectation for gatherings to submit pitiless endeavors will be seriously constrained. Blockchain's shared record sets the establishment for straightforward, auditable, believed business forms later on. Wide-arriving at potential crosswise over numerous open areas, it will clear that benefit the executives will pick up extraordinarily from blockchain innovation. Capacity to rapidly and successfully share data between a wide scope of effects will furnish organizations with the capacity to streamline the manner in which that they treat their information. Figure 9.7 shows safely moving resource with blockchain innovation.

9.3.1 Advantages of Blockchain for Asset Management

9.3.1.1 High Conventional Security Methodologies

As a matter of fact, distributed ledger technology (DLT) [26] accomplishes more than just improving the protection and security of information, it totally changes how information is put away and got to.

In a manner special to all customary security approaches, blockchain programming offers security, however a permanent record of everything being equal. By conveying records over different hubs, the chances of an information rupture on a focal database are killed.

Since DLT includes gathering exchanges into squares of information, encoding the information squares and connecting every datum square to each one of those

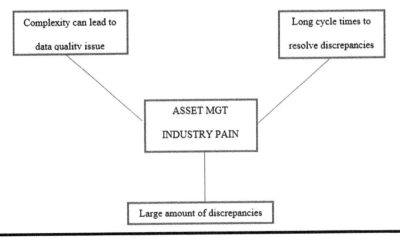

Figure 9.7   Securely transferring asset with blockchain technology.

before it and each one of those to pursue, information altering turns into a difficult process. Doing so would mean approaching the entirety of the private and open keys, and accessing the entirety of the hubs containing the blockchain.

9.3.1.2 High Speed in Real-Time Performance in Asset Viewing

Blockchain innovation verifies asset viewing and makes it quicker. A well-characterized resources blockchain can serve close constant execution in resource seeing, catching and giving administrative snappy bits of knowledge into information stockpiling and make changes that can influence their customers' portfolios.

9.3.1.3 Increased Operational Efficiency

On first idea, you may think about how repeating a database over different hubs can bring about higher effectiveness than can be accomplished with one focal database.

Albeit improving the speed at which information is followed up on has an immediate bearing on operational effectiveness; it isn't the essential factor.

As referenced, a blockchain is a database that is duplicated over numerous hubs. Those hubs are, above all else, just PC frameworks. In any case, since the hubs on which a blockchain exists are PCs worked by the entirety of the different foundations that are involved with the advantage the board business, the trading of information between establishments can happen in a split second. It implies, as opposed to one part passing data to another, that they basically alter their very own stockpiling records. The blockchain wraps up, naturally confirming the distinctions and altering the records on all other basic hub gatherings to coordinate each other. The dispersed structure of DLT offers an exponential increment in speed of B2B exchanges inside the advantage the board business.

9.3.1.4 Client Onboarding in Asset Management

In an exceptionally directed resource business, simply onboarding new customers is a tedious task. Approving customer recognizable proof, resource possession, riches sources, conjugal status, occupation, political ties, business premiums, and citizenship can take days or even weeks.

Blockchain doesn't inalienably summon these procedures, it gives the structure to advancement of arrangements that can do as such. With blockchain foundation hubs stretching out to the best possible segments, quick and permissioned access to the necessary data will become as ordinary as current credit checks. No single organization or innovation supplier can give such an answer; however, cooperating partners can construct foundations that encourage the quick sharing of data thus decreasing the onboarding procedure to a unimportant time period.

9.3.1.5 Streamlining Portfolio Management

Exhibitions based on blockchain innovation benefit from the exceptionally perceived information structures. Whatever conventions business eventually embraces, DLT will quicken interchanges between speculators, resource chiefs and outsider substances.

9.3.1.6 Clearance and Settling of Trades

Wastefulness in the present exchanging framework limits leeway and settling of exchanges to a few days. Since fulfillment of a blockchain exchange requires endorsement from every included gathering, DLT can dispense with the distinction between an exchange and the clearing of the exchange. This likewise dispenses with counterparty chance and improves capital accessibility.

In the long run, we could see blockchains supplant automated clearing house (ACH) [27] and Automated Customer Account move (ACAT) frameworks as the innovation develops.

9.3.1.7 Regulatory Compliance

Keys to fulfilling the regularly expanding weight to follow government and industry guidelines are three principle factors: speed, straightforwardness and recognizability. The structure of DLT naturally encourages every one of the three.

Each blockchain exchange is confirmed by every outsider and satisfying consistency needs gets easiest. Further, the unchanging nature of DLT makes making review trails a relic of times gone by. Each datum square turns out to be a piece of the review trail, giving an exchange's money related subtleties, yet in addition denoting each with an unalterable date and timestamp and an advanced mark.

9.3.2 Challenges of Adopting Blockchain for Asset Management

Despite the many benefits that DLT provides to executives and their businesses, it is not without its drawbacks. A portion of the difficulties that will slow down the selection are innovative, some are administrative, and some are basically mental in nature.

Here is our rundown of the top difficulties that must be overcome before DLT can raise its banner on the advantage the board slope [28].

9.3.2.1 Lack of Market Familiarity

Hazard isn't unfamiliar to resource supervisors. From multiple points of view, it is reason they have a vocation. On the off chance that there were no dangers in the administration of money-related resources, there would be little requirement for specialists to oversee portfolios. Then again, when dangers influence their vocation feasibility, they are justifiably less excited about tolerating them. Thus, it is with blockchain.

Are there drawbacks and even dangers to progressing to a blockchain stage? Certainly yes! Will there be misfortunes en route? We can rely on it. Be that as it may, the advantages of improved security, quicker exchanges, improved operational proficiency, and decreased consistence troubles incomprehensibly exceed the dangers of execution.

Ideally, articles, for example, this, and expanded uses cases, will settle on industry chiefs increasingly happy with grasping the DLT arrangements that are traveled their direction.

9.3.2.2 Limited History Processing Large Volumes of Data

Blockchain innovation has developed to be least difficult, simpler, quick, progressively vigorous, and more adaptable than numerous heritage frameworks. Notwithstanding, pundits contend that DLT presently can't seem to be tried on applications where billions of exchanges must be dealt with a high level of dependability and security. DLT is particularly untested in applications where emotional and nondirect increments in information volume can be experienced.

It's not that DLT can't oblige the rates and unwavering quality fundamental for the budgetary part, it's just that it still can't seem to be illustrated.

9.3.2.3 Lack of Experience in Smart Contract Security

The short street from DLT idea to appropriation has just been covered with instances of extortion coming about because of lack in keen agreement coding or outsider applications.

Pundits contend that the critical misfortunes experienced so far are reason enough to defer broad-scale selection by money-related parts. There may consistently be vulnerabilities in outsider parts of the blockchain biological system. Be that as it may, security is the greatest advantage of large-scale suppliers of big business DLT stages, for example, IMB and Amazon Web Services, so they will contribute whatever it takes to keep their foundation secure.

9.3.2.4 Regulatory Challenges Assured on Asset Blockchain

Blockchain guarantees to be more straightforward to get administrative consistence targets. Simultaneously, circulated records don't generally loan themselves to meeting the guidelines intended for siloed frameworks.

With the end goal for DLT to fulfill controllers, innovation suppliers, the money-related industry all in all, and government elements must cooperate to land at useful arrangements. Since controllers are not specialists on the innovation, and innovation suppliers are not specialists on administrative necessities, money-related organizations may end up at the junction except if participation happens on a great scale.

9.3.2.5 High Cost to Replace Legacy Systems and Processes

Blockchain consents to be about quick, quicker and radical changes to the defenseless money-related divisions whereupon we have come to stuck on as well. How fast and how radical the change might be is restricted, to some degree, by the expense of usage.

Despite the fact that change can and should continue circumspectly and through reasonable evidence of idea models, sooner or later substantial venture is important to clear the pathway for full reception.

Intending to address these cost difficulties is troublesome when an organization, or an industry, is on unfamiliar ground. Beating cost factor concerns will represent a test until adequate use cases develop. When an adequate measure of information is in, it will be simpler for chiefs to survey the expense of selection, and to get ready for it.

9.3.3 Road to Adoption for Asset Management Blockchains

The way to wide selection over the advantage the board division will incorporate a procedure like the accompanying: Consortium endeavors including government controllers, money-related organizations and innovation suppliers.

- POC testing of blockchain models
- Industry selection DLT innovation measures
- Interoperability with inheritance frameworks
- Successful uses cases
- Proof of adaptability
- Proof of security hardness

9.4 Coalition Scenarios in Asset Management

In an alliance setting, there are numerous sorts of benefits that may be shared among various accomplices. In this part we look forward to depend on three potential alliance situations and settings where the utilization of an innovation like blockchain can be improved. Alliances situations dependent on three ideas: (i) programming characterized alliances, (ii) dispersed resource task and (iii) data sharing on numerous different systems utilizing tear sheets.

9.4.1 Software-Defined Coalitions

In alliance activities [29], strategies frequently require the development of dynamic networks of interests (CoI) which are brief groups shaped including at least one

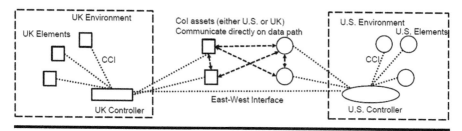

Figure 9.8   Software-defined coalition scenario.

alliance individuals. So as to help the dynamic CoIs, an IT framework which can bolster these gatherings is required. Since IT resources from various alliances may not generally be perfect with one another, a design for interoperability that obtains from the ideas of programming characterized systems administration has been proposed for empowering dynamic CoI and alluded to as a product characterized alliance. The structure of a software-defined coalition as verbalized in here appears in Figure 9.8, where the framework accepting that the advantages of CoI can emerge out of the United States.

The controller gives control data, for example, directing information, security data, strategy data and so on to their comparing nation components, consequently enabling them to speak with one another with the correct security approaches. The interchanges along the information way occurring between the CoI resources are indicated utilizing the thick run lines in the framework. This worldview, which depends on indistinguishable standards from that of SDN, enables alliance advantages for coordinate inside the rules and control components set out by their associations. Contingent upon the degree of trust between the two accomplices, the information correspondence may include sending bundles, sharing stockpiling, permitting offloading of figuring abilities, or sharing of detecting capacities between gadgets. Since there are various controllers engaged with a dynamic CoI, the distinctive control activities occurring among the controllers should be facilitated. In particular, if a control design for a CoI resource having a place with the United States originates from a UK machine, in light of the fact that the particular strategic being worked by the UK administrator, the exchanges mentioning the adjustment in direction and arrangement should be recorded, and can be utilized as the examination. Acquiring such circulated account would be a suitable case for utilizing blockchain innovations, since they forestall the requirement for another position which all alliance accomplices would need to trust so as to record the exchanges in this condition.

9.4.2 Dispersed Asset Assignment

One of the key difficulties in an alliance activity is to figure out which resources are accessible so as to lead a particular crucial. A case of a run of the mill task framework for the alliance activities is the sensor assignment to missions (SAM)

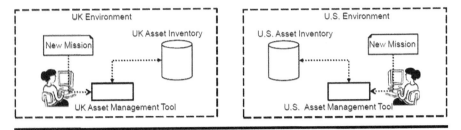

Figure 9.9   Distributed asset assignment scenario.

approach [30], which uses information portrayal and thinking innovations (ontologies and rules) to dole out advantages for strategic. At the point when a solicitation for a strategic got, the benefit the executives apparatus would see its arrangement of accessible advantages for figure out which resources can be best distributed to the mission. For sake of advantage to achieve its obligations, the benefit the executives device needs to have a stock of accessible and distributed resources, the missions to which the advantages are relegated, and the specialized part utilization of its dealings and semantic methods to plot the resources for the assigned missions.

An advantage task framework like SAM would be utilized by every one of the alliance accomplices to decide the way in which to best dole out their resources for the mission. In any case, when alliance tasks should be led, the overarching approach will be for every alliance to consider assignments freely for their own needs. This prompts a test on the grounds that the totality of the advantages isn't known to any individual accomplice and can't be utilized to share resources ideally over the missions of the whole alliance. That arrangement appears in Figure 9.9. It makes one of a kind if the guidelines pretty much every one of the benefits accessible to every alliance possessions could be kept up in a required focal stock, which would enable the resources for be utilized in the most ideal way for the missions that are to be directed. Be that as it may, in an alliance setting, where the trust between various accomplices isn't outright, it is difficult to get concurrence on who ought to claim and working this worldwide resource stock. Moreover, keeping up a focal asset is trying in such a domain as a result of the portable and transient nature of the earth.

9.4.3 Tear Sheets

The principle task in the alliance of the advantage stock is to deal with the task of resources for missions, choose whether a benefit should be reassigned from a crucial, to follow the strength of the advantage over its life cycle. The virtual registry model is presented in Figure 9.10. The stock administration in alliance conditions, just as in numerous different situations, various systems work with various degrees of security and each system works autonomously with an air hole between them,

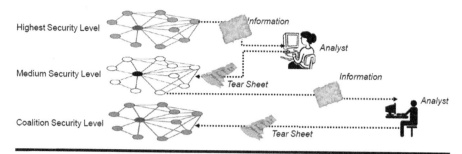

Highest Security Level

Information

Analyst

Medium Security Level

Information

Tear Sheet

Coalition Security Level

Analyst

Tear Sheet

Figure 9.10   Tear sheets among networks with multiple level of security.

for example, no gadget can be simultaneously associated with both of the systems simultaneously. Simultaneously, data some of the time should be passed between the distinctive secure systems.

The idea of tear sheets is utilized to empower the sending of data between the systems of various security levels.

Utilizing a tear sheet, a client with access to a system with a higher security level can extricate a snippet of data that should be given to a system at a lower security level. The snippet of data is separated from the more secure system will expel any data that is considered having an elevated level of security, and generally any insights regarding the root or the legitimacy of the data will be expelled. The sterilized data is known as a tear sheet from the past training of detaching some portion of a page from a book, and giving it over. The test in the less secure system is that there is no real way to follow the cause of the tear sheet which has been totally anonym zed, and even the guidance gave to the system that predefined the tear sheet is lost. Therefore, the legitimacy or genuineness of the tear sheets in the system with lower security is as often as possible lost. In a one of a kind structure, a focal vault framework that concentrates all tear sheets and participates them with the system they started from, alongside fitting subtleties that can be seen at a proper security level, would help in following and following tear sheets crosswise over various system security levels. In any case, the utilization of blockchain innovation may empower the formation of such a virtual vault without trading off the requirements of keeping up air holes between various systems. In the following barely any areas, we will talk about how a blockchain based arrangement can help in tending to the issues experienced in every one of the three settings.

9.5 Blockchain for Distributed Asset Assignment

On account of the appropriated physical resource task, the objective of utilizing blockchain is to make a virtual stock which traverses the entirety of the advantages accessible over the different alliance individuals. Each individual from the benefit would center its own stock of the various resources, the advantages may should be

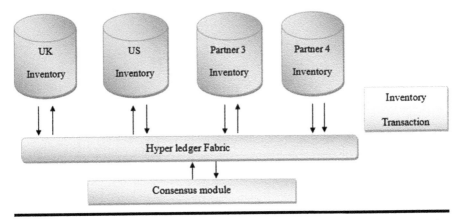

Figure 9.11   Blockchain-based solution for distributed asset assignment scenario.

shared crosswise over accomplices for a given arrangement of strategic converse with the hyperledge texture.

Agreement module that records exchanges pair-wise is required since stock exchanges would occur among two sets of gatherings. An exchange is viewed as last in the event that it is marked by both of the two gatherings engaged with the exchange. Figure 9.11 clarifies the hinders that can be spoken to utilizing a Merkle tree, made for a section of time and contain the hash of all exchanges that occur inside the given interim of time.

9.5.1 Challenges and Open Issues on Blockchain Advances

Blockchain innovation can be utilized to ad lib to some basic difficulties in alliance blended activity situations, a few difficulties stay in the execution and fulfillment of a last vision. Aside from the way that the application use is starter, and one may run into sudden difficulties during the execution of the methodologies portrayed over, a portion of the difficulties with blockchain sorted out are really being in this beginning period. In a remarkable blockchain usage, the surge of every exchange is disseminated with all the rose individuals in the blockchain biological system. This prompts two issues, the first is that of the measure of data transmission that is devoured because of all the message trades, and the other is the way that all individuals from the alliance can check the quantity of exchanges that are occurring. The previous might be an issue in conditions, for example, the strategic edge, where transfer speed is including some built-in costs. The last can be unwanted in conditions where a portion of the alliance individuals are less trusted than others. It might be conceivable to have usage of the circulated record that are more productive than those accessible in open source which consider the exceptional needs of the strategic condition. The product characterized alliances, impacts that it is useful to make a situation where an alternate blockchain is kept up for every assortment network of intrigue, in this manner taking out the need to communicate hashes to everybody. The methodology of characterizing specific agreement calculations gives a fractional arrangement; however, it might be conceivable to have significantly increasingly effective methodologies, which would need further investigation. It would have a teacher, that the nearness of the leader can be accustomed to centering a portion of the blockchain forms. The tear sheet model, which uses blockchain just as an information structure, can likewise be additionally enhanced if information can be transmitted without requiring an air-hole from the more elevated level of system security to a lower level of system security. At TCP layer, there is additionally an issue in dealing with the most basic and current blockchain executions that stuck on the utilization of TCP. TCP is commonly not reasonable for a strategic edge systems in light of the fact that the transient network of the companions regularly prompts various transmission disappointments, which TCP isn't intended to manage. For instance, Fabric uses Google RPC (gRPC), which is executed over HTTP/2 norms, based on TCP. One potential road for investigation here is to explore distinctive gRPC ties to increasingly effective conventions for example QUIC. QUIC is another vehicle which is intended to decrease idleness contrasted with that of TCP for such conditions, and has just observed some accomplishment in Android applications dependent on QUIC Chromium joining.

9.6 Conclusion

While blockchain's best-known, most utilized and most elevated effect application is Bitcoin, the potential effect of the innovation is a lot more noteworthy and more extensive than virtual monetary standards. Regardless of other assistance applications can 'piggyback' the Bitcoin blockchain, the most effective effects of Bitcoin might be found outside the money area. Exchanges of every sort of advantages are typically quick and less expensive for the clients when finished by means of a blockchain, and they likewise have benefit from the convention's security. The trading of advantage exchanges in Europe are frequently fast, modest and verified enough for most obvious purposes, clients and defenders of blockchain applications regularly observe extra advantages in its straightforwardness and unchanging nature. Without a doubt, there is a developing pattern towards less trust in monetary and administration establishments and more prominent social desires for responsibility and obligation. Obviously, for every exchange that uses an appropriated record rather than a customary concentrated framework, the delegates and arbiters are dislodged, passing up their typical wellspring of intensity and pay. For monetary standards these are the banks, for licenses the patent office, for races the discretionary commissions, for brilliant agreements the agents, and for open administrations the state specialists. A huge degree of development in the utilization of blockchain innovation, could see significant change in the substance and, maybe, amount of 'cubicle' work. For instance, a portion of crafted by middle people and agreement legal advisors could be supplanted by shared exchanges and brilliant agreements. Numerous pundits are loose about this possibility. Some contend that solitary a portion of the less fascinating assignments—for example, giving confirmation of affirmation—would be uprooted by blockchain, allowing for the center and high-esteem undertakings of giving bespoke administrations. While this may at present lead to some decrease in the complete amount of work, others reporters refer to likenesses with past influxes of computerization in industrial work—for example, mechanical generation lines—where dull errands were uprooted prompting work misfortunes, however new top notch occupations were made in the structure and upkeep of the vital frameworks. Regardless, while proof stays rare, most analysts expect an adjustment in the profile of undertakings performed by people with no general decrease in the total number of employments and, maybe, an expansion in their quality. Another clear effect of blockchain improvement could be proficiently expanded vitality utilization. In most recent years, the Bitcoin blockchain was liable for electrical and power utilization separating to that of Ireland, and has just expanded high since. The most significant calculations and equipment backend part could be built up; the vitality limit of blockchains may turn into an expanding issue later on. The most significant impact of blockchain improvement could be found in increasingly unpretentious effects upon wide social qualities and structures. These effects are related with the qualities that are installed inside the innovation. All specialized piece of the benefit innovation recognizes to have values and political legitimateness, really alluding the desire for their makers. In the understanding of this book, the reasons why customary record frameworks post their makers as the focal vaults are clear: since all every single terrific issue exchange go through them, the makers keep up their situation with most legat power and ideas to be handover to the client. In utilizing innovations, individuals reaffirm the qualities and governmental issues that they speak to, so each time these records are utilized to record an exchange, the centrality and imperativeness of the entertainer at its inside is reaffirmed. Obviously, a dispersed record without a focal middle person is likewise worth loaded and political, putting trust in encryption and systems administration innovation and redistributing power from focal specialists to non-progressive and distributed structures. In this unique situation, to utilize this sort of blockchain is to partake in a more extensive move that would decrease the trust in and intensity of conventional establishments, for example, banks and governments. The cases investigated in this report uncover a few instances of how blockchain applications typify these qualities. Obviously, for these progressions to be perceptible on a general social level would require extremely considerable advancement of blockchain to the point where it saturates everyday lives and commonplace schedules.

References

[1] Nagasubramanian, G., Sakthivel R.K., Patan R., Gandomi A.H., Sankayya M. and Balusamy B., Securing e-health records using keyless signature infrastructure blockchain technology in the cloud. Neural Computing and Applications pp. 1–9, 2018.

[2] Virtual Currencies and Beyond: Initial Considerations (PDF). IMF Discussion Note. International Monetary Fund. 2016. p. 23. ISBN 978-1-5135-5297-2. Archived (PDF) from the original on 14 April 2018. Retrieved 19 April 2018.

[3] Shah, R., 1 March 2018. How can the banking sector leverage blockchain technology?. PostBox Communications. PostBox Communications Blog. Archived from the original on 17 March 2018.

[4] Blockchain may finally disrupt payments from micropayments to credit cards to SWIFT. dailyfintech.com. 10 February 2018. Retrieved 18 November 2018.

[5] Blockchain disruptive use cases, 2016. https://everisnext.com/2016/05/31/blockchain-disruptive-use-cases/.

[6] Iansiti, M., Lakhani, K.R., The Truth About Blockchain. Harvard Business Review. Harvard University. Archived from the original on 18 January 2017. Retrieved 17 January 2017.

[7] Antonopoulos, A.M., Mastering Bitcoin: Unlocking Digital Cryptocurrencies O'Reilly Media, Inc. (2014), Google Scholar

[8] Zheng, Z., Xie, S., Dai, H.-N., Chen, X., Wang, H., Blockchain challenges and opportunities: a survey. International Journal of Web Grid Services. (2017), Google Scholar.

[9] V. Buterin, Ethereum white paper, 2013. Available online: https://github.com/ethereum/wiki/wiki/White-Paper.

[10] Androulaki E., Barger A., Bortnikov V., Cachin C., Christidis K., De Caro A., Enyeart D., Ferris C., Laventman G., Manevich Y., et al., Hyperledger fabric: A distributed operating system for permissioned blockchains, 2018, arXiv preprint arXiv:1801.10228.

[11] Kennedy, J., $1.4bn investment in blockchain start-ups in last 9 months, says PwC expert, 2016. Available online: http://linkis.com/Ayjzj.

[12] Eyal I., Gencer A.E., Sirer E.G., Van Renesse R. Bitcoin-NG: a scalable blockchain protocol 13th USENIX Symposium on Networked Systems Design and Implementation (NSDI 16), Santa Clara, CA, USA (2016), pp. 45–59. Litecoin, 2011. https://litecoin.org/.

[13] Sompolinsky Y., Zohar A. Accelerating bitcoin's transaction processing Fast Money Grows on Trees, Not Chains. IACR Cryptology EPrint Archive, pp. 1–31, Vol. 881 (2013).

[14] Decker C. and Wattenhofer R. A fast and scalable payment network with bitcoin duplex micropayment channels Symposium on Self-Stabilizing Systems, (2015), pp. 3–18 Springer, Edmonton, AB, Canada,.

[15] Stathakopoulou, C., Decker, C., Wattenhofer, R., A faster Bitcoin network, Tech. rep., ETH, Zurich, Semester Thesis, 2015.

[16] BigchainDB: The scalable blockchain database powering IPDB, 2017. Available online: https://www.bigchaindb.com/.

[17] Ipfs is the distributed web, 2017. Available online: https://ipfs.io/.

[18] Li, X., Jiang, P., Chen, T., Luo, X., Wen, Q., A survey on the security of blockchain systems. Future Generations Computer Systems, Vol. 107, pp. 841–853, 2017.

[19] Eyal I., Sirer E.G. Majority is not enough: Bitcoin mining is vulnerable International Conference on Financial Cryptography and Data Security, San Juan, Puerto Rico, Springer (2014), pp. 436–454 CrossRefView Record in ScopusGoogle Scholar.

[20] Bonneau, J., Felten, E.W., Goldfeder, S., Kroll, J.A. and Narayanan, A. Why Buy when You Can Rent? Bribery Attacks on Bitcoin Consensus Citeseer (2016)

[21] G. Karame, E. Androulaki, S. Capkun, Two bitcoins at the price of one? Double-spending attacks on fast payments in bitcoin, IACR Cryptology ePrint Archive 2012 (248), 2012.

[22] Bitcoin average transction confirmation time, 2017. Available online: https://blockchain. info/es/charts/avg-confirmation-time.

[23] H. Finney, The Finney attack(the Bitcoin Talk forum), 2011. Available online: https:// bitcointalk.org/index.php?topic=3441.msg48384.

[24] Heilman E., Kendler A., Zohar A., Goldberg S. Eclipse attacks on bitcoin's peer-to-peer network. USENIX Security Symposium, Washington, D.C., USA, USENIX Association (2015), pp. 129–144.

[25] SegWit2x backers cancel plans for bitcoin hard fork, 2017. Available online: https:// techcrunch.com/2017/11/08/segwit2x-backers-cancel-plans-for-bitcoin-hard-fork/.

[26] Sasson E.B., Chiesa A., Garman C., Green M., Miers I., Tromer E., Virza M., Zerocash: decentralized anonymous payments from bitcoin Security and Privacy (SP), 2014 IEEE Symposium on, San Jose, CA, USA, IEEE (2014), pp. 459–474.

[27] Miers I., Garman C., Green M., Rubin, A.D. Zerocoin: anonymous distributed e-cash from bitcoin Security and Privacy (SP), 2013 IEEE Symposium on, Berkeley, CA, USA, IEEE (2013), pp. 397–411.

[28] Monero, 2017. https://getmonero.org/. (Accessed 20 October 2017).

[29] Bitcoin Fog, 2017. Available online: http://bitcoinfog.info/.

[30] Maxwell G. CoinJoin: bitcoin privacy for the real world. Post on Bitcoin Forum (2013).

Chapter 10

Blockchain-Based Alleviation Measurement

L. Abirami and M. Iyapparaja

Contents

10.1 Introduction

Hyperledger is an open-source collaborative effort created to advance cross-industry blockchain technologies. It is a global collaboration hosted by the Linux Foundation, including leaders in finance, banking, Internet of Things, supply chains [1], manufacturing and technology.

10.2 Why Create a Hyperledger?

Not since the creation of Web itself has any technology emerged which promised broader and more fundamental revolution than blockchain technology. A blockchain is a peer-to-peer distributed ledger forged by consensus, combined with a system for 'smart contracts' and other assistive technologies. Together these can be used to build a new generation of transactional applications that establishes trust, accountability and transparency at its core, while streamlining business processes and legal constraints.

Think of it as an operating system for marketplaces, data-sharing networks, micro-currencies and decentralized digital communities. It has the potential to vastly reduce the cost and complexity of getting things done in the real world.

Only an open-source, collaborative software development approach can ensure the transparency, longevity, interoperability and support required to bring blockchain technologies forward to mainstream commercial adoption. That is what Hyperledger is all about—communities of software developers building blockchain frameworks and platforms.

10.2.1 Concept

A blockchain is made up of three things:

1. Ledger: It provides the place where transactions and contracts are digitally coordinated and encrypted. Ledgers are simultaneously and securely available to all participants with an audit trail.

Figure 10.1 Three stakeholders in the project.

2. Assets: These are things capable of being owned or controlled to produce value. Assets can be either digital or physical. A digital thumbprint (a permanent record) is created to connect the physical asset to the digital asset.
3. Business network: These represent ecosystems of exchange, a supply chain or a series of interconnected business transactions.

The use of a blockchain in our case should eliminate vulnerabilities through transparent transactions. All parties or stakeholders (i.e., government organizations, non-governmental organizations [NGO] and ground zero organizations, known as Global Citizen; Figure 10.1) should have access to a secure, synchronized record of transactions. The ledger records every sequence of transactions from beginning to end. It is shared and everyone has a copy available via peer exchange.

Blockchain should record the intention of donation, money transfer and distribution. A transaction's path can be traced from the donor to the ground zero team with security and transparency. As transactions in the chain occur, blocks are created in the ledger. Each block is connected to the previous block and the next block.

10.2.2 Blockchain Reference Architecture

1. A user of an application initiates a trade of a digital asset.
2. The user has a digital wallet with a wallet cloud provider. The user logs in to the wallet cloud with their user credentials and authorizes the blockchain cloud service to access his digital cash with the peer wallet cloud provider.
3. Edge services handle the request and route it to the security gateway. Edge services include a domain name server, content delivery network, firewall and load balancers.

IBM Cloud Architecture Center

Blockchain reference architecture

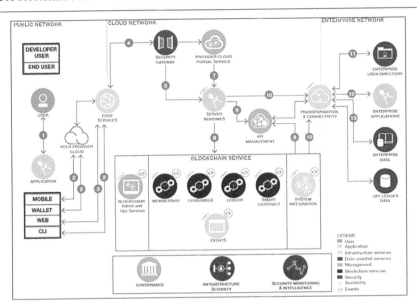

4. The security gateway establishes user identity and provides capabilities for authentication, authorization and integration. The security gateway ensures that participating users have permission and entitlements granted based on their roles in the blockchain trading network. The users are enabled to participate in a trade using web application programming interfaces (APIs).

5. From a web browser the user connects to the blockchain service of a provider cloud portal service.

6. An application request using the hyperledger fabric client (HFC) SDK goes to the membership services component. The membership services provide security, privacy and protection for the blockchain trading partners for their participating roles.

7. The HFC SDK runs in a server side web tier in the server runtimes. The request interacts with the hyperledger fabric membership services component.

8. The blockchain service receives the trading participant transaction request. The transaction is validated, the smart contract agreements are evaluated and enforced, and the validated transaction is committed to the ledger. The provider cloud portal service enables trading partners to exchange digital assets in a self-service, interactive manner using blockchain service. Events are generated from runtime at appropriate state changes to provide for integration and notification handling.

9. Smart contract provisions, back-end business data, and business logic are accessed in back-end systems by the API management capability.
10. The messages and data for the enterprise database are transformed from web formats to database formats. Secure reliable messaging is used to access the enterprise back-end system.
11. The user is authenticated in the user directory and permission rights are validated for smart contracts enforcement before accessing the back-end systems. Typically this is part of a login process that establishes a session used for a series of requests.
12. The enterprise application uses data from the client application, logs and analytics of the smart contracts and attributes. The client application updates the data and the enterprise applications process the changes.
13. Data is queried from the database to generate the requested response. The data is transformed appropriately to allow use by the application. The enterprise data includes logs and databases for analytics.

10.2.3 Transaction

What we want to achieve in our transactions is this that:

- The NGO should submit its intention to donate.
- The ground force should be notified and validate the stakeholder's identity and pledge.
- The government should be notified of the same.
- The government should approve the transactions and identity.
- The funds should be released as per the pledge.

We achieve this in our implementation as follows:
    Here, AidOrg is the NGO, Global citizen is the Ground Zero workforce.

1. Submit **SendPledgeToGlobalCitizen** transaction to send the pledge to global citizen to get the funds for the project.
2. GC reviews the pledge and after successful verification, submits a **SendPledgeToGovOrg** transaction to get funds for the project pledge from government organization.
3. Government organization reviews the pledge. After reviewing they submit an **UpdatePledge** transaction to update the project pledge asset.
4. Government organization submits **TransferFunds** transaction.

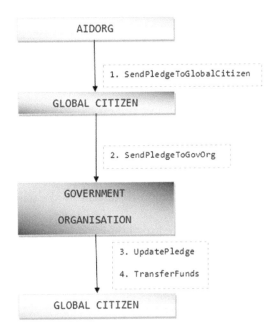

Code snippets and Transactions on our application:

```
{
  "$class": "org.global.citizens.net.
SendPledgeToGlobalCitizen",
  "citizenId": "resource:org.global.citizens.net.
GlobalCitizen#gc",
  "pledgeId": "resource:org.global.citizens.net.
ProjectPledge#p1"
}
```

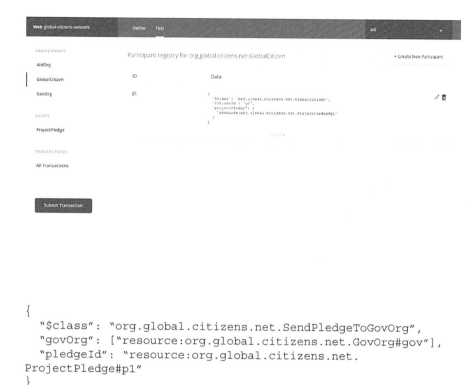

```
{
  "$class": "org.global.citizens.net.SendPledgeToGovOrg",
  "govOrg": ["resource:org.global.citizens.net.GovOrg#gov"],
  "pledgeId": "resource:org.global.citizens.net.
ProjectPledge#p1"
}
```

```
{
    "$class": "org.global.citizens.net.UpdatePledge",
    "govOrgId": "resource:org.global.citizens.net.GovOrg#gov",
    "pledgeId": "resource:org.global.citizens.net.
    ProjectPledge#p1",
    "fundingType": "WEEKLY",
    "approvedFunding": 100000,
    "fundsPerInstallment": 1000
}
```

```
{
"$class" : "org.global.citizens.net.TransferFunds",
"govOrgId" : "resource:org.global.citizens.net.GovOrg#gov",
"pledgeId" : "resource:org.global.citizens.net.
ProjectPledge#p1"
}
```

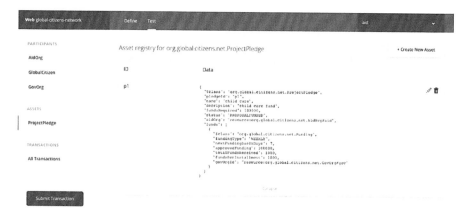

As you can see, we were successful in creating the user interface (UI). It was done by hyperledger composer playground which easily generates it; it is described below. Also, to deploy it we needed an ecosystem and applications. So we describe the IBM CLOUD's blockchain ecosystem and the algorithms used with proper diagrams for architecture as revealed by the IBM company.

10.3 The Blockchain Ecosystem and the IBM Cloud

The following are the key components of a blockchain ecosystem.

10.3.1 Blockchain Node Application

Every computer that is part of a blockchain ecosystem must install and run an application. For example, in the Bitcoin network every computer must install and run the Bitcoin wallet application.

10.3.2 Shared Ledger

Shared ledger is the data structure (blockchain) that is distributed across all the nodes of a blockchain network. The shared ledger can be managed and viewed through the node application that runs on every computer in the network.

10.3.3 Consensus Algorithm

Consensus algorithm is an algorithm implemented as part of the node application which provides the rules on how the blockchain network arrives at a single view of the shared ledger. Other important technical concepts are shown below.

Peers are the networked services that maintain ledger state and run smart contracts

Channels are defined subsets of the peer network that share a single ledger

Certificate authorities provide identity services to participants on the network

Smart contracts constitute the transaction logic whose output is agreed by the peer network

Consensus is the process by which agreement is obtained on the peer network

The **Ordering Service** agrees transaction sequence and distributes blocks to peers

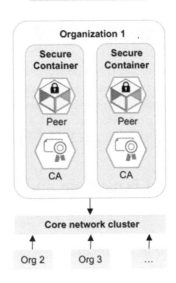

IBM CLOUD Blockchain Platform is a fully integrated enterprise-ready blockchain platform designed to accelerate the development, governance and operation of a multi-institutional business network. It has:

1. Developer tools that make use of Hyperledger Composer to quickly build a blockchain application.

2. Hyperledger fabric provides the ledger, which is managed through a set of intuitive operational tools.
3. Governance tools for democratic management of the business network.
4. Flexible deployment options, including a highly secure and performant IBM Cloud environment.

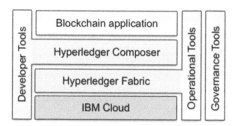

10.4 Distributed Ledger

A distributed ledger (DLT) is a type of database that is shared, replicated and synchronized among the members of a decentralized network. The distributed ledger records the transactions, such as the exchange of assets or data, among the participants in the network.

Participants in the network govern and agree by consensus on the updates to the record in the ledger. No central authority or third-party mediator, such as a financial institution or clearinghouse, is involved. Every record in the distributed ledger has a timestamp and unique cryptographic signature, thus making the ledger an auditable, immutable history of all transactions in the network.

A DLT can be considered a first step toward a blockchain, but importantly it won't necessarily construct a chain of blocks. Rather, the ledger in question will be stored across many servers, which then communicate to ensure the most accurate and up to date record of transactions is maintained.

10.5 Working (How It Interacts)

The DLT database is spread across several nodes (devices) on a peer-to-peer network, where each replicates and saves an identical copy of the ledger and updates itself independently. The primary advantage is the lack of central authority. When a ledger update happens, each node constructs the new transaction, and then the nodes vote by consensus algorithm on which copy is correct. Once a consensus has been determined, all the other nodes update themselves with the new, correct copy of the ledger. Security is accomplished through cryptographic keys and signatures. The hyperledger fabric framework supports distributed ledger solutions on permissioned networks, where the members are known to each other, for a wide range of industries. Its modular architecture maximizes the confidentiality, resilience and flexibility of blockchain solutions. Hyperledger Composer is a set of free, open-source tools for quickly prototyping, defining and testing a hyperledger fabric blockchain network and writing applications to interact with it.

The IBM CLOUD Blockchain Platform runs on the hyperledger fabric framework and integrates the Hyperledger Composer toolset as the 'IBM CLOUD Blockchain Platform: Develop' tools.

10.6 Consensus Algorithm

In general, a consensus algorithm is a process in computer science used to achieve agreement on a single data value among distributed processes or systems. Consensus algorithms are designed to achieve reliability in a network involving multiple unreliable nodes. Solving that issue—known as the consensus problem—is important in distributed computing and multi-agent systems.

10.6.1 Merkle Trees

- Content address
- Using hash function(one way function)
- No 2 inputs generate the same output
- Unique ID for a piece of content

10.6.1.1 How It Enables the Decentralized Web?

- It is a binary tree
- Nodes stores hashes instead of data
- Leaf stores hashes of chunks of data
- Parent are rest of concatenating the child and then applying the hash function
- Four chunks of data, determining the leaf nodes
- Apply the hash function
- Root hash or root node (important role in P2P network)
- Partial verification

In various distributed and peer-to-peer systems, data verification is very important. This is because the same data exists in multiple locations. So, if a piece of data is changed in one location, it's important that data is changed everywhere. Data verification is used to make sure data is the same everywhere.

However, it is time-consuming and computationally expensive to check the entirety of each file whenever a system wants to verify data. So, this is why Merkle trees are used. Basically, we want to limit the amount of data being sent over a network (like the Internet) as much as possible. So, instead of sending an entire file over the network, we just send a hash of the file to see if it matches.

10.6.1.2 Why a Merkle Tree?

Merkle trees are used because they:

1. Significantly reduce the network I/O packet size to perform consistency and data verification as well as data synchronization.
2. Significantly reduces the amount of data that a trusted authority has to maintain to proof the integrity of the data.
3. Separates the validation of the data from the data itself—the Merkle tree can reside locally, or on a trusted authority, or can itself reside on a distributed system (perhaps you only maintain your own tree). Decoupling the 'I can prove the data is valid' from the data itself means you can implement the appropriate and separate (including redundant) persistence for both the Merkle tree and the data store.

10.6.1.3 Merkle Trees in Action

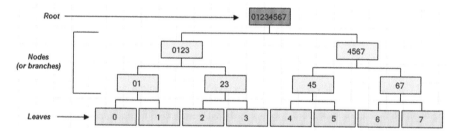

A Merkle tree is typically a binary tree in which each leaf represents the hashed value of the record associated with that leaf. The branches are the hash of the concatenated hashes of the two children. This process of rehashing the concatenation of the child nodes to create the parent node is performed until the top of the tree is reached, called the 'root hash'.

10.6.1.4 How Does Data Verification Work?

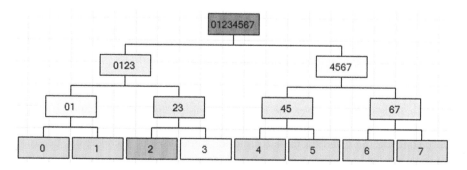

Let's say you are the owner of the record '2' in the above diagram. You also have, from a trusted authority, the root hash, which in our simulation is '01234567'. You ask the server to prove to you that your record '2' is in the tree. What the server returns to you are the hashes '3', '01', '4567' as illustrated here:

Using this information (including the right-left flags that are sent back along with the hashes), the proof is that:

- 2 + 3 from which you compute 23
- 01 + 23 from which you compute 0123
- 0123 + 4567 from which you compute 01234567

Since you know the root hash from your trusted authority, the proof validates that '2' exists in the tree. Furthermore, the system from which you have obtained the proof is proving to you that it is an 'authority' because it is able to provide valid hashes so that you can get from '2' to your known root hash '01234567'. Any system pretending to validate your request would not be able to provide you with the intermediate hashes since you're not giving the system the root hash, you're just telling it to give you the proof—it can't invent the proof because it doesn't know your root hash, only you know that.

10.7 Practical Byzantine Fault Tolerance

The validating peers run a Byzantine fault tolerance (BFT) consensus protocol for executing a replicated state machine that accepts three types of transactions as operations:

1. **Deploy transaction:** Takes a chaincode (representing a smart contract) written in Go as a parameter; the chaincode is installed on the peers and ready to be invoked.
2. **Invoke transaction:** Invokes a transaction of a particular chaincode that has been installed earlier through a deploy transaction; the arguments are specific to the type of transaction; the chaincode executes the transaction, may read and write entries in its state accordingly, and indicates whether it succeeded or failed.
3. **Query transaction:** Returns an entry of the state directly from reading the peer's persistent state; this may not ensure linearizability.

Each chaincode may define its own persistent entries in the state. The blockchain's hash chain is computed over the executed transactions and the resulting persistent state. Validation of transactions occurs through the replicated execution of the chaincode and given the fault assumption underlying BFT consensus, i.e., that among the *n* validating peers at most f < *n*/3 may 'lie' and behave arbitrarily, but all others execute the chaincode correctly. When executed on top of PBFT consensus, it is important that chaincode transactions are deterministic, otherwise the state of the peers might diverge. A modular solution to filter out non-deterministic transactions that are demonstrably diverging is available and has been implemented in the SIEVE protocol.

Membership among the validating nodes running BFT consensus is currently static and the setup requires manual intervention. Support for dynamically changing the set of nodes running consensus is planned for a future version. As the fabric implements a permissioned ledger, it contains a security infrastructure for authentication and authorization. It supports enrollment and transaction authorization through public-key certificates, and confidentiality for chaincode realized through in-band encryption.

More precisely, for connecting to the network every peer needs to obtain an enrollment certificate from an enrollment CA that is part of the membership services. It authorizes a peer to connect to the network and to acquire transaction certificates, which are needed to submit transactions. Transaction certificates are issued by a transaction CA and support pseudonymous authorization for the peers sub-mitting transactions, in the sense that multiple transaction certificates issued to the same peer (that is, to the same enrollment certificate) cannot be linked with each other. Confidentiality for chaincodes and state is provided through symmetric-key encryption of transacations and states with a blockchain-specific key that is available to all peers with an enrolment certificate for the blockchain. Extending the encryption mechanisms towards more fine-grained confidentiality for transactions and state entries is planned for a future version.

10.8 Consensus in IBM Cloud Blockchain Service (Hyperledger Fabric)

The consensus in hyperledger fabric network is a process where the nodes in the network provide a guaranteed ordering of the transaction and validating those block of transactions that need to be committed to the ledger. Consensus must ensure the following in the network:

1. Confirm the accuracy of all transactions in a proposed block, according to endorsement and consensus policies.
2. Agree on order and accuracy and hence on results of execution (implies agreement on global state).
3. Interface and depend on a smart-contract layer to verify the accuracy of an ordered set of transactions in a block.

10.8.1 Consensus Properties

Consensus must satisfy two properties to guarantee agreement among nodes: safety and liveness.

1. Safety means that each node is guaranteed the same sequence of inputs and results in the same output on each node. When the nodes receive an identical series of transactions, the same state changes will occur on each node. The algorithm must behave identical to a single node system that executes each transaction atomically one at a time.
2. Liveness means that each non-faulty node will eventually receive every submitted transaction, assuming that communication does not fail.

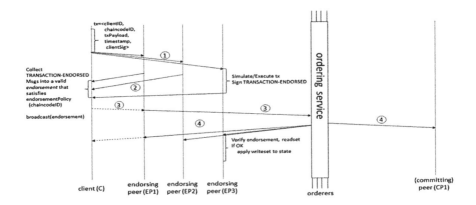

10.8.2 How IBM Cloud Is Doing It Differently

Hyperledger fabric uses a new execute-order-validate architecture, which lets transactions execute before the blockchain reaches consensus on their place in the chain. Furthermore, it supports modular consensus protocols and lets distributed applications be written in standard programing languages.

Hyperledger fabric is the first blockchain system that runs distributed applications written in general-purpose programming languages (such as Go, Java, Node.js), without systemic dependency on a native cryptocurrency. This is a significant advancement to existing blockchain platforms, which require code to be written in a domain-specific language that requires specific training.

The execute-order-validate architecture departs radically from the order-execute paradigm in that it separates the transaction flow into modular building blocks and includes elements of scalable replicated databases. Fabric pioneers a hybrid replication approach, combining passive and active replication in the Byzantine model [2]. Fabric's replication is passive in the sense that every transaction is executed or endorsed by a subset of peers only, which allows for parallel execution and non-determinism. And because the effects of transactions on the ledger state are written only after a consensus is reached on their order, Fabric also uses active replication.

Essentially, this hybrid replication design supports a flexible endorsement policy in any given smart contract and simultaneously allows Fabric to respect application-specific trust assumptions according to the transaction endorsements. In other words, the transactions don't have to be constructed all in one order, as long as they are consistent with each other and come together at the right time. Since the consensus is modular, its implementation can be tailored to the assumption of a specific deployment. This adds a great deal of flexibility and lets the system rely on well-established toolkits and protocols for crash fault-tolerant (CFT) or BFT [3] ordering.

After fleshing out their initial ideas and creating a design document on the 'consensus architecture', the researchers convinced their colleagues in the community of open-source developers behind fabric to adopt this model [4].

10.9 Advantages in a Nutshell

Due to its innovative architecture, hyperledger fabric has the ability to deliver unique network capabilities such as enhanced privacy and confidentiality, efficient processing, scalability, standard programming languages and a modular structure that can be customized for individual deployments. Such capabilities make fabric a suitable blockchain platform for businesses.

The flexibility is almost endless. One could even apply an additional layer of permission through the platform's identity management service. As an example, a specific user ID could be permitted to invoke a smart contract application but be blocked from deploying a new one [5].

10.9.1 Hyperledger Composer and Node.js Application

Hyperledger Composer is an extensive, open development toolset and framework to make developing blockchain applications easier. The framework makes it easier to integrate the blockchain applications with the existing business systems. We can use Composer to rapidly develop use cases and deploy a blockchain solution in weeks rather than months. Composer allows you to model your business network and integrate existing systems and data with your blockchain applications.

Hyperledger Composer **supports** the existing **hyperledger fabric** blockchain infrastructure and runtime, which supports pluggable blockchain consensus protocols to ensure that transactions are validated according to policy by the designated business network participants.

- Everyday applications can consume the data from business networks, providing end users with simple and controlled access points. We can use Hyperledger Composer to quickly model our current business network, containing our existing assets and the transactions related to them; assets are tangible or intangible goods, services, or property.
- As part of our business network model, we define the transactions which can interact with assets.
- Business networks also include the participants who interact with them, each of which can be associated with a unique identity, across multiple business networks.
- Hyperleder Composer generate business network archive (BNA) file which you can deploy on existing hyperledger fabric network

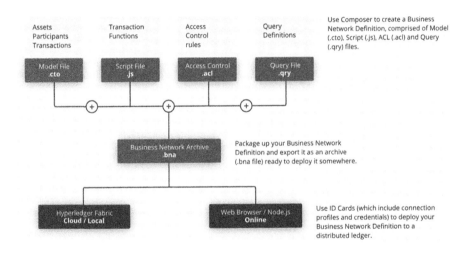

10.9.2 *How Does Hyperledger Composer Work in Practice?*

We can quickly model the business network as such:

- **Assets:** The donation money
- **Participants:** The stakeholders described above: government, NGO and global citizen
- **Transactions:** As described above

Participants can have their access to transactions restricted based on their role and the application can be created via the composer where are the stakeholder interact and view all the transactions.

The Hyperledger Composer Playground provides a user interface for the configuration, deployment and testing of a business network. Advanced Playground features permit users to manage the security of the business network, invite participants to business networks and connect to multiple blockchain business networks. We use the composer-client npm module to programmatically connect to a deployed business network, create, read, update and delete assets and participants and to submit transactions.

10.10 Business Network Definition

The Business Network Definition is a key concept of the Hyperledger Composer programming model. They are represented by the **BusinessNetworkDefinition** class, defined in the **composer-common** module and exported by both **composer-admin** and **composer-client**.

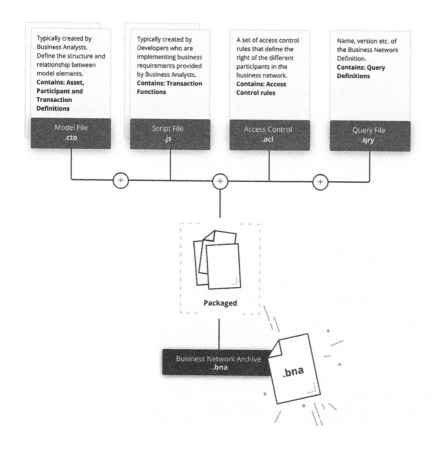

Business Network Definitions are composed of:

1. A set of model files

> ▲ models
>> ☰ org.global.citizens.net.cto

CODE:

```
namespace org.global.citizens.net
enum Status{
  o INITIALSTATE
  o GLOBALCITIZENREVIEW
  o GOVORGREVIEW
  o PROPOSALFUNDED
}
enum FundingType{
  o WEEKLY
  o MONTHLY
  o SEMIANNUALY
  o ANNUALY
}
enum FundingStatus{
  o COMPLETE
  o INCOMPLETE
}
enum MessageStatus{
  o NOTREVIEWED
  o REVIEWED
}
concept Funding {
  o FundingType fundingType
  o Integer nextFundingDueInDays
  o Double approvedFunding
  o Double totalFundsReceived
  o Double fundsPerInstallment
  --> GovOrg govOrgId
}
asset ProjectPledge identified by pledgeId {
  o String pledgeId
  o String name
  o String decription
  o Double fundsRequired
  o Status status
  --> AidOrg aidOrg
  o Funding[] funds
}
```

```
abstract participant User {
  --> ProjectPledge[] projectPledge
}
participant GovOrg identified by govOrgId extends User {
  o String govOrgId
  --> ProjectPledge[] fundedPledges
}
participant AidOrg identified by aidOrgId extends User {
  o String aidOrgId
}
participant GlobalCitizen identified by citizenId extends
User {
  o String citizenId
}
transaction CreateProjectPledge {
  o String pledgeId
  o String name
  o String decription
  o Double fundsRequired
  --> AidOrg aidOrg
}
transaction SendPledgeToGlobalCitizen {
  --> GlobalCitizen citizenId
  --> ProjectPledge pledgeId
}
transaction SendPledgeToGovOrg {
  --> GovOrg[] govOrg
  --> ProjectPledge pledgeId
}
transaction UpdatePledge {
  --> GovOrg govOrgId
  --> ProjectPledge pledgeId
  o FundingType fundingType
  o Double approvedFunding
  o Double fundsPerInstallment
}
transaction TransferFunds {
  --> GovOrg govOrgId
  --> ProjectPledge pledgeId
}
```

2. A set of JavaScript files

```
1    'use strict';
2    /**
3     * Write your transction processor functions here
4     */
5    var NS = 'org.global.citizens.net';
6    /**
7     * createProjectPledge
8     * @param {org.global.citizens.net.CreateProjectPledge} createProjectPledge
```

```
 9   * @transaction
10   */
11   function createProjectPledge(txParams) {
12     if(!txParams.name || (txParams.name && txParams.name === "")) {
13       throw new Error('Invalid Pledge Name!!');
14     }
15     if(!txParams.aidOrg) {
16       throw new Error('Invalid Aid Org!!');
17     }
18     var factory = getFactory();
19     var pledge = null;
20     return getAssetRegistry(NS + '.ProjectPledge').then(function (registry) {
21       pledge = factory.newResource(NS, 'ProjectPledge', txParams.pledgeId);
22       pledge.name = txParams.name;
23       pledge.decription = txParams.decription;
24       pledge.fundsRequired = txParams.fundsRequired;
25       pledge.status = 'INITIALSTATE';
26       pledge.funds = [];
27       pledge.aidOrg = txParams.aidOrg;
28       return registry.add(pledge);
29     }).then(function () {
30       return getParticipantRegistry(NS + '.AidOrg');
31     }).then(function (aidOrgRegistry) {
32       // save the buyer
33       txParams.aidOrg.projectPledge.push(pledge);
34       return aidOrgRegistry.update(txParams.aidOrg);
35     });
36   }
37   /**
38    * SendPledgeToGlobalCitizen
39    * @param {org.global.citizens.net.SendPledgeToGlobalCitizen} sendPledgeToGlobalCitizen
40    * @transaction
41    */
42   function sendPledgeToGlobalCitizen(txParams) {
43     if(!txParams.citizenId || !txParams.pledgeId) {
44       throw new Error('Invalid input parameters!!');
45     }
46     txParams.pledgeId.status = 'GLOBALCITIZENREVIEW';
47     txParams.citizenId.projectPledge.push(txParams.pledgeId);
48     var factory = getFactory();
49     return getAssetRegistry(NS + '.ProjectPledge').then(function (registry) {
50       return registry.update(txParams.pledgeId);
51     }).then(function () {
52       return getParticipantRegistry(NS + '.GlobalCitizen');
53     }).then(function (registry) {
54       return registry.update(txParams.citizenId);
55     });
56   }
57   /**
58    * SendPledgeToGovOrg
59    * @param {org.global.citizens.net.SendPledgeToGovOrg} sendPledgeToGovOrg
60    * @transaction
61    */
62   function sendPledgeToGovOrg(txParams) {
63     if(!txParams.pledgeId || !txParams.govOrg || (txParams.govOrg && txParams.govOrg.length === 0)) {
64       throw new Error('Invalid input parameters!!');
65     }
66     var factory = getFactory();
67     txParams.pledgeId.status = 'GOVORGREVIEW';
68     return getAssetRegistry(NS + '.ProjectPledge').then(function (registry) {
69       return registry.update(txParams.pledgeId);
70     }).then(function () {
```

```
71       return getParticipantRegistry(NS + '.GovOrg');
72    }).then(function (registry) {
73      for(var i = 0; i < txParams.govOrg.length; i++) {
74        txParams.govOrg[i].projectPledge.push(txParams.pledgeId);
75      }
76      return registry.updateAll(txParams.govOrg);
77    });
78  }
79  /**
80   * UpdatePledge
81   * @param {org.global.citizens.net.UpdatePledge} updatePledge
82   * @transaction
83   */
84  function updatePledge(txParams) {
85    if(!txParams.govOrgId) {
86      throw new Error('Invalid user type!!');
87    }
88    var factory = getFactory();
89    var funding = factory.newConcept(NS, 'Funding');
90    var daysToAdd = 0;
91    switch(txParams.fundingType) {
92    case 'WEEKLY':
93      daysToAdd = 7;
94      break;
95    case 'MONTHLY':
96      daysToAdd = 30;
97      break;
98    case 'SEMIANNUALY':
99      daysToAdd = 180;
100     break;
101   case 'ANNUALY':
102     daysToAdd = 365;
103     break;
104   }
105   funding.fundingType = txParams.fundingType;
106   funding.nextFundingDueInDays = daysToAdd;
107   funding.approvedFunding = txParams.approvedFunding;
108   funding.totalFundsReceived = 0;
109   funding.fundsPerInstallment = txParams.fundsPerInstallment;
110   funding.govOrgId = txParams.govOrgId;
111   txParams.pledgeId.status = 'PROPOSALFUNDED';
112   txParams.pledgeId.funds.push(funding);
113   txParams.govOrgId.fundedPledges.push(txParams.pledgeId);
114   return getAssetRegistry(NS + '.ProjectPledge').then(function (registry) {
115     return registry.update(txParams.pledgeId);
116   }).then(function () {
117     return getParticipantRegistry(NS + '.GovOrg');              ) {
118   }).then(function (registry) {
119     return registry.update(txParams.govOrgId);
120   });
121 }
122 /**
123  * TransferFunds
124  * @param {org.global.citizens.net.TransferFunds} transferFunds
125  * @transaction
126  */
127 function transferFunds(txParams) {
128   if(!txParams.pledgeId || !txParams.govOrgId) {
129     throw new Error('Invalid input parameters!!');
130   }
131   var factory = getFactory();
132   var valid = false;
133   for(var i = 0; i < txParams.govOrgId.fundedPledges.length; i++) {
134     if(txParams.govOrgId.fundedPledges[i].pledgeId === txParams.pledgeId.pledgeId) {
135       valid = true;
136       break;
137     }
138   }
139   if(!valid) {
```

```
140      throw new Error('Pledge not funded!!');
141    }
142    for(var i = 0; i < txParams.pledgeId.funds.length; i++) {
143      if(txParams.pledgeId.funds[i].govOrgId === txParams.govOrgId) {
144        var daysToAdd = 0;
145        switch(txParams.pledgeId.funds[i].fundingType) {
146          case 'WEEKLY':
147            daysToAdd = 7;
148            break;
149          case 'MONTHLY':
150            daysToAdd = 30;
151            break;
152          case 'SEMIANNUALY':
153            daysToAdd = 180;
154            break;
155          case 'ANNUALY':
156            daysToAdd = 365;
157            break;
158        }
159        txParams.pledgeId.funds[i].nextFundingDueInDays = daysToAdd;
160        txParams.pledgeId.funds[i].totalFundsReceived += txParams.pledgeId.funds[i].fundsPerInstallment;
161        break;
162      }
163    }
164    return getAssetRegistry(NS + '.ProjectPledge').then(function (registry) {
165      return registry.update(txParams.pledgeId);
166    });
167  }
```

3. An Access Control file

```
21
22    rule Default {
23        description: "Allow all participants access to all resources"
24        participant: "ANY"
25        operation: ALL
26        resource: "org.global.citizens.net.*"
27        action: ALLOW
28    }
29
30    rule SystemACL {
31      description:  "System ACL to permit all access"
32      participant: "ANY"
33      operation: ALL
34      resource: "org.hyperledger.composer.system.**"
35      action: ALLOW
36    }
37
```

■ The model files defined the business domain for a business network, while the JavaScript files contain transaction processor functions. The transaction processor functions run on a hyperledger fabric and have access to the asset registries that are stored in the world state of the hyperledger fabric blockchain.

- The model files are typically created by business analysts, as they define the structure and relationships between model elements: assets, participants and transactions.
- The JavaScript files are typically created by developers who are implementing business requirements provided by business analysts.
- The Access Control file contains a set of access control rules that define the rights of the different participants in the business network.

Once defined, a Business Network Definition can be packaged into an archive using the composer command line interface. These archives can then be deployed or updated on a fabric, using the AdminConnection class from the composer-admin module.

global-citizens-network@0.0.1.bna   U

10.10.1 Business Network Cards

A business network card provides all of the information needed to connect to a blockchain business network. It is only possible to access a blockchain business network through a valid business network card. A business network card contains identity for a single participant within a deployed business network. Business network cards are used in the Hyperledger Composer Playground to connect to deploy business networks. You can have multiple business network cards for a single deployed business network, where those business network cards belong to multiple participants.

Business network cards are grouped under a Connection Profile, and each card shows the business network that may be accessed using the displayed Identity via the *Connect now* option. A business network card may be deleted or exported using the icons present on the card.

A business network card can be created when an identity is issued within the Playground. This business network card can then be exported and shared with others, allowing them to connect to the business network using the issued identity. If a user is provided with an enrollment ID and secret by an administrator, which corresponds to a valid Identity within a business network, then a business network card may be directly created in the Playground. It is also possible to manually create a business network card.

10.10.2 The Business Networks Page

The **Business Networks** page is the default Playground landing page. Here all the business network cards you have are available for use. Each business network card provides all of the information needed to connect to a blockchain business network. It is only possible to access a blockchain business network by using a valid business network card. Once connected to a deployed business network, you will be taken to the **Define** page.

10.11 Conclusion

Using blockchain, we were able to transparently conduct transactions related to donations during a natural calamity. Because of the features of a block-chain-based solution the irregularities were prevented. We used IBM CLOUD's blockchain services on bluemix for the implementation using which we were able to streamline the development process. IBM CLOUD also helped us by providing sample code for blockchain and the documentation and the support team on their slack channel for code2create provided us with invaluable support for which we are grateful.

References

[1] K. Korpela, J. Hallikas, T. Dahlberg, "Digital supply chain transformation toward blockchain integration," In: Proceedings of the 50th Hawaii International Conference on System Sciences, 2017.

[2] Y. Amir, B.A. Coan, J. Kirsch, and J. Lane. Prime: Byzantine replication under attack. IEEE Transactions on Dependable and Secure Computing, vol. 8, no. 4, pp. 564–577, 2011.

[3] C. Cachin, S. Schubert, and M. Vukoli´ c. Non-determinism in Byzantine fault-tolerant replication. e-print, arXiv:1603.07351 [cs.DC], 2016. URL: http://arxiv.org/abs/1603.07351.

[4] B. MBeamon, "Supply chain design and analysis: Models and methods," International Journal of Production Economics, vol. 55, no. 3, pp. 281–294, 15 August 1998.

[5] M. Vukoli´ c. The quest for scalable blockchain fabric: Proof-of-work vs. BFT replication. In: Open Problems in Network Security, Proceedings of IFIP WG 11.4 Workshop (iNetSec 2015), volume 9591 of Lecture Notes in Computer Science, pages 112–125. Springer, 2016.

Chapter 11

Blockchain versus IoT Architectural Styles

M. Vivek Anand and S. Vijayalakshmi

Contents

Machine to machine (M2M) is expected to increase dynamically from 780 million in 2016 to 3.3 billion in 2021. This shows the enhancement of Internet of Things (IoT) in different aspects with respect to their applications. IoT is applied in various applications such as smart home, wearable's, emergency, smart agriculture and supply chain management, etc. IoT is entirely changing the world through modern devices and data communications. IoT is making virtualization in the applications by applying the network function Virtualization and minimizing the storage of data in the client by applying software-defined networks where the control plane and data plane are separated in the network.

Though IoT is providing good service in every aspect, the Architecture of IoT is failed to provide security in the network. Although various architecture styles have been proposed for IoT such as client-server architecture, cloud-based architecture, Fog computing architecture, they are deficient to handle data breaching. IoT is not only involved in a sophisticated application but it is also involved in the emergency application. The data breaching in emergency applications such as a remote patient health monitoring system where the patient's health condition is monitored through a wearable chip kept inside the patient's body. The wearable chip will send the notification to the hospital when there is a change in the patient's body condition. Based on the data analytics, hospital management will call for the ambulance in a critical situation to save the life of the patient. In this case, IoT is contributing to majorly monitoring health conditions through the sensor and giving the notification to the device that is embedded in the hospital. (In this kind of scenario, if IoT is failing to perform the task because of data breaching, the patient life would not be saved. The failure of IoT in this task may lead the patient's life in a dangerous state.)

IoT is based on a centralized server such as client-server architecture, cloud-based architecture and fog computing architecture. In a client-server architecture, a client requests for every process to the server where the server is having the big data storage. If the server is affected by any unauthorized person, the entire system will fail to do the task. In cloud-based architecture, the application residing on the Internet and the data are stored online. The request will be given by the client whenever the data is required. The privacy of data is questionable in public cloud architecture.

A small organization cannot maintain the hardware and data storage in a private cloud. Security tools cannot be maintained by a small organization. In the case of the public cloud, the data may be misused by cloud service providers. Centralized server architecture is vulnerable to data breaching through the Internet. IoT devices will not perform the task without receiving commands and associated data from the centralized server. The entire system will fail if the server is hacked by an unauthorized person. This will lead to the misuse of data by hackers by tampering the data intentionally to spoil the system. Fog computing is rectifying some of the issues addressed in cloud computing such as latency, volume, etc., that also works in the base of cloud servers.

Various security measures proposed for security in centralized servers are not enough to secure the system and also the maintenance of the server is expensive because of upgraded security tools and techniques in the network. Since the centralized server architecture is not enough to handle data breaching, the important challenge is to propose the new architectural styles that are saving the data from an unauthorized person. In a decentralized architecture, the maintenance of the server is not required. In the way of looking for an architecture that is free from hacking and decentralized in nature, many suggestions are given by experts to go for blockchain.

The blockchain is a peer-to-peer decentralized network, where the users who are involved in the network will have the responsibility of controlling their own peers only. The blockchain is an anonymous network where the user can hide their identity from the remaining peers in the network. Transactions over the network are recorded and transmitted to their terminals. Tampering with data in the distributed ledger is highly impossible because it has to get approval from most of the peers. Blockchain performance can be identified by the study on the impact of blockchain in various applications. The blockchain is successfully implemented in cryptocurrency networks where the first cryptocurrency is called bitcoins.

Bitcoins are a digital cryptocurrency that is working in the concept of the blockchain. In bitcoins, all the transactions are stored in the network as a ledger that will be available to all the peers in the network. All the users are anonymous, they can hide their identity and one person cannot control others' transactions. The new user can enroll in the network through various types of cryptocurrency wallets such as web wallet, a desktop wallet, mobile wallet, etc. The user can do a transaction by creating the transaction address that is known as a public key that can be shared with people who are in the network to transfer bitcoins. Creations of user ID in the cryptocurrency wallets will also generate the transaction address. The user can generate different transaction address for different transactions. The users who want to do the transaction can broadcast the message in the network which will be visible to all the miners involved in the network. Bitcoin network will validate all the transactions to ensure the security. If any abnormality is found, then all are resolved using specified resources and a unit is created.

Miners will validate a unit by finding the cryptographic hash that is associated with the blockchain network. Units associated hash has to be coinciding with hash of the existing unit. Hash of the block has to be matched with the previous block. Miners are finding the hash by having high-power computational resources. Miners will get the reward by adding the block of transactions into the previous block after finding the hash and getting approval from most of their peers. Tampering with transaction data is not possible in blockchain because a cryptographic key is associated with every transaction. Private key of the bitcoin users will be used for receiving the bitcoins that have been sent to the bitcoin address.

The blockchain is providing security to the application by anonymity and peer-to-peer distributed network. The blockchain is using the consensus algorithm to make it more complex for breaching by getting the approval of every transaction from most of the peers. The blockchain is a well-formed architecture that can provide security; this can be applied to various applications to hold the security against threads. Blockchain can be applied to IoT for making security in IoT applications thereby providing a good impact on the applications in the world.

Integrating the IoT and blockchain opens a door for IoT applications in a different perspective in terms of security. An application such as supply chain management from marketing to the delivery of the product can be monitored by all the peers if the IoT is backboned with the blockchain. Stored data in IoT devices should be protected to make a secure environment in applications.

The blockchain is not only applied in cryptocurrency. Blockchain-based IoT applications are evolving with ensured security. Blockchain can be applied in various IoT applications such as voting system, supply chain management, emergency applications, smart home, education, academia, etc. Adapting the blockchain into the IoT application is a major challenge nowadays in the industry. Industries are looking for a smooth way of running applications that are free from hacking by embedding blockchain architecture into IoT applications.

Though the challenges that are raised while integrating blockchain and IoT, blockchain is inevitable nowadays in the IoT industry to make security in their applications. Finally, blockchain and the IoT will lead to a healthy environment in industry and developers, service to the people with ensured security.

11.1 Introduction

IoT is creating communication facilities in all the environment with connecting devices such as mobile, PC, network devices, communication devices, etc. [1]. In the real world, we cannot avoid the uses of IoT devices to connect each device through the Internet. The Internet is everywhere in the modern world with Internet connecting devices. The actual IoT allows individuals as well as things to be related at anytime, anywhere, connecting with something as well as anybody, accessing any kind of network. IoT is designing with regular organizations to function for a particular environment in order to perform a certain task quickly and easily through connecting devices.

11.2 Evolution of IoT

The computer network made communication between two computer machines possible in the 1960s. TCP/IP stack was introduced in the 1980s. The Internet is changing the world and growth rapidly after the inauguration of World Wide Web in 1991s. Later, devices like mobile phones, personal computers are interacted with World Wide Web to share messages. The user started connecting the Internet and making the relationship on social networking websites through devices such as mobile, PC, etc. The machine connected with another machine making communication through network and understanding and processing data has happened while the technology was evolving in the world. This communication technique is referred to as M2M communication. The next innovation of technology is IoT where an object will connect to each other making communication via the Internet.

The development in Internet technologies is expanding the boundaries of Internet as the connectivity is becoming cheap and pervasive, even in rural areas. Devices require more consumption of power and energy to fulfill their assigned tasks in an environment. According to the requirement, the devices are equipped with powerful storage and energy devices such as sensors and actuators to become active on the Internet and become smaller in size to accommodate small space in the environment to perform moving of objects from one place to another without interrupting the Internet connectivity.

Well-equipped devices are able to connect and communicate over the Internet, have the ability to sense, compute, and communicate through the Internet. Some of the physical objects are modernly equipped with Radio-Frequency Identification (RFID) to identify the product details or the device details by scanning through RFID scanner and Near Field Communications (NFC) to read the electronic bar code that can be scanned by smart devices, the connections are made when the devices are moving near to the devices. See Figure 11.1.

Things to be identified as smartphones, tablets, digital cameras, smart watch, game consoles, etc... Environmental elements and other electronic equipment are embedded with either RFID or NFC tags which able to connect the Internet via the gateway device. According to the word "Things" mentioned above, the numerous

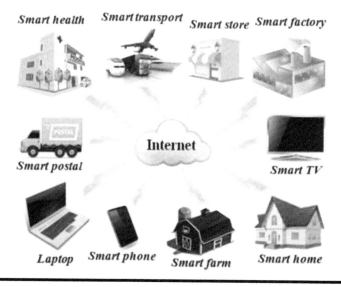

Figure 11.1   IoT scenario.

devices and things will be connected to the Internet almost simultaneously and each element providing gathered data and information, even services. The IoT completely changes the connectivity from "any-time, any-where" for "any-one" into "any-time, any-where" for "anything" [2]. The IoT is able to connect real-world elements and embeds the intelligence in a communication system to smartly process its specific information and autonomous decision. Hence, IoT is a key enabling the different types of beneficial applications and services that can sustain our economies, transportation, environment and health that we never expected before.

11.3 IoT Elements

Components of IoT are shown in Figure 11.2. There are six components which are described below.

Identification: Identification of IoT used to detect with the help of electronic product codes and ubiquitous codes. It helps to address the issues of the identification process in the IoT.

Sensing: Sensing IoT is used to collect the data from warehouses which will be stored using a cloud computing system. The application involving the sensing IoT environment is smart Hub, Smart mobile communications.

Communication: Communication taken place in IoT using only the Internet that may be different communication mediums such as RFID, 802.11, WLAN, WIFI, WIMAX, and ultra-wideband communication. Here, communication should lie between the RFID transmitter and RFID receiver. Near field, communication covers only 246kbps and wireless fidelity has given a 100m wide range for efficient communication. Ultra-wideband communication provides high bandwidth utilization for communication. Bluetooth provides low power control and short distance communication. Zigbee occupies more distance compared to Bluetooth and lesser distance compared to WIFI.

Computation: Computation is related to computational software like Arduino, raspberry pi, cupboard, gadget, coated sky for efficient performance. It relates to the brain and it gives the condition to do the activities of the system.

Services: IoT services will be offered by various services for administrative purposes like collaborative services, identity services, fundamental services and aggressive services.

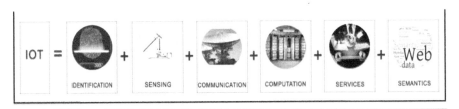

Figure 11.2 Six components of Internet of Things.

Semantics: Semantics is the most important task in IoT and it helps to find out the reliable and efficient communication between ontology services. It supports decision-based services for the searching algorithms. It works with various machines to support to perform necessary algorithms.

11.3.1 Architecture

Architecture styles that are proposed for the IoT are from the generic architecture forms, and styles of the architecture are changing for the day to day requirement and now it becomes useful to use certain architecture in place of the application requirement.

11.3.1.1 IoT Architecture

IoT functionality has been classified into five major layers including business layer, application layer, middle layer, network layer and perception layer (see Figure 11.3).

Perception layer: The perception layer is the first layer of the IoT architecture which has various environmental elements and sensors. As like physical layer in OSI architecture, it has the same operational procedure. The layer has the

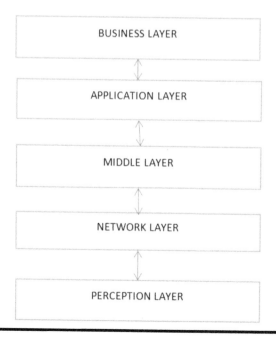

Figure 11.3 IoT architecture.

sensors and managerial elements which coordinate the complete system, and as discussed earlier, it has sensor so it collects the information from the environment. For example, the collected data may be water level, temperature, volume of noise in air, humidity, speed of the air flow, etc. These data are proceeded to the next level called the network layer.

Network layer: It is obvious that IoT provides the secure communication over the networks which have been ensured in network layer. This is layer which is responsible for secure Message passing over the network. The data observed by sensors are sent via the network layer by either wired or wireless medium which is based on the sensor. To ensure the security of IoT, it is important to secure the data which is transferred through the mediums. Hence, it is playing a sensitive role in the architecture.

Middleware layer: Based on the connected devices, IoT will provide different services. This middleware layer has the gateway to connect the different devices to the IoT. There are two fundamental tasks that middleware layer performs. One is service management which is to accept the various devices into IoT. Another one is transferring lower layer data to the central database. In addition, it maintains the data processing, data retrieval, data computation and decision making.

Application layer: Application layer controls the various applications that are connected to the IoT. It controls the applications based on information retrieved from the middle layer. The connected applications may be smart health, smart transportation, smart car, smart postal smart home, smart independent living, smart glasses, etc.

Business layer: Business layer maintains the entire layers of this architecture. It cumulates the data from the entire lower layer and generates the report. Repots may be in the form of diagram, graph or tables. The accuracy of the system depends on analysis efficiency of the above lower layers. Based on the accuracy of reports, decision making and business planning will be more effective.

There we have more verity of IoT models [3–7] because of the flexibility. This characteristic is because the devices that are connected to IoT have same service and architectures. Because of the characteristic there is stable architecture that highlights all the phases of IoT.

11.3.1.2 Client Server Architecture

In client-server architecture, the client is requesting the server and the server replies to the client's request. Devices are communicating through the server; a node cannot make any own decision because everything is controlled by the server. The server plays a major role in serving the data to the client whenever it requires. The initial version of client-server architecture gets all the input from outside storage such as databases for processing the client request. The server is having all the logic to perform client requests. Client-server architecture starts from a single tier to multitier. In single-tier architecture, both client and server are the same machines. In two-tier architecture, the client and server are in the different location, client requests to the server from different location and server replies to the client accordingly. In two-tier, all the data are stored in the server and it will have the program to process the client's request. The server is deficient to handle the client's request if all the data stored in the server itself. In three-tier architecture shown in Figure 11.4, the server will have only the logic and the data will be stored in the database. The server gets the data from the database for the processing client request, whenever it requires.

11.3.1.3 Cloud Architecture

Cloud architecture is used in IoT where all the applications are residing online, requesting the service to the cloud server and all the data is stored online as cloud storage. IoT devices are performing the task by getting the command from cloud servers. Devices that are connected in the real world are getting the command from the server and do the required work for their environment. Cloud-oriented IoT models are Service-oriented because the cloud itself is service oriented. In case of any breaching of data from cloud storage, the entire IoT devices will not get any command from the server. It will fail to do the required work in the given environment.

Cloud-based architecture is not reliable for the IoT environment. Maintaining the cloud servers is very difficult in a private cloud. Maintenance is costly in private cloud because making security for cloud servers we need to buy malware protectors, antivirus, firewalls, etc. Small organizations cannot maintain the server properly in

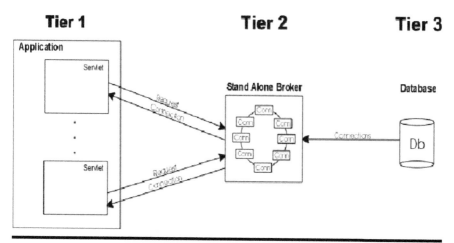

Figure 11.4 Three tier architecture.

the private cloud. In the public cloud environment, data may be misused by cloud service providers. Keeping essential data in a private cloud is a must in this scenario. Data can be breached in any way if it is found online. This type of architecture is vulnerable to threats.

11.3.1.4 Pros of Cloud for IoT

Improved performance: The communication between IoT sensors and data processing systems is faster

Storage capacities: Highly scalable and unlimited storage space is able to integrate, aggregate and share the enormous amount of data

Processing capabilities: Remote data centers provide unlimited virtual processing capabilities on-demand

Reduced costs: License fees are lower than the cost of the on-premise equipment and its continuous maintenance

11.3.1.5 Cons of Cloud for IoT

High latency: More and more IoT apps require very low latency, but the cloud can't guarantee it because of the distance between client devices and data processing centers.

Downtime: Technical issues and interruptions in networks may occur for any reason in any Internet-based system and make customers suffer from an outage; many companies use multiple connection channels with automated failover to avoid problems.

Security and privacy: Your private data is transferred through globally connected channels alongside thousands of gigabytes of other user's information; no surprise that the system is vulnerable to cyberattacks or data loss; traditional cloud-centered IoT architectures have certain inherent vulnerabilities, being most relevant the fact that the cloud is a point of failure: if the cloud is down due to cyberattacks, maintenance or software problems, the whole system stops working. It leads to the damage of data or misguiding of services if a device in IoT gets disturbed. This misleading may be happened by eavesdropping of unauthorized data, denial service attaches which leads to the service collapse. As in centralized severs architecture, if the server is interrupted, then the terminals connected get affected, the same will happen to IoT architecture. To address this issue, blockchain network is not employed on centralized server architecture of cloud architecture. Also the transactions over the networks are monitored and validated by the encryption and decryption method. Data is not updated in database if abnormality is found in the transactions.

It is necessary to enhance the efficiency of cloud server if connected terminals are enlarged linearly because it multiplies the amount of communication over the network. If failed to enhance the efficiency, it leads to transaction failure and data loss. To address this issue, fog computing is used which manages the transaction traffic and reduces the load of network. Basically, the function of fog computing is load balancing and enhancement of Quality of Service

11.3.1.6 Introduction to Fog in IoT

Cloud computing is a faster growing technology which is introduced initially. But, it is too away from the end users; to avoid this issue, fog computing has been introduced. In 2014, the term fog computing was coined by Cisco and it is new for the general public. Fog and cloud computing [8] are interconnected. In nature, fog is closer to the earth than clouds; in the technological world, it is just the same, fog is closer to end-users, bringing cloud capabilities down to the ground.

The considerable processing power of edge nodes allows them to perform the computation of a great amount of data on their own, without sending it to distant servers. However, the fog IoT architecture is envisioned to be user centric, whereby interactions between devices, exchange of control messages, and data flow are governed by user-centric policies. For example, a user decides on the granularity of services and data they wish to access and the associated monetary and energy cost of probing the provisioned resources.

While this entails more processing and power at the edge, it builds on many advantages in privacy-preserving mechanisms, mobility control, and elastic offloading when the need arises. The granularity of data handled by users could further be controlled from both the user to reduce access latency and from the cloud.

Fog computing [9] is actually considered a subset of edge computing, which has recently been presented as a valid architecture for supporting blockchain and blockchains Directed Acyclic Graph (DAG) IoT applications. BIoT architecture should be as close as possible to the Fully Distributed approach, but in some scenarios, where computational power or cost are limiting factors, other approaches may be more appropriate. Even though, there are miles to go to reach user's expectations in terms of mobile world.

11.3.1.7 Fog Architecture through IoT Architecture

As we advocate for moving from a service-centric to a user-centric approach to IoT systems for smart cities, we focus on the architectural components that will enable such a progressive framework. At its core, a user-centric architecture must utilize the context as well as resources of local fog and establish real-time management modules that will tap into the potential of neighboring resources in the mist, as well as cloudlet/edge-level resources when needed. Thus, service matching, mobility monitoring, and overall offloading granularity are largely served within the bounds of the fog network rather than the cloud. On an architectural level, we advocate for establishing an IoT-in-the-fog controller that is able to probe local resources and communicate directly with a local fog mediator, which could be the cloudlet/

edge access point. The controller operation could be deployed on a dedicated device placed for that purpose or delegated to high-end resources

The core operational mandate of this controller would be to respond to policies mandated by the fog mediator, as passed down from respective cloud services but matching the current resources in the fog zone. This includes catering to mobility and resource volatility, especially in utilizing mobile/vehicular resources in urban environments. Figure 11.5 overviews the interactions between cloud variants and what they are dubbed in current literature, highlighting the reach/scale of each cloud variant. A simple scenario for e-health applications is presented in Figure 11.5, whereby classes of e-health applications running on each tier of the fog-IoT architecture are overlaid and explained.

11.3.1.8 Pros of Fog Computing

1. **Low latency:** Fog is able to provide instant responses.
2. **No problems with bandwidth:** Pieces of information are aggregated via one channel.
3. **Loss of connection is impossible:** Multiple interconnected channels are used.
4. **High security:** Data is processed by a huge number of nodes.
5. **Enhanced user experience:** Not in recent times.
6. **Power-efficiency:** Edge nodes run power-efficient protocols such as Zigbee, Bluetooth, or Z-Wave.

11.3.1.9 Cons of Fog Computing

1. **A more complex architecture:** Fog computing architecture has data processing and storage management system in addition.
2. **Expensive:** Companies should buy edge devices: gateways, hubs, routers,
3. **Fixed size:** Integration of resources is restricted.

11.3.1.10 Fog Computing versus Cloud Computing: Key Differences

Cloud vs. fog concepts are very similar to each other. Fog architecture consists of millions of small nodes located as close to client devices as possible. Fog acts as a mediator between data centers and hardware. Fog layer is used as an intermediate for communication otherwise it is a time-consuming communication. In cloud computing, data processing takes place in remote data centers. Fog processing and storage are done on the edge of the network close to the source of information, which is crucial for real-time control. Cloud is more powerful than fog in the case of computing capabilities and storage capacity. The cloud consists of a few large server nodes but fog includes millions of small nodes. Fog performs short-term edge analysis due to instant responsiveness but the cloud aims for long-term deep

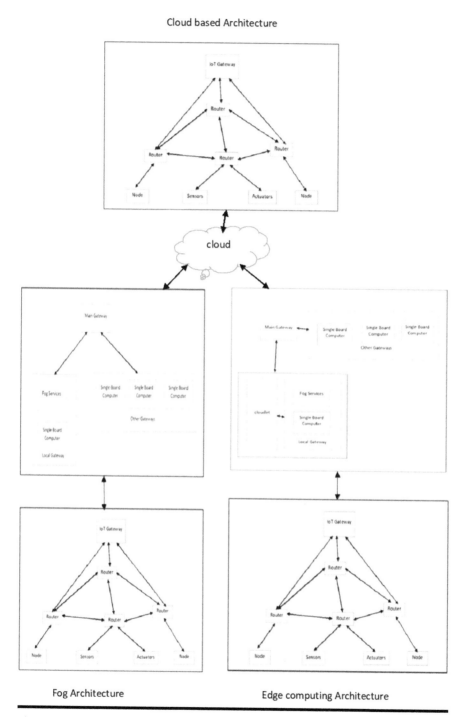

Figure 11.5 Fog, Cloud and Edge Computing-Based Architecture.

Table 11.1 Relationship between Fog Computing and Cloud Computing

	Cloud	Fog
Architecture	Centralized	Distributed
Communication with devices	From a distance	Directly from the edge
Data processing	Far from the source of information	Close to the source of information
Computing capabilities	Higher	Lower
Number of nodes	Few	Very large
Analysis	Long-term	Short-term
Latency	High	Low
Connectivity	Internet	Various protocols and standards
Security	Lower	Higher

analysis due to slower responsiveness. Fog provides low latency and cloud provides high latency. A cloud system collapses without an Internet connection. Fog computing uses various protocols and standards, so the risk of failure is much lower. Fog is a more secure system than the cloud due to its distributed architecture.

Table 11.1 helps to better understand the differences between fog and cloud, summarizing their most important features [9].

11.4 Blockchain

IoT is modernizing the world with devices such as tablet, pc, mobile, etc., where many of our daily objects will be connected and making communication with their environment in order to collect information and perform certain tasks. It has the following characteristics: error-free, user-free, easy maintenance, data authenticity, privacy and security. Though different architectural styles have been proposed for IoT, but fail to keep the security in the IoT. We require a different architecture that has to be proposed to the IoT to free from breaching of data. Blockchain is a secure network that will provide security to the application that is already proved with Cryptocurrencies. The study about implementing blockchain as IoT architecture is required. Adaptation of blockchain to the specific needs of IoT in order to develop Blockchain-based IoT applications is a major challenge appearing in the world. This study is about an explanation of blockchain and how blockchain architecture is implemented for IoT systems.

The IoT is expanding at a fast pace and some reports predict that IoT devices will grow to 26 billion by 2020. Moreover, some forecasts anticipate a fourfold growth in M2M connections in the coming years (from 780 million in 2016 to 3.3 billion by 2021), which may be related to a broad spectrum of applications like home automation, transportation, defense, and public safety, wearable's or augmented reality.

In order to reach such huge growth, it is necessary to build an IoT stack, standardize protocols and create the proper layers for an architecture that will provide services to IoT devices. Currently, most IoT solutions rely on the centralized server-client paradigm, connecting to cloud servers through the Internet. Although this solution may work properly nowadays, the expected growth suggests that new paradigms will have to be proposed. Among such proposals, decentralized architectures were suggested in the past to create large Peer-to-Peer (P2P) Wireless Sensor Networks, but some pieces were missing in relation to privacy and security until the arrival of blockchain technology. Therefore, the new architecture is evolving from past and present as illustrated in Figure 11.6. Blockchain is the next step for IoT because of security issues in the previous architecture. Own control of peers in blockchain technology can help the system to run anonymously and securely.

The technology has the ability to organize and monitor the transmission of data, extracting information from the various nodes and making the services based on the non-federal cloud. Some companies like IBM go further and talk about blockchain as a technology for democratizing the future IoT since it addresses the current critical challenges for its massive adoption.

Many IoT solutions are still expensive due to the architecture that has been proposed, costs related to the development, deployment and maintenance of centralized clouds and server farms with various antivirus and malware protection. When such architecture is not created in design, the cost comes from middlemen. Maintenance of servers is a big problem when having to distribute regular software updates to millions of smart devices. After the Edward Snowden leaks, it has been difficult for IoT adopters to trust technological partners who, in general, give device access and control to certain authorities (i.e., governments, manufacturers

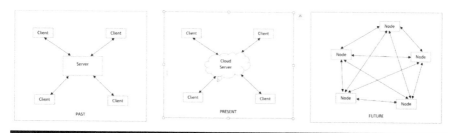

Figure 11.6   Past, present and future IoT architectures.

or service providers), allowing them to collect and analyze user data. In such a case, privacy and anonymity should be at the core of future IoT solutions. Privacy is questionable when we trust centralized architecture.

Lack of trust in centralized architecture will lead to a distributed architecture. It is important to maintain the transparency in order to enhance the security and reliability. Hence, while thinking for the future, it is mandatory to use the open-source methods.

Moreover, open source has more advantages over the traditional systems like finding an error, debugging, etc. Each transaction in open sources was monitoring by several users over the environment and debugged by any of the absorbers. It is less prone to malicious modifications from third parties. The control is given to all the peers in the network in P2P distributed architecture.

Reach of the blockchain over the last 2 years was remarkable. In 2016, venture capital reserves were around $550 from $93. Moreover, the market for blockchain technology became worldwide because of the architecture style of P2P distributed architecture. In 2021, blockchain is a project to raise $2.3.

According to McKinsey & Company, although it is still in a nascent stage, blockchain technology may reach its full potential within the next 4 years based on its current pace of evolution. In addition, as of writing, there are over 1,563 digital coins, just a few years after Bitcoin, the cryptocurrency that originated the block-chain, was born.

Bitcoin is a digital coin whose transactions are exchanged in a decentralized trustless way combining P2P [10] sharing with public-key cryptography. Public keys are alphanumeric strings formed by 27 to 32 characters that are used to send and receive Bitcoins, avoiding the necessity of making use of personal information to identify users. One feature that characterizes Bitcoin is miners, who receive coins for their computational work to verify and store payments in the blockchain. Such payments, like in any other currency, are performed in exchange for products, services or money.

The use of cryptocurrencies based on blockchain technology is said to revolutionize payments, thanks to their advantages with respect to traditional currencies. Since middlemen are removed, merchant payment fees can be reduced below 1% and users do not have to wait days for transfers and receiving funds.

Modern cryptocurrencies can be divided into three elements: blockchain, protocol and currency. In cryptocurrency, a coin can implement its own currency and protocol, but its blockchain may run on the blockchain of another coin like Bitcoin or Ethereum. Ethereum is used for a smart contract in blockchain, each member of the blockchain will receive the contract details and who are all interested they can proceed with the transaction.

As discussed earlier, all transactions have a coin that has been maintained in blockchain logs. Multiple transactions can be taken as a block and the block will be verified by the miners by verifying the cryptographic hash associated with that. If the block is matched with the previous block, the block will be added into the previous block. Otherwise, the blockchain will be integrated periodically and integrate the novel blocks in a timestamp.

A full node is a computer that validates transactions, owns a copy of the whole blockchain and also contains information about user's addresses and balances. If the blockchain is public, it can be queried through a block explorer like Blockchain.info in order to obtain the transactions related to a specific address.

Blockchain technology enables a path to all the transaction without any third-party entity or the node. This is possible, thanks to many decentralized miners who evaluate and authorize each transaction.

This contribution allowed the Bitcoin blockchain to provide a solution to the Byzantine Generals Problem since it is able to reach an agreement about something (a battle plan) among multiple parties (generals) that do not trust each other when only exchanging messages, which may come from malicious third parties (traitors) that may try to mislead them. In the case of cryptocurrencies, this computational problem is related to the double-spend problem, which deals with how to confirm that some amount of digital cash was not already spent without the validation of a trusted third party (i.e., usually, a bank) that keeps a record of all the transactions and user balances.

IoT with blockchain needs to be considered for privacy and security architecture without the third party, no centralized authority and transparency from distributed P2P transactions. During the process, there are many nodes that need to relay on each other in IoT.

However, there are several aspects that differentiate IoT from digital currencies, like the amount of computing power available in the nodes or the necessity for minimizing the energy consumed in devices powered with batteries. Adapting IoT in the blockchain environment is also a big deal while making blockchain IoT applications. Few applications of blockchain IoT are available and are adapted to the blockchain environment.

11.5 Blockchain Basics

A blockchain is a distributed ledger in which data are shared among all the peers of a network. It is contributed more to Bitcoin because it solved a longer-lasting financial problem known as the double-spending problem. The solution for this problem is proposed by Bitcoin consisted of looking for the consensus of most mining nodes, who append the valid transactions to the blockchain.

The concept of blockchain was originated and it successfully implemented for a cryptocurrency, it is not necessary to develop a cryptocurrency to use a blockchain and build decentralized applications. A blockchain, as its name implies, is a chain of timestamped blocks that are linked by cryptographic hashes. To introduce the reader into the inner workings of a blockchain, the next sections describe its basic characteristics and functioning.

11.5.1 Blockchain Basic Functioning

In order to use a blockchain, it is required to create a P2P network with all the nodes interested in making use of such a blockchain. Every node of the network receives public key which is used by the other users for encrypting the messages sent to a node, and a private key, which allows a node to read such messages. Therefore, two different keys are used, one for encrypting and another for decrypting. In practice, the private key is used for signing blockchain transactions (i.e., to approve such transactions), while the public key works like a unique address. Only the user with the proper private key is able to decrypt the messages encrypted with the corresponding public key. This is known as asymmetric cryptography.

The transactions are disseminated in this way and that are considered valid by the network are ordered and packed into a timestamped block by special nodes called miners. The election of the miners and the data included in the block depend on a consensus algorithm.

The blocks packed by a miner are then broadcast back into the network. The blockchain nodes verify that the broadcast block contains valid transactions and whether it references the previous block of the chain by using the corresponding hash. If such conditions are not fulfilled, the block is discarded. If both conditions are verified successfully, the nodes add the block to their chain, updating the transactions and making the chain by adding the block.

Bitcoin is a P2P transaction. It does not require any third party. It works on the concept of blockchain. The blockchain is a new era in which all transactions are treated as a chain of blocks and if the transaction has to be performed that will be added to the blockchain network. In blockchain, all communications are recorded in an unrestricted register and anyone can refer. The bitcoin blockchain is a decentralized P2P network; it does not require authorization from any trusted third party for processing the transactions.

In blockchain, the nodes communicate over a network without relying on a trusted third party. Bitcoin communications can be completed throughout bitcoin wallets. Bitcoin wallets are available in the form of desktop wallet, web wallet, mobile wallet, hardware wallet, etc. Installation of bitcoin wallets will provide the service for a transaction. In every transaction, the user can generate the transaction address that is called a public key. The public key or the transaction address can be distributed to the user in the blockchain network to send bitcoins to the corresponding transaction address. The private key is used for accessing their own account to receive the bitcoins or send bitcoins. The private key provides anonymity over the network and the blockchain is having only the transaction address instead of a name.

Bitcoin miners are implicated in the progression of Bitcoin communication. Miners collect no transaction request from the network and make it as a block and this has to be added into the previous block with matching hash values. To solve the Hash puzzle, a large amount of power supply and nodes are required. Miners will automatically get the reward as bitcoin if the block is added to the existing block. The miner must follow a set of rules specified in the consensus protocol. Bitcoin's objective is fulfilled by the distributed consensus by using the Proof of Work based consensus algorithm.

The Bitcoin blockchain is considered robust and secure because of its consensus model. In the consensus algorithm, the participants do not require authentication to join the network. It makes the Bitcoin consensus model extremely scalable regarding supporting thousands of network nodes. The design of the bitcoin is open to all in the blockchain network and nobody can control it.

Bitcoin provides a cryptographically secure environment over the network. Bitcoin is denoted in BTC. Since it deployed, it has attracted more people and has reached 375,000 confirmed transactions per day in December 2017. It provides theft resistance, anonymity, no third party influence, transparency, no taxes, and lower transaction fees. The distributed ledger is helping the user to see all the transactions on the network. Awareness is required to access while storing the private key because that will lead to the loss of Bitcoins.

11.6 Determining the Need for Using a Blockchain

Before delving into the details on how to make use of a blockchain for IoT applications, it must be emphasized that a blockchain is not always the best solution for every IoT scenario. Traditional databases or DAG-based ledgers may be better for certain IoT applications. Specifically, in order to determine if the use of blockchain is appropriate, a developer should decide if the following features are necessary for an IoT application:

Decentralization: IoT applications demand decentralization when there is no trusted centralized system. However, many users still trust blindly certain companies, government agencies or banks, so if there is mutual trust, a blockchain is not required.

P2P exchanges: In IoT, most communications go from nodes to gateways that route data to a remote server or cloud. Communications among peers at a node level are actually not very common, except for specific applications, like in intelligent swarms or mist computing systems. There are also other paradigms that foster communications among nodes at the same level, as it happens in fog computing with local gateways.

Payment system: Few IoT applications may require to perform economic transactions with third parties of centralized authority, but many applications do not have the transaction. Moreover, economic transactions can still be carried out through traditional payment systems, although they usually imply to pay transaction fees and it is necessary to trust banks or middlemen.

Unrestricted chronological communication logging: Many IoT networks collect data that need to be timestamped and stored sequentially in such needs that may be easily fulfilled with traditional stored databases, especially in that cases where security will be guaranteed or where attacks are rare.

Micro-transaction collection: Some IoT applications may need to keep a record of every transaction to maintain traceability, for auditing purposes or because Big Data techniques will be applied later. In these situations, a side chain may be useful but other applications do not need to store every collected value. In remote agricultural, IoT nodes wake up every hour to obtain environmental data from sensors. Here, a local system may collect and store the data, and once a day it transmits the processed information all together in one transaction.

Figure 11.7 shows a generic diagram that allows for determining the type of blockchain that is necessary depending on the characteristics of an IoT system.

Etherium is used for smart contracts. Moreover, updating the code on Ethereum modifies the behavior of the IoT devices, which simplifies maintenance and bug corrections.

11.7 Implementation of Optimized BIoT Applications

IoT will produce large applications along with IoT, still they are interlinked with the IoT platform because various interfaces that are needed to make it complete. In order to optimize them, people are suggesting that BIoT (Blockchain Internet of Things) will give good performance in different scenarios. They analyzed a number of essential aspects, but they mainly focus on the performance of consensus algorithms.

A consensus algorithm could be a bottleneck in networks with a large number of peers. Actually, the tests described making use of up to 100 peers that interact with a blockchain-based on IBM's Bluemix.

11.8 Blockchain Architecture

The architecture that supports a blockchain [11] used for IoT applications should have to be adapted to the amount of traffic that such applications usually generate. This is a concern for traditional cloud-based architectures, which evolved toward the more complex edge and fog computing-based architectures. In such an architecture it can be observed that three architectures depend on a cloud, although, in practice, the dependency degree varies a great deal. In the case of cloud-based architecture, the data collected by the node layer are forwarded directly to the cloud through IoT gateways without further processing the one needed for protocol conversion. There are also gateways that perform more sophisticated tasks (e.g., sensor fusion), but in most cloud-centered applications, most processing is carried out in the cloud. However, note that traditional cloud-centered IoT architectures have

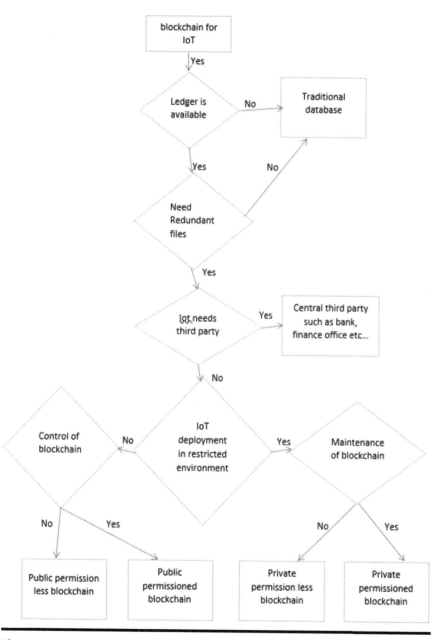

Figure 11.7 **Flow diagram for deciding when to use blockchain in an IoT application.**

certain inherent vulnerabilities, being the most relevant the fact that the cloud is a point of failure: if the cloud is down due to cyberattacks, maintenance or software problems, the whole system stops working.

In addition, it is important to emphasize that if a single IoT device is compromised, it may disrupt the whole network by performing Denial of Service attacks, eavesdropping private data, altering the collected data or misleading other systems. Therefore, once an IoT device connected to the cloud or to a central server is breached, the rest of the nodes may be compromised. In contrast, blockchain-based systems do not rely on a unique central server or cloud. Moreover, transactions are verified cryptographically, so when malicious activities from a compromised device are detected, the system can reject its blockchain updates.

The other two architectures are more recent and of load part of the processing from the cloud to the edge of the network. This loading is key for IoT applications since it is estimated that if the number of IoT connected devices keeps on growing at the same rate, the cloud network capacity will have to be expanded. Thus, Edge and fog computing can be used to support physically distributed, low-latency and QoS-aware applications that decrease the network traffic and the computational load of traditional cloud computing systems.

Fog computing is based on a set of local gateways able to respond fast to IoT node requests through specific services. Such nodes can also interact with each other and, when required, with the cloud (for instance, for long term storage). In fog, local gateways are represented by Single-Board Computers (SBCs), which are low-cost and low-energy consumption computers that can be installed easily in a reduced space. Examples of popular SBCs are the different versions of Raspberry Pi or BeagleBone.

Fog computing is actually considered a subset of edge computing, which has recently been presented as a valid architecture for supporting blockchain and blockchain DAG IoT applications. In the Edge Computing Layer, besides fog gateways, there is a cloudlet, which in practice consists of one or more high-end computers that act as a reduced version of a cloud. The main advantage of cloudlets is that they can provide high-speed responses to compute-intensive tasks required by the Node Layer.

An interesting platform that promotes decentralization for IoT systems is IBM's ADEPT. Such a platform was conceived for secure, scalable and autonomous P2P IoT telemetry. Mining is necessary for Bitcoin to restrict currency issuance, but IBM considers that such a limitation restricts scalability and imposes an increased computational cost. Therefore, ADEPT uses Proof-of-Stake and PoW, which guarantee network integrity and security, but which do not impose additional limitations.

The reduction in overhead is carried out by removing the PoW consensus mechanism, so every block is mined and appended to the blockchain without additional efforts. Every transaction is also appended to a block and it is assumed that it is a true transaction, being the owner the one responsible for adding/removing devices. This simplification eases the blockchain functioning and, although the researchers studied the impact of different attacks on the system, it is not clear that the proposed scheme would withstand attacks performed by compromised IoT nodes whose contribution (e.g., collected sensor values), which is assumed to be true by default, may alter the behavior of other subsystems.

IoT is also gaining traction, thanks to its global vision where devices are interconnected seamlessly among them and with the environment. For such a purpose, a theoretical blockchain-based architecture focused both on providing IoT services and connecting heterogeneous devices is presented. The proposed architecture makes use of hierarchical and multi-layered blockchains, which enable building a contextual service discovery system called CONNECT.

The proposed architecture [12] decreases the complexity of deploying a blockchain by dividing the IoT ecosystem into levels and making use of the blockchain in each one. The researchers state that the architecture harnesses both the power of a cloud and the security and reliability of the blockchain.

A slightly different approach is presented in [13–16], where the use of a cloud and a fog computing architecture to provide BIoT applications it is evaluated. Many authors indicate that architecture is proposed because it is really difficult to host a regular blockchain on traditional resource-constrained IoT devices [17]. Thus, the researchers measure empirically the performance of the system proposed by using IoT nodes based on Intel Edison boards and IBM's Bluemix as blockchain technology. The obtained results show that, under high transaction loads, the fog system latency response is clearly faster than in a cloud-based system.

Software-Defined Networking (SDN) has been also suggested for implementing BIoT architectures. For instance, it is proposed a novel blockchain-based architecture that makes use of SDN to control the fog nodes of an IoT network.

11.9 Conclusion

Blockchain can offer to IoT a platform for distributing trusted information that defies non-collaborative organizational structures. But it should also give emphasis on scenarios for BIoT applications in fields like healthcare, logistics, smart cities or energy management. These BIoT scenarios face specific technical requirements that differ from implementations involving crypto currencies in several aspects like energy efficiency in resource-constrained devices or the need for a specific architecture. Well-formed architecture will not lead to waste of resources, latency, and huge storage. Adapting blockchain in IoT application is possible with some changes in architecture according to the applications and scalability of the blockchain should be considered to avoid huge data storage in IoT peers.

References

[1] Gartner. Report: "Forecast: The Internet of Things, Worldwide, 2013," Nov. 2013.
[2] L. Atzori, A. Iera, and G. Morabito, "The internet of things: a survey," Computer networks, vol. 54, no. 15, pp. 2787–2805, 2010.

[3] P. Datta and B. Sharma, "A survey on iot architectures, protocols,security and smart city based applications," in Computing, Communication and Networking Technologies (ICCCNT), 2017 8th International Conference on. IEEE, 2017, pp. 1–5.

[4] D. Singh, G. Tripathi, and A. J. Jara, "A survey of internet-of-things: Future vision, architecture, challenges and services," in 2014 IEEE World Forum on Internet of Things (WF-IoT), March 2014, pp. 287– 292.

[5] B. Dhanalaxmi and G. A. Naidu, "A survey on design and analysis of robust iot architecture," in Innovative Mechanisms for Industry Applications (ICIMIA), 2017 International Conference on. IEEE, 2017, pp. 375–378.

[6] S. Kraijak and P. Tuwanut, "A survey on iot architectures, protocols, applications, security, privacy, real-world implementation and future trends," in 11th International Conference on Wireless Communications, Networking and Mobile Computing (WiCOM 2015), Sept. 2015, pp. 1–6.

[7] S. Kraijak and P. Tuwanut, "A Survey on IoT Architectures,Protocols, Applications, Security, Privacy, Real-World Implementation and Future Trends," 16th International Conference on Communication Technology (ICCT), 2015.

[8] S. Sarkar, S. Chatterjee, and S. Misra, "Assessment of the Suitability of Fog Computing in the Context of Internet of Things," IEEE Trans. Cloud Computing, Oct. 2015, pp. 1–14.

[9] F. Bonomi et al., "Fog Computing and Its Role in the Inter-net of Things," ACM Wksp. Mobile Cloud Computing, Aug. 2012, pp. 13–16.

[10] Nakamoto, S. "Bitcoin: A Peer-to-Peer Electronic Cash System," Available online: https://bitcoin.org/bitcoin.pdf (Accessed on 10 April 2018)

[11] Zheng, Z., Xie, S., Dai, H., Chen, X., Wang, H. "An Overview of Blockchain Technology: Architecture, Consensus, and Future Trends," in Proceedings of the IEEE International Congress on Big Data (BigData Congress).

[12] Yli-Huumo, J., Ko, D., Choi, S., Park, S., Smolander, K. "Where Is Current Research on Blockchain Technology? - A Systematic Review," in PLOS ONE, vol.11, no. 10, pp.1–27, 2016.

[13] Conoscenti, M., Vetrò, A., De Martin, J. C., "Blockchain for the Internet of Things: A systematic literature review," in Proceedings of the IEEE/ACS 13th International Conference of Computer Systems and Applications (AICCSA), Agadir, Morocco, 29 Nov. - 2 Dec. 2016.

[14] Han, D., Kim, H., Jang, J. "Blockchain based smart door lock system," in Proceedings of the 2017 International Conference on Information and Communication Technology Convergence (ICTC), Jeju Island, South Korea, pp. 1165–1167, Dec. 2017.

[15] Kshetri, N. "Can Blockchain Strengthen the Internet of Things?," in IT Professional, vol. 19, no. 4, pp. 68–72, 2017.

[16] Samaniego, M., Deters, R. "Blockchain as a Service for IoT," in Proceed-ings of the IEEE International Conference on Internet of Things (iThings) and IEEE Green Computing and Communications (GreenCom) and IEEE Cyber, Physical and Social Computing (CPSCom) and IEEE Smart Data (SmartData), Chengdu, China, 15–18 Dec. 2016

[17] Li, C., Zhang, L.-J. "A Blockchain Based New Secure Multi-Layer Network Model for Internet of Things," in Proceedings of the IEEE International Congress on Internet of Things (ICIOT), Honolulu, United States, 25–30 June 2017.

Chapter 12

The Role of Blockchains for Medical Electronics Security

C. Poongodi, K. Lalitha and Rajesh Kumar Dhanaraj

Contents

12.1 Introduction

Effective medical exercise involves several instances where critical data must be perfectly exchanged for communication. Lack of communication yields circumstances where medical faults may happen. These faults probably result in serious injury or unexpected consequences with patient condition. These data errors, particularly those triggered by a failure in communications, are a persistent problem in healthcare organizations nowadays. Essentials of providing effective collaborative treatment for this lack of communications, healthcare decisions for affected patients and then the role of blockchain in providing collaborative treatment are to be addressed.

12.1.1 Culture of Healthcare

Medical professionals are not operating collaboratively across various disciplines in traditional healthcare systems. Healthcare nurses and physicians taking care of the same patients regularly are not able to recognize each other and have multiple priorities, suggesting that collaborative care was less than optimal. Few other cultural barriers also occur among them and only a little experience with each other's role and perspective. This fosters miscommunication, conflict, mistrust and lack of collaboration. Traditionally, physicians are dominant and autonomous compared to other health professions, rather than being collaborative. Patients also are not given a part of the decision making associated with their healthcare [1]. There are conflicts to adopt, as healthcare professionals might be unwilling to change for a collaboration culture. Other barriers for collaboration among the healthcare professionals are listed as follows:

- Personal ethics and expectations
- Dissimilarities in payment, accountability and rewards
- Disruptive behavior
- Culture and ethnicity
- Worries of diluted professional identity
- Concerns related to clinical responsibility
- Importance on rapid decision making
- Generational differences
- Difficulty of care
- Historical inter and intra-professional rivalries
- Different levels of training, status and qualifications
- Differences in regulations, requirements and norms of professional education
- Variation in schedules and everyday routines

Safer health system identified that between 44,000 and 98,000 persons die every year because of medical faults in U.S. clinics, which was reported in the Institute of Medicine (IOM) report 1999 [2]. Communication negligence is the core root cause of the sentinel events stated to the Joint Commission from 1995 to 2004. It also refers to communication failures as they are the source of medication faults, treatment delays, operative and postoperative actions and fatal falls.

Conventional education in medical field highlights the significance of error-free follow, employing intense peer pressure to attain excellence throughout each diagnosis and medication. Faults are so perceived normally as associate degree expression of failure. This creates an atmosphere of associate degree that precludes the truthful, open discussion of mistakes mandatory if organizational education is to take place and has deep consequences on the method of healthcare delivery. It is necessary to make team collaboration and communication in helping to scale back medical faults and increase the safety of patient [3].

The issues in implementing collaboration in the healthcare system are to be addressed as they impact many systems. There are national organizations that compute and promote best practices for collaboration, but what works in one healthcare setup does not necessarily apply to another. This chapter is intended to report this issue with concrete ideas of how to make collaborations.

12.1.2 Collaborative Decision Making

Delivery procedures in the healthcare system nowadays involve several applications and patient handoffs between many healthcare physicians with various stages of educational and professional exercise. A person may communicate with 10–15 different employees, including doctors, nurses, technicians and others during the course of a few days hospital visit. Effective medical practice will be given when critical information is accurately communicated and crucial to have team collaboration [4]. When healthcare specialists are not interacting productively, safety of patients is in danger for numerous reasons: absence of critical information, wrong interpretation of data, vague orders over the phone and unnoticed alterations in status.

An attractive property of joint decision making is that the patients are involving in decisions about their own health. It is certainly tough to debate against struggles that highlight the necessity to current treatment choices to patients and consider their preferences. It seems apparent that mostly all the patients like to be up-to-date and most of them would wish to join in collaborative decision making when multiple diagnostic or therapeutic option is offered. Preference of patient selections and choices will be explored by the clinical experts. The minimum need for an expert and a patient to join in collaborative decision making is the chance to have an unhurried discussion about the multiple options available and should be willing to hear and consider each other's values, views and preferences.

Regardless of its theoretical appeal, joint decisions do not seem to have been decoded into practices in clinics every day. Patients who also act as clinicians have showed that they are enthusiastic to play an energetic role in the shared decision-making process initially. But it decreases when the condition of disease increases. In all the cases, patient's contribution in the shared decision-making method is either not imaginable when selecting among any of the multiple options that could lead to diverse risks of mortality and adverse events when it is like only one option is offered or appropriate but with a partial value like.

Patients might change their chosen collaboration made over the usual history of major diseases, matching the fluctuating degrees of significance of their health conditions. The important barrier to joint decisions is the time limitation challenged by professionals in hectic clinical situations. Unfortunately, only a few clinical settings are beneficial for updating patient data in a method that is unhurried easily understood, timely and jargon-free. Not many medical experts are provided with the skills and tools that are essential to encourage patients to consider outcomes, clarify values and ask questions and to express their preferences about treatment or diagnostic options within usual consultation times. Instead, many of the consulting duration tends to be finished to define the problem rather than proposing treatment options, thereby hindering the capability of collaborative decision making. Knowledge building develops a social movement by which communities generate novel knowledge through a procedure of collaborative, repeated idea improvement.

Along with ubiquitous Wi-Fi networks and other mobile communication tools along with Internet, it can stimulate collaboration, costs consumption and remove traditional barriers, predominantly those associated with data interoperability and physical location. The practice of these collaborative mechanisms will soon become additional nature for patients and clinicians alike. This will occupy time as all people involved turn familiar to such innovations in developments as a part of healthcare revolution efforts at all levels.

12.2 Consumer Medical Electronics

Technology has been criticized nowadays for stress, but smart devices such as meditation apps, fidget gadgets and stress-tracking devices have also proven themselves in helping people to reduce anxiety and promote feelings of positivity. All health institutions have acknowledged that the transformational role of modern tools can play important role in helping practitioners to treat patients in more effective and less expensive ways and all while creating better patient outcomes. These innovations in services and products have been intended especially for medical environments. These are often used only in some places, like ICUs or operating theaters. It leaves numerous arenas in need of trending tools to help them to operate more efficiently, run smarter and better serve patients. But progressively, providers are revolving to digital consumer tools that we use already in everyday life.

The modern tools and smart devices are given a new role in the healthcare field. Virtual reality deals with new, cost-effective, non-addictive treatment choices for patients with a variety of conditions. How consumer devices are varying the future of healthcare is discussed further.

12.2.1 Home Connected Devices and Tablets

Senior citizens affected with chronic illness or disability needs in-person home care. It would be unpleasant as well as costlier when it is to be given with 24 hours, and ineffectual when executed for brief daily periods. Wearable personal devices and smart homes can be leveraged to improve daily living. They also attach the healthcare workers for real-time care and patients to their relatives without the charges and hassle typically related to in-home visits.

Nowadays, sensors with Internet of Things (IoT) systems have been prepared easier and effective than ever for medical care teams to confirm that elderly people and disabled people can enjoy the best living conditions in their homes. Electronic appliances, thermostats and other utilities can inform automatically care teams during a potentially hazardous incident. IoT-enabled sensors have been tactically placed in the bathroom, bedroom and other areas of home, can recognize slow changes in baseline movements and enable proactive involvement when an individual's complaint is worsening.

12.2.2 Smartphones

More smart mobile consumers are utilizing their devices to monitor their own health through mobile solutions. Monitoring health circumstances becomes easier with diverse alarms at many points in our lives. Kids may want fast check-ins once a fever soars or a severe cough persists, whereas the patients with prolonged illnesses would need more straight, continuing collaboration and attention from providers. Here's the practice of mobile devices become even more vital. A smart mobile has become the primary necessary device in everyone's life. It is now helping us to live healthier, better lives, by providing us with the mechanisms for detecting the status of the health and by linking us with medical experts with the easy touch of a button.

12.2.3 Driving the Future of Healthcare

The new trending tools aren't new apparatuses or robotic surgical procedures, but the pervasive consumer devices which are already own by many of us. Healthcare solutions installed in client side are remodeling care and creating it affordable and proficient for patients to share healthcare data and for healthcare authorities to cope with their patients' requirements. Remodeling the medical services market is done with advanced semiconductor technology by sanctioning a replacement of technology solutions that pull the recent markets of client physical science, while supplying the medical compliance and robustness ordinarily related to costly capital instrumentation. This trending technology is a method of wireless observing of the people's body, judiciously and at a reduced price. Revolutions in modern technology are sanctioning the event of latest smart devices with its applications and interface through plenty of healthcare organizations. Microchip-sized intelligent personal body observation systems are fixed to change the prosperity of the latest trending application programs, bio-chemical and genomic data for healthcare authorities providing quality of life for customers and providing important physical activity monitoring.

12.2.4 Converge to a New Vision

Convergence is the push of the development of the most recent worldwide advanced medication showcase. Advanced data measures currently empower X-beams and examined pictures to be put away, recovered, conveyed and broke down utilizing Picture Archiving and Communication Systems. Improvement of interoperable norms of Electronic Health Records (EHRs) is additionally opening the path for more prominent patient/doctor access to information and the arrangement of patient decisions. Doctors, drug stores and medical clinics can share data and convey opportunely, understanding focused and versatile consideration through interoperable EHRs [5, 6, 7].

The universality and pervasive nature of remote and portable Mobile GSM (Global System for Mobile communication) are motivating the unmistakable pattern for connecting the medicinal services and the expanding interest for smartphone-based arrangements. It is helpful when all is said in done ward clinic conditions just as in out-patient and caring home situations. Semiconductor innovations are additionally empowering these united patterns to meet up and make a nexus for significant developments in diagnostics and medication. Exchange of this kind of information permits the benefit of economies of measure that semiconductor industries and it is to be agreed onto social healthcare markets.

12.2.5 Intelligent Wireless Infrastructure for Healthcare and Lifestyle Management

System-on-chip with ultra-low power mechanisms is empowering an innovative group of low-cost wireless body-worn vital signs which monitors the professional healthcare and medical services. As shown in Figure 12.1, these new technologies offer a complete wireless communication arrangement to permit healthcare suppliers to monitor the human body from a distant place through smart devices, such as PDAs and smartphones. An intellectual data acquiring framework and the whole solution for taking care of patients – enabling the pervasive observation of physiological efforts from ambulatory as well as from non-ambulatory patients – can also be implemented.

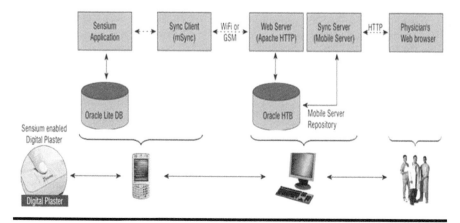

Figure 12.1   Intelligent wireless infrastructure for healthcare.

Along with fitting some external sensors, like electrodes, three-pivot temperature sensors, accelerometers, strain gauges, amperometric sensors, pressure sensors, etc, this platform expertise permits nonstop, smart observing of different essential signs, for example, temperature, ECG pulse, body breath and action level continuously permitting prior recognition and expectation of unfriendly occasions, for example, respiratory failure, falls or hypoglycemia.

Along with cheap and thin sized batteries, body-worn devices can operate and concentrate on highlights of information and wisely coordinate within an EHR. It is done through a base station gadget with a power-optimized remote networking system. Healthcare experts can convey exceptional opportunities for proactive observing and better nature of care at a significantly reduced expense. The current healthcare devices and systems are essentially not prepared to deal with this degree of constant consideration aside from costly ICU settings [8]. This trending innovation opens a greater arrangement of individualized patient considering all through the diagnostic and treatment cycle from the clinic until returning to the home. This changes the opportunities for the patients for way of life perfect, customized medicinal services as well as better therapeutic outcomes.

12.2.6 Personalized Healthcare with Endless Opportunities

As perceived by the digitization of the telecom business, combination makes unheard of technological changes. Today, well-known social networking websites such as Facebook and MySpace are altering the human texture of accessing the Internet. This advancing long-range interpersonal communication model may even give the best approach to new patterns, human service measurements later on. Aggregating information from search engines like Google or from these sites creating this accessible or available, EHRs could see the development of different online networks that empower clients to choose clinical treatments, training in-person or recuperation scheme, and even access way of life.

With a developing spotlight on cost-effective preventive care models, interest for customized human services and nonstop body observing will encounter exponential development. The development of a replacement breed of service supplier association is set up explicitly to convey coordinated patient data and bio-sensor organize watching facilities to the expert medicinal services and wellbeing marketplace. These monitoring services will fuse a wide scope of arrangements, comprising checking, medical information or buzzer services and linking to devoted call centers or SMS to registered mobiles and email functions.

As of now, remote personal monitoring equipments are varying attitudes and suppositions about healthcare services. A definitive objective is for ill-health to turn out to be generally unsurprising and fit for being overseen, in attention to anticipation than symptomatic and event-driven therapeutics. It is presently giving the stage to healthcare officials to work on data in an embedded matrix and also patients turning out to be partners in dealing with their own health.

Moving toward this computerized clinical future makes new patterns. Converging of the purchaser gadgets and healthcare industries make immense market open doors for makers. This is doubtlessly just the beginning of an overall healthcare revolution.

12.3 Internet of Medical Things

The Internet of Medical Things (IoMT) is the gathering of clinical electronic gadgets and application programs that link to healthcare systems frameworks via online PC-networked systems. Clinical gadgets furnished with Wi-Fi or Bluetooth permit the machine-to-machine communication with premise of IoMT. Gadgets of IoMT connect to cloud data platforms, for example, Amazon Web Services, on which the collected data can be put away and examined [9, 10]. Healthcare IoT is the other name for IoMT.

IoMT gadgets are, for example, remote monitoring of individuals with chronic diseases; following patient medicine guidelines and the place of admitted patients to emergency clinics; and patients' wearable portable healthcare gadgets, which can send data to healthcare providers. Pumps that infuse drugs are appended to examination e-dashboards and clinic beds fixed with body sensing units that measure patient's crucial signs are clinical gadgets that can be deployed as IoMT technology.

There are more potential utilizations of IoMT than before in light of the fact that many consumer portable devices are assembled with Near Field Communication (NFC). Radio Frequency Identification (RFID) is a label that permits the gadgets to impart data to IT frameworks. RFID is fixed on each clinical hardware and to be provided with the goal that emergency clinical workers can be aware of the quantities available in stock.

The act of utilizing IoMT gadgets to find the status of patients in their homes in remote spot is otherwise called telemedicine. This treatment uses the patient's time from heading out for an emergency to clinic or doctor's place at whatever point they have a clinical inquiry or change in their condition. The market for IoMT comprises of keen gadgets like wearable gadgets and clinical/essential screens, carefully for social insurance for the body parts, in the home, or network, center or emergency clinic settings; related telehealth, real-time locality based and other services

12.3.1 On-Body Segment

This segment can be extensively partitioned as consumer healthcare wearables and clinical-grade wearables. In which consumer health wearables incorporate gadgets for individual health or wellness, for example, movement trackers, groups, wristbands, sports watches, and Consumer health wearable devices. These gadgets are not controlled by specialists yet might be supported by specialists for explicit well-being applications dependent on casual clinical approval and consumer studies.

Organizations working in this environment include Fitbit, Withings, Samsung Medical and Misfit (Fossil Group).

Clinical-grade wearable gadgets comprise regulated tools and supportive platforms that are usually certified for the usage by at least anyone administrative or health officials, for example, the U.S. Food and Drug Administration. The gadgets are employed with a help of expert's guidance or doctor recommendation. Models from Active Protective incorporate a smart belt that distinguishes falls and sends assurance for old wearers; Halo Neuroscience's Halo Sport smart headset is worn during physical preparing and exercises to inspire mind zones liable for strength, endurance and muscle memory. Neurometrix's Quell is a neuro-modulation gadget which is wearable that takes advantage of tactile nerves to sensory nerves to release from chronic illness.

12.3.2 In-Home Segment

The smart home incorporates remote checking, Personal Emergency Response Systems (PERS) and telehealth online visits. A PERS incorporates portable gadgets and transfer units and a call center service to build confidence for homebound or elderly people. These packages permit clients to convey rapidly and get crisis clinical consideration.

Remote patient monitoring comprises of smart gadgets for monitoring home, relays, sensors, actuators utilized for chronic disease management. It includes consistent checking of physiological parameters to help continuous care in the home of patients with a goal to slow down the sickness movement; intense observing, for persistent perception of released patients and prescription administration, to give clients drug updates and dosing data to advance adherence and results.

Virtual telehealth appointments incorporate online meetings that assist patients dealing with their conditions and acquire remedies and suggested care plans. Models are video discussions and assessment of manifestations or wounds through video perception and computerized tests.

12.3.3 Community Segment

Five components of this segment are:

- Mobile services permit traveler automobiles to follow healthcare measurements during travel.
- Emergency intelligence response is intended to help first responders, emergency department care providers in hospitals and paramedics.
- Kiosks are physical arrangements, regularly in connection with PC shows, that can manage items or offer services such as connectivity to healthcare providers.
- Point-of-care gadgets are used by a supplier external to the home or customary medicinal services, for example, at a clinical camp.

- Logistics includes the conveyance of human services merchandise and ventures including pharmaceuticals, clinical and careful supplies, clinical gadgets, apparatus and other products wanted by healthcare providers. IoMT gadgets embedded with sensors for medicinal deliveries that monitor humidity, temperature, tilt and shock; a complete solution that provides personalized medicine for a particular disease utilizing RFID, NFC and scanner tags; and automatons that offer quicker last-minute convenience.

12.3.4 In-Clinic Segment

This incorporates IoMT gadgets that are utilized for authoritative or clinical capacities in the center and telehealth system or for the purpose of healthcare. Point-of-care gadgets contrast to those in the network section as one key perspective, rather than the consideration supplier truly utilizing a gadget where it is utilized, the supplier might be situated at remote spot while the gadget is utilized by trained staff. Rijuven's Clinic is a model gadget in which a cloud-based stage is a Bag for clinicians to monitor patients' case any time. ThinkLabs' computerized Tytocare's comprehensive patient inspection device and stethoscope using telehealth for the skin, heart, throat, ears, lungs and midsection, which can also monitor temperature.

12.3.5 In-Hospital Segment

The in-hospital is categorized into IoMT devices and a bigger set of solutions in numerous management areas:

- Asset management system monitors high-esteem capital apparatus and portable resources, for example, infusion pumps and wheelchairs, throughout the facility.
- Monitoring of a patient's appearance times from an enquiry to present consideration on a wardroom are improved by streaming the executives and it prevents bottlenecks and improves office tasks and upgrading understanding experience.
- Inventory the board for emergency clinics smoothes out requesting, stockpiling and utilization of clinic supplies, consumables, pharmaceuticals and clinical gadgets to diminish stock expenses and improve effectiveness.
- Temperature and stickiness for environment and energy observing oversee power usage and guarantee ideal conditions in storage rooms and patient areas.
- Creative IoMT gadgets incorporate Zoll's wearable defibrillator. It constantly observes patients at hazard of fibrillation or ventricular tachycardia [11]. Another is Stanley Healthcare's hand hygiene system, in which it joins an inhabitant

sensing and a locality system recipient alongside ongoing to follow the character of representatives with the allocator and utilization information investigation to decide if the workers are following cleanliness convention. Boston Children's Hospital's application called MyWay guides guests to their goal utilizing the fastest route.

Around 60% of worldwide healthcare associations have executed IoT advancements and 27% are expected to do so by 2019. Conventional healthcare is changing to totally computerized and places technologically advanced items with shoppers and gives doctors and patients even in the least fortunate and most distant areas better accessing to healthcare facilities [12].

12.3.6 Examples of IoMT Devices

12.3.6.1 Dexcom G5

Dexcom G5 is a smart glucose monitor that a diabetes patient wears to monitor their glucose levels. This wearable gadget is associated with a remote system and cell phones so it can show consistent glucose-level checking. Consumer is made aware of spikes in glucose levels through a cell phone application. The subtleties can likewise be sent to their primary care physician, other medicinal services suppliers, and relatives so everybody is educated regarding potential unsafe circumstances

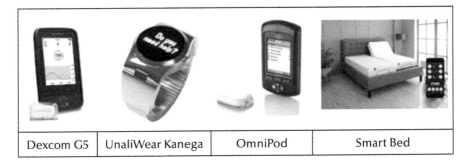

| Dexcom G5 | UnaliWear Kanega | OmniPod | Smart Bed |

12.3.6.2 UnaliWear Kanega

UnaliWear Kanega is again a compact gadget intended for use in elderly populations. Wearable gadgets for older generations are turning out to be progressively mainstream since they permit senior residents to stay autonomous, while additionally looking after security. Kanega will screen an individual's crucial signs, yet additionally has an accelerometer and GPS empowered tracker to constantly screen an individual's area.

This gadget can be especially valuable for seniors which are inclined to falling or have memory issues. Kanega can likewise identify the client's falls and sends alarms to relatives with their area. The equivalent goes for if the older individual finds themself in a new area. The area data is sent to a relative so they can be recovered securely.

12.3.6.3 OmniPod

The OmniPod is utilized for remote clinical treatment. This bit of innovation is a wearable clinical insulin pump. It works in combination with a glucose monitor to ensure the patient is given the right dose at some random time. The information gathered will be advised to the specialist or other medicinal services supplier when the measurement was regulated and what amount was taken to the patient.

12.3.6.4 The Smart Bed

The BAM Labs Smart Bed is an IoMT smart gadget. This gadget is a cloud-associated bed that screens fundamental signs/biometric data. It assists with forestalling the advancement of bed ulcers for patients who need to remain in bed up to 85.4%. This can likewise follow pulse patterns, breath trends, the span of the patient stays out of the bed and can likewise follow the patient's rest designs. The entirety of this data can be utilized by healthcare providers to ceaselessly follow a patient's advancement, difficulty and changes in their condition for a superior in general human services understanding. The security of sensitive information, for example, protected health data managed with the Health Insurance Portability and Accountability Act (HIPPA) which goes via the IoMT is an emerging concern for healthcare providers. HIPPA is examined in segment 5.

12.4 Barriers of the Technical Infrastructure in Medical Electronics Systems

E-health and healthcare information technology have become a key distraction of human services frameworks around the world [13, 14]. An audit of the writing uncovers that there is a critical accord that the usage of EHR and health IT frameworks is considered among the most elevated needs of present-day healthcare frameworks.

A current investigation upheld a job for health IT in improving the nature of pediatric consideration. The capacity of EHRs to improve the nature of care in wandering consideration settings was shown in a few investigations. These investigations additionally examined upgrades in supplier execution when clinical information management and decision support tools were made accessible inside an EHR framework. Be that as it may, there was deficient information on the cost viability of these frameworks and it was impractical to decide the degree to which the showed benefits were generalizable. In any case, the analysts presumed that health IT can probably empower a sensational transformation in the conveyance of medicinal services, building it more secure, progressively effective, and increasingly proficient. Few associations also have just acknowledged significant increases through the usage of interoperable multifunctional healthcare IT frameworks operated around an EHR.

EHR is repository of standard medical information accumulated in one provider's office, and EHR is planned to enclose and share data from all providers engaged with a patient's consideration. The most significant advantages of EHR innovation are as follow:

- Maximized cost reduction
- Standardization of care
- Long-term information monitoring
- Chronic disease management and preventative care
- Enhanced immunization rates

The most important barriers are identified to adopt EHR technology and are listed below.

12.4.1 Economic Barriers

Time: EHR framework learning may require significant time. The EHR is amazingly exploring but contrasting expenses and time incurred becomes an overhead and numerous family doctors don't possess the energy. Nonetheless, when an EHR has been chosen, utilization of it needs careful training, a few physicians don't feel they can manage the cost of added time for that.

Cost: Physicians must pick between buying an EHR framework from a seller or dispatching custom frameworks for their practices. In any case, use and upkeep of an EHR framework collects costs that come from buying the framework, yet in addition from preparing, IT support, data storage, system upgrade, and administration and movement costs. In this way for small measured practices, these costs accumulate to make critical obstruction of the appropriate innovation, as advantages of EHR reception would take longer time to even consider reaping.

12.4.2 Barriers to Adoption for Clinicians

Poor plan: The popular legacy EHR frameworks in North America were organized with the essential helpfulness of record saving for charging patients. Therefore, the usefulness isn't intended to aid a doctor in most model patient consideration, encouraging difficult connections among framework and doctor. Likewise, sellers will, in general, think little of intricacy of patient appraisal and care work processes and systems. Talking and directing consideration to patients is an exceptionally fragile association, and additional overhead of cooperation with difficult interfaces to record data is frequently prevented. A few doctors revealed that they, in some cases, quit utilizing EHRs in light of the fact that chasing for menus and catches disturbs the clinical experience and hinders doctor-patient interaction.

Absence of adaptability: Physicians regularly keep away from reception of EHR arrangements as each training has various procedures and work processes that work, and physicians would prefer not to be forced by rigid software systems.

12.4.3 Infrastructure and Regulations

■ Privacy and security: Non-adopters of EHR innovation frequently accept that utilization of EHR arrangements endangers patient privacy. This isn't an altogether unwarranted conviction, as Forbes reports that in 2015 alone there were extra 112 million information penetrates in human services archives in the United States alone.

■ System reliability: Physicians need dependable access to their patient's data consistently, and they pressurize that persistent information can be incidentally isolated at a crucial point in time or even lost if PCs crash, infections assault or the force falls flat. Notwithstanding these obstructions, appropriation of EHR innovation by doctors and wellbeing associations, for example, emergency clinics and centers is consistently growing. This regularly occurs because of force from organization or government to reform care, and not on the grounds that barriers for technology adoption by doctors have been survived. Doctors are compelled to utilize items that they discover are tedious or problematic for patient's consideration, leaving numerous with distaste and distrust for the technology.

Having outlined the barriers to adopt the technology in healthcare, then it is to be discussed the actions that can be taken to overcome those barriers.

■ Security and protection measures and awareness: Patient's clinical information must be treated with high protection and security norms, regardless of whether in EHRs or RPMs. As of now, while EHR arrangements ordinarily utilize high-security guidelines, numerous RPMs are as yet deficient. Governments should unmistakably plot and authorize security desires and healthcare providers must convey their privacy requirements to help carriers.

■ Integration and interoperability norms: Private and public sectors need to cooperate to create and drive the steady particular and usage of principles that empower interoperability and guarantee information security in both EHR and RPM innovations. Such norms explain the necessities and desires for security and expectations for secure and trusted exchange of data and empower engineers to incorporate distinctive programming arrangements quicker and more financially effective than previously.

■ Accountability and liability standards: The rising responsibility and liability concerns for RPM frameworks can be predominantly tended to with either government guidelines or by following clear rules for officially characterizing and conveying duties and liabilities merchants and caregivers are happy to acknowledge and those they anticipate that patients should acknowledge.

■ Health IT certification surveillance: All innovations utilized in healthcare settings are carefully managed by government and should be confirmed. Some industry chiefs have reacted to government calls for interoperability and are starting to adhere to norms that make their items genuine. EHR merchants that don't matter to principles (e.g., impose contractual or technological restrictions on use or access of patient information) are being de-guaranteed as sellers.

■ Setting performance incentives and mandates: It has been discovered that financial payback to practices for accomplishing quality improvement or orders for IT use expands the selection and utilization of EHRs. This speeds up adoption by decreasing expenses and conceivably additionally energizes interoperability and incorporation.

■ Personalization of software: Many clinics don't utilize full abilities of their EHR programming as they are unyielding or don't line up with procedures and work processes followed by healthcare personnel. Permitting personalization of software, while costly, will guarantee higher and progressively exhaustive reception of EHRs, releasing their maximum capacity.

■ Make healthcare practitioners first class citizens: Requirement-driven structure of MRs and RPMs by healthcare professionals and patients are to be planned properly and the software should be utilized with the full ability. This necessitates an iterative plan process with consistent input. While costs will increment because of a progressively convoluted structure process, the advantages are certainly unique, as frameworks are bound to be utilized to their maximum capacity, and information gathered will be richer and more useful.

■ State-of-the-art infrastructure: Physician's desire for reliable and accessible framework can be met with cloud administrations and numerous interface plan. This will lead clinician adoption and help make frameworks more integration friendly, however it additionally makes vital expense and intricacy on foundation like security, organize network, information encryption, trained personnel and so on. In addition, state-of-the-art frameworks in their early stages may be progressively helpless, including information security concerns.

■ Open information activities: As security is primary concern in human services, scientists frequently complain about lack of information to drive cutting edge innovative work and assessing current frameworks. The WHO perceives these and expresses that putting resources into information accessibility, quality and usage are important for productive and coordinated efforts in improving health.

12.5 Privacy Rules for Electronic Medical Records

Individually Identifiable Health Information of measures privacy and sets up a lot of national guidelines for the safety of certain health data. The Health and Human Services of U.S. Division distributed the Privacy Rule to perform the prerequisite of the HIPAA of 1996 [15]. The principles for privacy manage the exploitation and exposure of people's health information which is called as ensured health data by associations subjected to the protection rule and termed as covered entities just as ethics for people's security rights to understand and control how their health data is exploited.

The aim of the privacy standard is to promise that people's health information is appropriately confirmed when permitting the progression for healthcare data expected to offer and encourage high quality and forestall the general fitness and prosperity. Privacy rule offers parity that permits significant data employments, when guarding the shield of individuals who request for care and recovering. The rule is proposed to be flexible and exhaustive to fulfill the variety of uses and disclosures those are to be addressed given that the healthcare marketplace commercial center is diverse.

All healthcare providers ought to follow the HIPAA, a government law for security that sets a standard of assurance for a few separately recognizable healthcare information. The Privacy Rule licenses when it is required to cover the healthcare suppliers to afford the options with regards to whether the patient's health data might be revealed to others for certain key purposes. These reasons may incorporate treatments, payments and human services activities.

Social insurance suppliers may choose to depend on the necessity to offer patients a choice with respect to whether the health data might be traded electronically, either straightforwardly or through a Health Information Exchange Organization. Many of the security laws ensure that data is identified with health conditions and is considered sensitive by many people.

HIPAA created a baseline of privacy protection and overrides other security laws that are less defensive. In any case, HIPAA makes different laws to remain that are more privacy-protective. Healthcare providers and different implementers must keep on following other relevant government and state laws that require patient's assent before uncovering their wellbeing data.

HIPAA was planned to prevent sensitive personal health data. Clinical records were both composed and put away in file organizers. Progress to electronically kept data hasn't altered the protection and security commitments of healthcare suppliers, in any case, which implies that all EHR frameworks should guard healthcare data safe according to the act.

HIPAA forms the industry standards that should happen to shield Protected Health Information, and it could be in oral, electronic or on paper. HIPAA compliance relates to:

- Covered entities offer treatment, tasks and payment. It incorporates specialists, facilities, dental specialists, clinicians, nursing homes, chiropractors, clearinghouses, pharmacies, health insurance organizations, employer supported health plans and Health Monitoring Organizations (HMO).
- Business partners that use patient data and offer help. This incorporates lawyers, specialists, CPA firms, pharmacy benefits managers, third-party supervisors and autonomous clinical transcriptionists.

HIPAA violations penalties are sudden. Before 2009, a single abuse could bring about a fine of $100. When the Clinical Health Act (HITECH) became effective in 2009, its cost bounced to $50,000 [16].

EHR's regularly incorporate the accompanying health data:

- Appointments
- Complete clinical history
- Physician notes
- Prescriptions
- Contact and charging data
- Consent to discharge data
- Personal data like weight, weight record (BMI) and internal heat level
- Allergies
- Discharge rundowns and treatment plans

The entirety of these delicate information need to be put away to consent to HIPAA guidelines.

12.5.1 The Dangers of EHR

EHR systems increase the standard of care for the patients but there are few safety risks, including:

- Hacking that destroys the healthcare system
- Expose data that can be used by cybercriminals to steal identity of patient's
- Make certain information public
- Alter patient data
- Embedded devices that can be taken away and controlled remotely

The expired software application makes it easy to take sensitive information. Security risks can be prevented by these safety risks by building the EHR with HIPAA compliant that are as follows:

- Use passwords and PIN numbers to reduce the access to health data
- Build firewalls to cut the network intruders like hackers and data thieves
- Record who is accessing data, as well as what alterations are made
- Encrypt the data to change the data illegible by unauthorized entities
- Should keep the antivirus software up to date

12.6 Recent Research Records for Applying Blockchain Technology in Biomedical Data

It is acceptable to join healthcare and Information Technology to make EHRs as HIPPA complaint. Because of progressions in genetic research and accuracy medication, healthcare is providing a creative way for disease prevention and treatment, which adapts a particular patient's genetic, way of everyday life and environment situation. At the same time, development in the IT field has brought enormous databases of clinical data, offered apparatuses to follow health data and illustrated information to the people about their own healthcare. These trends can be consolidated in data innovation and social insurance to advance transformative change in the field of healthcare.

Blockchain is proposed to address the interoperability issues that are present in recent healthcare frameworks. It is the specific standard that authorizes people, healthcare suppliers, human services elements and clinical scientists to safely share electronic health information. A national health IT foundation dependent on square chain can possibly improve the accuracy of medication, advances in clinical research and want the patients to be progressively accountable for their health [17, 18].

12.6.1 Blockchain Basics

Blockchain is an invention that believably helps the customized, secure and reliable healthcare, association with every ongoing medical and clinical information of patients and introducing it as a recently protected healthcare setup and its features are shown in Figure 12.2. Basically, it tends to be expressed as that it is a system of PCs along with an indistinguishable duplicate of the database and varying its state (records) by a common agreement based on complete mathematics.

Blockchain act as the ledger available in public for all Bitcoin exchanges that have ever been executed. Miners consistently add new blocks to it (like clockwork) to ledger the latest exchanges and it develops. The blockchain blocks are connected

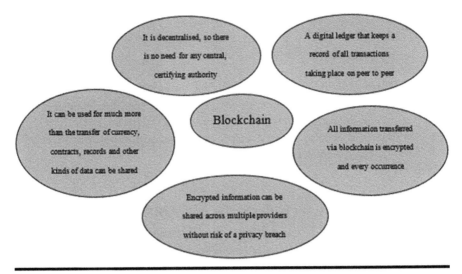

Figure 12.2   Features of a blockchain.

in a linear, chronological order. Every PC associates with a Bitcoin arrangement, exploiting a consumer that plays the mission of acknowledging and transferring information. The process of transaction in a blockchain is shown in Figure 12.3. Stored information is transferred naturally while the miner joins into the Bitcoin. It has entire data about addresses and equalizations from the beginning block with the absolute first exchanges executed at any point and to the most as of late finished block. An open ledger like blockchain implies that it is difficult to inquiry any explorer about block for exchanges related to a specific Bitcoin address.

It is a solitary Linked List of a block, with every block consisting of numerous exchanges. It produces assets and work as a mutual dark book that archives all exchanges with a decentralized and permanent data stored which can be utilized

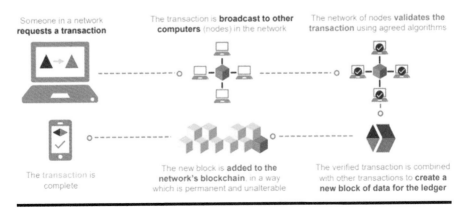

Figure 12.3   Process of transaction in a blockchain.

over a structure of clients. Blockchain exchanges can be successfully questioned, bearing more prominent truthfulness and faith to all gatherings included. The blockchain is changeless in which data stays in a similar state as long as the network exists.

Any consumer who wants to write or update the blockchain requires a public address and also a private key. Each transaction must be retained with the private key and it becomes an encrypted message. Every time a Bitcoin is bought or sold, a transaction is further included to the Bitcoin and disseminated to each node in the blockchain network. The entire system would be safe as the data is duplicated multiple times throughout different nodes. A hacker has to control 51% of the nodes in the network to alter an existing record and it is unfeasible.

The blockchain ledger is retained by a network of connected computers rather than as a central entity such as bank which has several consequences:

- In any bank system, the customer knows only his own debits, credits and balances whereas in the blockchain everyone can see each other's transactions.
- Customers can normally trust any nationalized banks but the Bitcoin is distributed and if anything is not correct then there is no one to call to sue.
- Intended design of the blockchain is that no trust is needed, reliability and security are attained via pure mathematical functions and a lengthy hash code.

For initiating the transactions on the blockchain network, a *wallet is essential and is* a program that permits to keep and exchange the Bitcoins. A client can apply his own Bitcoins and so every *wallet* is secured by a distinct cryptographic technique that utilizes a unique pair of diverse but linked keys called as a public and a private key.

If data is encoded using an explicit public key, the source of the paired private key can only decode and go through the message. If data is encoded with a private key then the paired public key can only be applied to decode it. When Ragav likes to supply Bitcoins, he requests transmission of a message encoded with his wallet private key, so he can only employ the Bitcoins. Ragav is the only person to identify his private key which essential to reveal his *wallet*. Every node can verify that the transaction appeals whether it comes from Ragav by decoding the transaction of appeal message with the public key.

If any transaction is encoded with a private key of wallets then a digital signature is produced which is utilized by blockchain nodes to cross verify the source for the authenticity of the transaction. The produced digital signature is a combination of strings and it cannot be utilized for other transactions because it is the outcome of a mixture of transaction appeal and the private key. If there is a slight change in the transaction appeal message, the digital signature will vary, so no possible attacker can modify the transaction needs or adjust the count of Bitcoins that is sent.

Encoding keeps the data and digital signatures privately to confirm integrity, authenticity and non-repudiation of stored data. Blockchains try to resolve the problem of trusting third parties.

12.6.2 Advantages of Blockchain

- Blockchain negotiates a single joint view of the accuracy in the network, decreasing data entry duplication and compromise
- Reducing data duplication
- Speeding up transactions
- Cutting costs and complexity
- Increasing resilience
- Blockchain verification procedure has the potential to support near to or real-time handling and settlement of transactions
- Due to the distributed nature of blockchain, there is no single point of failure. This makes it considerably stronger than existing systems
- Blockchain can be applied to orchestrate and automate communications with external parties, also within own processes

12.6.3 Blockchains in EHR

The need for sheer growth in computerized EHRs was produced by hospitals, medical professionals and healthcare devices, as computerized healthcare data permits easy access and distribution and also provides improved and quick decision making as shown in Figure 12.4. The most common and important benefit of blockchain technologies in healthcare is presently in the area of EHRs [19].

EHRs are never produced to hold lifetime records among many healthcare organizations. Patients leave their data disseminated among various healthcare institutions as life situations dispersed them from the data of any healthcare provider's data to another; in this way, they fail easy accessing to past history of data. To face a crisis of an innovative way to hold EHRs in a way that inspires patients to involve in their present and historical healthcare data, many researchers have carried up the blockchain in preserving the EHRs.

Figure 12.4 An illustration of interaction among mobile health applications, EHR, blockchain technology and preventative care.

EHR mostly consists of highly sensitive and serious information related to patients, which is often shared among healthcare providers, pharmacists, clinicians, radiologists and researchers for efficient analysis and treatment. When storing, broadcasting and disseminating this highly sensitive patient data among several entities, the patient's treatment data can be compromised, and it can pose heavy threats to patients and in preserving the patient history from past to present. When patients struggling with a chronic illness like (e.g., HIV and cancer), the occurrence of these risks can be more due to a lengthy history of pre- and post-behavior, rehabilitation and follow-up procedures. Upholding a patient's history becomes more vital to provide treatment effectively. To avoid those limitations, a framework like blockchain-based is suggested to maintain, manage and share the EHR of severe cases like chronically ill patients. A permission blockchain technology can be adopted to manage and collect encoded healthcare data of patient. Such structures can be applied to blockchain technology basically for accessing and handling the safety and privacy of history of patient data in clinical practices.

The Estonian medical record blockchain-based project in the year 2016 is developed with global leadership, where it is a planned to possess millions of private medical records and also to make them commonly accessible to healthcare suppliers and other insurance corporations.

Blockchain applications in medical field are growing globally and it is a strong promise to patients, using this technology to create their healthcare data is inviolable and immutable. Any change or alteration in data can be rapidly identified and renowned all through the blockchain.

This is going to be beneficial for data integrity, but it also recognizes any illegal exercises, including adulteration or wholesale scam of data. Furthermore, permitted medicinal facility data sharing and evaluation would be considered very simple. When a patient visits the clinic often, it is likely to be seen by the suppliers quickly. Medication hypersensitivities, drug and bugs solutions can be lodged without the necessity for difficult pharmaceutical compromise forms through appropriate patient-caring algorithms over all blockchain records rapidly. The exploitation of blockchain technology innovation will consequently inspire improved access to care, expanded security, prompt clinical data confirmation, medical record management and more effective arrangement of care.

12.6.4 Blockchains in Clinical Research

A range of security issues including sharing, privacy, integrity of data and record keeping, patient enrolling may also arise in clinical treatments. Blockchain is the next Internet generation and can deliver viable keys to these problems [20]. The storm of applications of blockchain will soon be occupied in the healthcare industry accompanied with artificial intelligence and machine learning. Timothy et al. [21] proposed a permissioned Ethereum that offers a smart contract functionality which is used in parallel to clinical- and medical-based data management systems. The focus was to address the challenges in the patient enrolment problem. The study showed that Ethereum causes quick transactions, as related to bitcoin, and hence the resulting decision planned the use of smart contracts in Ethereum for transparent nature of data management systems in medical data trials. Hence, in clinical research, the patient registration becomes the existing systems in using blockchain [22, 23].

12.6.5 *Advantages of Blockchains*

Blockchain technology has more rewards to be offered to the medical industry. Internet transformed the way of healthcare and presented telemedicine, likewise, the blockchain may yield medical sciences to their next level, by low-cost monitoring, arrangement and having a centralized server to store and for the management of the medical data [24]. Engaging blockchains in medical contexts will considerably drop the treating time, because whenever a patient records in a study, whole gathering of data will be accessible at once, due to convenience on the distributed ledger.

Due to their ability to get the original, authentic and qualified source-documented data in real time, decreasing any probable medical errors, the doctors need not to bother about the patient and their honest medical history. Likewise, due to the transparent data, the patients need not to bother about having a second consultation from another physician.

Having the data on a blockchain may rise to people knowing and relating with various other persons everywhere. It will not only be helpful for their healthcare, but effect the patients feeling supported, and to strengthen them to handle the illness. Patient has ample autonomy on their data, and they can choose whom to share their data.

The practical use of blockchain will profit a huge number of individuals, healthcare entities and providers, medical practitioners and biomedical researchers to efficiently distribute huge number of shared clinical knowledge, data and connect recommendations with enhanced certain privacy and security protection [25, 26]. The fruitful implementation of blockchain in healthcare would confidently open new research opportunities for the biomedical application research. The secure, safe and storage, scalable acquisition and sharing medical data would aid in evolving potential plans for the treatment of diseases in precision medicine applications [27].

A computerized brain could be shared on a blockchain and it can be programmed for neural-control systems. Neurotechnology is at a starting phase, and only a nominated few industries have taken so far as to apply blockchain technology in their development [28]. The decentralized and apparent type of blockchains would surely escape data from being changed or stolen, but other general concerns with respect to large-scale data gathering still apply: That data which is very sensitive may end up being traded to other parties for problematic advertising resolutions. Those users may still be incidentally identifiable via pseudonymous identifiers or with strategies of data. Accordingly, healthcare with blockchain design will occupy persons more in their safety and usage of data, which will eventually enhance the quality of life in a more profitable manner.

12.7 Research Issues and Challenges in Blockchain-Based Medical Electronics Security

Due to the use of proprietary systems by the hospitals, software revolutions are separated by the side of organization level. A digital resolution may enable many hospitals to get the complete observation of the patients and the patients still have certain amount of control on their data, since digital records can be wrong like paper-based records.

Payers, providers, experts and researchers are capable to communicate with the patient data, as well as protecting their privacy. Data safety and privacy are major concern that slices across almost every healthcare issue. This may often come with the high expense of good organized communication and data coordination amongst companies [29].

The public register concept introduces first-hand challenges for privacy of data. Initially, public blockchains may looks like the better answer for patient's data because they are in need of all entities within the network and all join together on sharing data and each block has the similar record and account.

All blockchain platforms are now trying to give solution for safety by adding layers to distinguish private data in order to prevent publicly spoiled data. Nevertheless, if the diverse privacy layers don't interact with others, all that is generated are new storage of data and the careful problem of blockchains promises to solve. All these factors creates the need to envisage a near future with highly effective impact on communication between several stakeholders, like providers, payers, pharmaceutical manufacturers, patients, etc., in which privacy should be a core decision in the design [30, 31].

The issues in employing blockchain technology in healthcare categorized as people, process and technology are listed as follows.

12.7.1 People

Blockchain is a technology that enables unified, secured and interoperable view and interchange of health records electronically. Patients are provisioned with handling their medical records on their own in spite of storing this sensitive information separately on the networks of various healthcare providers. Since it's a unique data, any further updates to be completed globally. Up-to-date data is available as and when required. In addition to the data privacy, patients also select people to share the data. The mechanism concentrates more on consumer point of view while having balance with other players in the system. Blockchain gives the authorities the ability to get the health records whenever needed. If the provider has gathered all patient's data once, they can retain it permanently even though the patients don't want it.

12.7.2 Processes

Privacy and security are a predominant issue to be solved for healthcare progressions. This technology provides great tamper resistance and henceforth vulnerable healthcare data might be assured to maintain with top-level security. Since the health records from various sources can be deposited on the distributed blockchain that does not rely on one central storage facility, government and other organizations would be liberated from the liability of handling enormous amounts of data. Applying blockchain technology provide solutions for verifying eligibility verification, validation of automated claims; and preauthorization that might increase the transparency, authenticity, security and efficiency of the process. Because of transparency in the shared infrastructure, a new confidence level would be attained among patients and medical stakeholders in addition to the increased security. Blockchain technology also has some cons. There is a great deal of hype and ambiguity about the evolving of this technology. It may poses the problems based on the legitimacy about this technology (e.g., for access management). In order to make the changes in the current infrastructure required for this technology, it must be legally approved first.

While information within the blockchain can be de-identified and encrypted, the security still may be vulnerable due to poorly preserved or outdated codes in an incident involving a decentralized autonomous organization. Even though a user is anonymized by a hash value, the user can still be identified through inspection and analysis of the publicly available transaction information, and therefore provides only pseudonymity instead of anonymity [32]. Blockchain can prevent data block fraud but it remains a challenge to guarantee the identity and authenticity of the informant and stakeholders. The transparency makes it difficult to guard data against mischievous traffic analysis while retaining accountability and privacy of transactions.

Transition to the blockchain technology in healthcare processes has other problems. Healthcare providers and patients are to be provided with a sufficient amount of training. Users have to be skilled on how to plan and manage the distributed controllers and network functions to guarantee vertical and horizontal scalability. Users should also know to autonomously adapt network functions and services across the softwarized middleware. There are a lot of difficulties in the processes and the transition may take a long time. For example, self-reporting the symptoms of the patients for their sickness is application specific. It means patients can only be permitted for this option if their healthcare provider's medical system implements it. Therefore, this kind of issues should be resolved to make the transition smooth. There is still requisite for metrics to measure the efficiency of this technology in healthcare. Some researchers propose to include metrics such as policy compliance, high-level computation ability, authentication, interoperability, scalability, cost-effectiveness and domain-specific healthcare requirements.

12.7.3 Technology

The blockchain technology has adaptable, agile, flexible and secure infrastructure with highest performance and low latency [33]. It is more appropriate for healthcare sector as it does for other sectors too. With the aid of decentralized technology, resource-intensive and time-consuming authentication and processing information can be avoided which creates healthcare procedures quicker. Blockchain has been started in practice. Software is coded to confirm the transparency of manufacturing process of medicine to follow medical distribution and confirm the authenticity of medical prescriptions for compliance with the Drug Supply Chain Security Act.

The implementation cost and complication can cause adverse consequences for stakeholders of healthcare. Because of the cost of data centers, many EHR services may transfer to third-party providers, which, in turn, healthcare workers may need to pay for accessing the data. The difficulty of the cryptography and networking involved would be challenging to recognize for all stakeholders. Patients may be reluctant to share their records owing to the complication of blockchain setup. Also, blockchain is not ideal for information like high historical resolution and also issues with handling multi-dimensional data, such as complex images, text and graphs. It is also an open and public network that anyone can join but it necessitates massive processing power for effective tamper resistance.

12.7.4 Challenges and Opportunities

The following challenges are to be solved for blockchain to be accepted and implement. Although substantial issues can be solved with the maturity and also with more development of the tools in near future, it becomes significant for discussion.

12.7.4.1 Scalability

The blockchain will become increasingly colossal in size when aggregating the volume of blockchain usage and the rush in the sheer number of transactions every day. All transactions in each node are to be authorized for storing. Authorization is to be done first for the source of recent transaction before it is to be validated. The limited block size and the time interval for generating a new block also shows that a part in not satisfying the necessity of processing millions of transactions concurrently in real-time scenarios. At the same time, the block size in blockchain might generate an issue of delay in case of small transactions, and miners would choose to authenticate transactions with more transactional payment. The scalability problem in blockchains is categorized into two: optimization in storage and reshaping of blockchains. This data would withstand remaining of the non-empty addresses. A consumer with small transactions can also be used as a substitute to solve the issue of scalability. In reforming, the blockchain could be broken into a micro block and a key block, with the key block being accountable for leader selections while the micro block would be accountable for transaction storage.

12.7.4.2 Privacy Leakage

Due to the fact that the particulars and balances of all public keys are observable to everybody in the network, the blockchain is more susceptible to leak of privacy in transactions. The suggested solution is to attain anonymity is that categorizing into anonymous solution and mixing solution. Transmitting funds from multiple input addresses to multiple output addresses is the process of mixing to deal with anonymity. Anonymous removes the payment sources for a contract to avoid transaction analysis.

12.7.4.3 Selfish Mining

Selfish mining is an additional issue encountered. A blockchain block is vulnerable to fraud if a minor share of hash code power is applied. The selfish miners preserve the mined blocks by not distributing to the network and generate a private branch that gets transmitted only after certain necessities are encountered. In other cases, honest miners spends more time and resources, at the same time the private blockchain is mined by selfish blockchain miners.

12.7.4.4 Personal Identifiable Information

Personal Identifiable Information (PII) is any kind of data that is used to extract an identity of an individual. The PII in addition to exchange of data and locality privacy are to be explored.

12.7.4.5 Security

Security is discussed in terms of integrity, availability and confidentiality. It is always an issue in open and free networks like public blockchains. Confidentiality is not available in distributed schemes that replicate data over its network. The next one is integrity which is the trade of blockchains although there exist several research challenges. Availability in blockchains is more with respect to readability due to wide duplication compared to write availability. There are 51% of majority attack issues that are more theoretic in a massive blockchain because of these properties.

12.7.5 Research in Healthcare

Research is another important aspect of blockchain in medical electronics that benefits the healthcare sector in many ways. It is a distributed approach to manage permissions, authorization, absolute audit trail and to provide protected access to research data. Blockchain technology may improve the manufacturing of drugs and medical devices and can reduce the counterfeit clinical and medicine trials by reducing the amount spent currently by the third party on confirmation. Blockchain can benefit from emerging new software and hardware for improving healthcare. It can handle the issue of proper usage and integrating new portable gadgets into the existing network that has sensitive health records.

Blockchain makes healthcare developments easier and robust. In blockchain, information is kept in a single layout and interconnected between other organizations, no matter in which place the health data record was handled. This reduces the complexities of preserving and sharing EHRs. The human mistakes and processing times would be less because the scheme could decrease human association with data. The features such as robustness and availability offer the preservation of records by keeping a whole copy of history of data record on each node and building them accessible to the users at all times. The resources and their origin is traceable, thus the reusability and robustness of verified data increases. This is also mentioned as data source and is important for some healthcare processing like insurance policies and their transactions. It is also expected that in the future, healthcare application users may receive financial benefits for their data provided for medical research.

12.8 Conclusion

From the organized analysis of literature review for blockchain in medical electronics, evidently, this technology offers many advantages for healthcare. Being an open-source technology and its promise in providing high-level security and transparency during data sharing and financial transactions, the interest in adapting blockchain into electronic healthcare has been increasing exponentially. However, despite the hype and gaining popularity, we have identified some principle research gaps that need to be addressed in this field. First, although blockchain technology promises secure sharing through a distributed network, there is always a possibility that hackers may find a way to break the security system.

Research studies say that having 51% malicious nodes would make blockchain vulnerable to security threats. In this perspective, profound research has to be done on how to combat if such a situation was to occur in the real-time environment. Second, if the blockchain technology were to implement worldwide across all the health providers, it should handle the intense data traffic while still maintaining the speed and scalability. Third, maintaining high-cost data centers that require vast amount of energy is another cost-related challenge. Patients would not be ready to share the financial burden, considering the fact that the medical costs are already very high. Fourth, legal issues, access management, regulatory issues should be made taking all nation's medical policies into consideration. Alternatively, the notion of having an integrated data storage and sharing system would be very far from reality. Training the stakeholders to use this new complex system would be also another grave challenge. There are many more challenges to be addressed. However, the above issues are to be solved before investing in this technology.

References

[1] R. Kravitz and J. Melnikow, "Engaging patients in medical decision making," *BMJ*, vol. 323, no. 7313, pp. 584–585, 2001. Available: 10.1136/bmj.323.7313.584.

[2] B. Chaudhry, et al., "Systematic review: impact of health information technology on quality, efficiency, and costs of medical care," *Annals of Internal Medicine*, vol. 144, no. 10, p. 742, 2006. Available: 10.7326/0003-4819-144-10-200605160-00125.

[3] J. Baggs and M. Schmitt, "Collaboration between nurses and physicians," *Image: the Journal of Nursing Scholarship*, vol. 20, no. 3, pp. 145–149, 1988. Available: 10.1111/j.1547-5069.1988.tb00055.x.

[4] C. Christensen and J. Larson, "Collaborative medical decision making," *Medical Decision Making*, vol. 13, no. 4, pp. 339–346, 1993. Available: 10.1177/0272989x9301300410.

[5] D. Randall, P. Goel, and R. Abujamra, "Blockchain applications and use cases in health information technology," *Journal of Health & Medical Informatics*, vol. 08, no. 03, pp. 8–11, 2017. Available: 10.4172/2157-7420.1000276.

[6] D. R. Kumar, T. A. Krishna, and A. Wahi, "Health monitoring framework for in time recognition of pulmonary embolism using Internet of Things," *Journal of Computational and Theoretical Nanoscience*, vol. 15, no. 5, pp. 1598–1602, 2018.

[7] M. Salahuddin, A. Al-Fuqaha, M. Guizani, K. Shuaib, and F. Sallabi, "Softwarization of Internet of Things infrastructure for secure and smart healthcare," *Computer*, vol. 50, no. 7, pp. 74–79, 2017. Available: 10.1109/mc.2017.195.

[8] T. Heston, "Establishing a regional blockchain innovation cluster in health care," *SSRN Electronic Journal*, 2017. Available: 10.2139/ssrn.3077020.

[9] T. Fernandez-Carames and P. Fraga-Lamas, "A review on the use of blockchain for the Internet of Things," *IEEE Access*, vol. 6, pp. 32979–33001, 2018. Available: 10.1109/access.2018.2842685.

[10] A Gopu and V Neelanarayanan, "Multiobjective virtual machine placement using evolutionary algorithm with decomposition," In: Proceedings of 6th International Conference on Big Data and Cloud Computing, 2020.

[11] M. Mettler, "Blockchain technology in healthcare: The revolution starts here," In: 2016 IEEE 18th International Conference on e-Health Networking, Applications and Services (Healthcom),. 2016.

[12] P. Zhang, J. White, D. Schmidt, G. Lenz, and S. Rosenbloom, "FHIRChain: Applying blockchain to securely and scalably share clinical data," *Computational and Structural Biotechnology Journal*, vol. 16, pp. 267–278, 2018. Available: 10.1016/j.csbj.2018.07.004.

[13] K. Stroetmann, A. Dobrev, S. Lilischkis, and V. Stroetmann, "eHealth priorities and strategies in european countries," eHealth ERA report, European Commission Information Society and Media, European Communities, Brussels, Belgium, 2007, pp. 7–16. http://www.ehealth-era.org/documents/2007ehealth-era-countries.pdf. [Accessed April 15, 2009).

[14] Kevin Peterson, Rammohan Deeduvanu, Pradip Kanjamala, and Kelly Boles Mayo Clinic "A blockchain-based approach to health information exchange networks", 2016.

[15] R. Miller and I. Sim, "Physicians' use of electronic medical records: Barriers and solutions," *Health Affairs*, vol. 23, no. 2, pp. 116–126, 2004. Available: 10.1377/hlthaff.23.2.116.R.

[16] N. Rifi, E. Rachkidi, N. Agoulmine, and N. C. Taher, "Towards using blockchain technology for eHealth data access management," In: Proceedings of the 2017 Fourth International Conference on Advances in Biomedical Engineering, Beirut, Lebanon, 19–21 October 2017, pp. 1–4.

[17] J. Tung and V. Nambudiri, "Beyond Bitcoin: potential applications of blockchain technology in dermatology," *British Journal of Dermatology*, vol. 179, no. 4, pp. 1013–1014, 2018. Available: 10.1111/bjd.16922.

[18] S. Angraal, H. Krumholz, and W. Schulz, "Blockchain technology, circulation: Cardiovascular quality and outcomes," *Blockchain Technology*, vol. 10, no. 9, 2017. Available: 10.1161/circoutcomes.117.003800.

[19] D. Protti, T. Bowden, and I. Johansen, "Adoption of information technology in primary care physician offices in New Zealand and Denmark, part 5: final comparisons," *Journal of Innovation in Health Informatics*, vol. 17, no. 1, pp. 17–22, 2009. Available: 10.14236/jhi.v17i1.710.

[20] R. Herr, "HIPPA loosens regulations for release of patient information," *Journal of Emergency Nursing*, vol. 29, no. 1, p. 7, 2003. Available: 10.1067/men.2003.32.

[21] H. Gerlach and M. J. Tobin, "Principles and practice of intensive care monitoring," *Intensive Care Medicine*, vol. 24, no. 6, pp. 647–647, 1998. Available: 10.1007/bf03035543.

[22] FT. Nugent, D. Upton, and M. Cimpoesu, "Improving data transparency in clinical trials using blockchain smart contracts," *F1000Research*, vol. 5, p. 2541, 2016. Available: 10.12688/f1000research.9756.1.

[23] A. Omar, M. Bhuiyan, A. Basu, S. Kiyomoto and M. Rahman, "Privacy-friendly platform for healthcare data in cloud based on blockchain environment," *Future Generation Computer Systems*, vol. 95, pp. 511–521, 2019. Available: 10.1016/j.future.2018.12.044.

[24] D. Kennedy, "Better never than late," *Science*, vol. 310, no. 5746, pp. 195–195, 2005. Available: 10.1126/science.310.5746.195.

[25] P. Robinson, "Using Ethereum registration authorities to establish trust for Ethereum private sidechains," *The Journal of the British Blockchain Association*, vol. 1, no. 2, pp. 1–7, 2018. Available: 10.31585/jbba-1-2-(6)2018.

[26] Sahla Sherin O, Anna Joshy, Neethu Subash. "Ethereum blockchain based secure e-voting system," *International Journal of Innovative Technology and Exploring Engineering*, vol. 9, no. 5, pp. 1677–1681, 2020. Available: 10.35940/ijitee.e2542.039520.

[27] A. Siyal, A. Junejo, M. Zawish, K. Ahmed, A. Khalil, and G. Soursou, "Applications of blockchain technology in medicine and healthcare: Challenges and future perspectives," *Cryptography*, vol. 3, no. 1, p. 3, 2019. Available: 10.3390/cryptography3010003.

[28] T. Kuo, H. Kim and L. Ohno-Machado, "Blockchain distributed ledger technologies for biomedical and health care applications," *Journal of the American Medical Informatics Association*, vol. 24, no. 6, pp. 1211–1220, 2017. Available: 10.1093/jamia/ocx068.

[29] D. Rajesh Kumar, and A. Shanmugam, "A hyper heuristic localization based cloned node detection technique using GSA based simulated annealing in sensor networks." In: *Cognitive Computing for Big Data Systems Over IoT*, (pp. 307–335), 2017, Springer, Berlin, Heidelberg.

[30] Sathish and D. R. Kumar, "Dynamic detection of clone attack in wireless sensor networks," In: 2013 International Conference on Communication Systems and Network Technologies, 2013.

[31] M. Benchoufi, R. Porcher, and P. Ravaud, "Blockchain protocols in clinical trials: Transparency and traceability of consent," *F1000Research*, vol. 6, p. 66, 2017. Available: 10.12688/f1000research.10531.4.

[32] S. Lee, "Blockchain-based framework for medical data management," *International Journal of Advanced Research in Big Data Management System*, vol. 3, no. 2, pp. 31–36, 2019. Available: 10.21742/ijarbms.2019.3.2.05.

[33] I. Radanović and R. Likić, "Opportunities for use of blockchain technology in medicine," *Applied Health Economics and Health Policy*, vol. 16, no. 5, pp. 583–590, 2018. Available: 10.1007/s40258-018-0412-8.

Index

Note: Page numbers in *italics* indicate figures and **bold** indicates tables in the text.

Printed and bound by CPI Group (UK) Ltd, Croydon, CR0 4YY

24/10/2024

01778307-0008